KINGSTON DEVERILL

Watercolour of Kingston Deverill Church, by Chris Littlemore, 2006 (detail)

Kingston Deverill

A SOUTH WEST WILTSHIRE VILLAGE

Julian Wiltshire

First published in the United Kingdom in 2016, and reprinted with minor changes, 2021 for the Author, Julian Wiltshire,
by The Hobnob Press, 8 Lock Warehouse, Severn Road,
Gloucester GL1 2GA

www.hobnobpress.co.uk

© Julian Wiltshire, 2016, 2021

The Author hereby asserts his moral rights to be identified as the Author of the Work.

All rights reserved. No part of this publication may be reproduced, stored in a retrieval system, or transmitted in any form or by any means, electronic, mechanical, photocopying, recording or otherwise, without the prior permission of the publisher and copyright holder.

British Library Cataloguing in Publication Data
A catalogue record for this book is available from the British Library

ISBN 978-1-906978-41-9

Typeset in Adobe Garamond Pro 11/14 pt. Typesetting and origination by John Chandler.

Contents

Introduction   6

1 'East of Selwood'   9
2 The Church and the Clergy   28
3 Kingston Deverill School   86
4 Farming in the Upper Deverills   122
5 The Social Scene   145

Appendices
    A Kingston Deverill Clergy   223
    B Kingston Deverill WW1 War Memorial   228
    C Architect's Plans for Church Restoration, 1842   231
    D KD School Admissions 1949-1969   232
    E KD Field Names   236
    F 1782 Map and Key to Occupants   238
    G Old Village Customs of Kingston Deverill   240
    H KD Evacuees   242
    J Longleat Estate Map of Kingston Deverill, 1748   244
    K Kingston Deverill Old and New Rectories   246

Bibliography   250
List of Illustrations   252
Index   255

Introduction

When I was struggling to translate the Anglo-Saxon Chronicle during my first term at university in 1953, I came across the passage which describes King Alfred's arrival in 878 at the point where the three counties of Dorset, Wiltshire and Somerset meet. The account goes on to describe his march from there to 'Egbert's Stone, East of Selwood' and on to 'Ethandun' where he defeated the Danish army. Forty-eight years after I first wrestled with that text, I found myself living in the village through which Alfred passed, and only a few miles from that conjunction of county boundaries where he gathered his forces. When the opportunity arose, this particular coincidence of past and present became the focus for an attempt to write a fairly comprehensive history of the village of Kingston Deverill.

I realise that all the other villages in the Deverill Valley have their own story to tell, and were also on Alfred's route. The importance of each individual village became even more evident when I was introduced to the excellent collection of essays published in 1982 under the title 'The Deverill Valley' and popularly referred to as 'The Green Book'. A glance at the unique past history of each these villages indicated immediately that a detailed survey which included all the Deverills – Longbridge, Hill, Brixton and Monkton as well as Kingston- was out of the question. This realisation was underlined when I started looking at the huge amount of information relating to Kingston church and the local school, let alone the Longleat records concerning the village, and the 'social scene' as revealed by the census returns and by the series of books published by the Wiltshire Record Society, quite apart from the extensive archive held at the History Centre at Chippenham.

For these reasons I have had to concentrate on the village in which I live. However, this is not to say that I have left out all reference to our neighbours, and when I reach the twentieth century it becomes

INTRODUCTION 7

obvious that the Deverill Valley is gradually approaching the current situation when it might be described as a unified entity, brought about by increased ease of access, and in particular by the sad but inevitable closure of two of the churches, all the schools and shops and the survival of only one pub.

Any errors and omissions in the following text are entirely my responsibility, and I am greatly indebted to all those who have written up aspects of the village history in the past or have given me oral or photographic evidence.

I must single out two people without whom the production of this book would not have been possible, namely John Chandler and Alison Cameron. John is well-known in the county both as a writer and publisher of a large number of books on an amazingly varied array of Wiltshire subjects, and it is a great privilege to have been given the offer of his editorship, and subsequent publication of my KD book by the Hobnob Press. John is also well-known as an accomplished historian, and has pointed me in the direction of many archive sources of which I was unaware, as well as correcting a number of errors. Similarly, without Alison's enthusiasm and expert knowledge, the book would lack the splendid illustrations which help bring the text to life. Her expertise in genealogy has also been invaluable.

I list below the names of those whose assistance has also been greatly appreciated: Kevin Abraham, Lady Clare Asquith, Virginia Bainbridge, Dinah Barnes, John Budgen, Crispian Beattie, Olivia Clifton-Bligh, Karen Dunford, Carol Fear, Ted and Gillian Flint, David Fuller, Richard Harbud (evacuee), Betty Kent, Bill Knowles, John Lea, Andrea Llewellyn, Davina Miles (nee Trollope), Eddie Mirzoeff, Tim Moore, Judy Munro, David O'Connor, Chris Ralph, Jill Russell, Robert Shuler, John Skibiak, Tim Spinney, Richard Stratton, Sylvia Titt, Joyce Turner (nee Harbud, evacuee), Sheila White.

I should also like to thank the Longleat archivist, Kate Harris; the archivists at the Wiltshire History Centre, Chippenham, Robert Jago, Steve Hobbs and Helen Taylor; the staff at the museums in Devizes, Salisbury and Warminster and at the National Archive at Kew; The Commonwealth War Graves Commission; the Headmistress and administrative staff at the Beckford School, West Hampstead.

Very special thanks are due to David Stratton, who has added a sequel to his father Richard's 'Green Book' essay on the history of farming in the valley. This gives details of all the many changes which have taken place at Manor Farm over the past thirty-five years since the earlier essay was completed, and both accounts form Chapter 4 of this book.

Finally, without the co-operation and encouragement of my wife Anne, this book would never have happened.

Julian Wiltshire,
Cold Kitchen Cottage, Kingston Deverill
July 2016

Julian Wiltshire can trace his family back to the 15th century in the north of Wiltshire. Despite the misfortune (as he sees it) of having been born outside the county – his parents having left Salisbury shortly before that crucial event – his father passed on to him his own enthusiasm for the county, and spoke with a Wiltshire burr to the end of his life. Julian also spent long periods of his childhood at his great-grandfather's home in Devizes, and insofar as he could decipher the Wiltshire dialect and intonation of his very elderly relation, much of his devotion to the area dates from this early encounter. He has lived for the past 31 years in west Wiltshire and his interest in the history and topography of the county is unwavering. His involvement in the story of Kingston Deverill ultimately derives from his tutors in Anglo Saxon at Oxford, where a study of the Anglo Saxon Chronicle resulted in a very much later connection with the village through which King Alfred passed on his way to defeating the Danes in the 9th century.

Julian is also an enthusiastic amateur musician, and this activity still takes up much of his spare time. Nonetheless, his future plans include the writing up of his 'eccentric' walk (in both directions) round the boundary of Wiltshire which he undertook between 1999 and 2004.

1 'East of Selwood'

Kingston Deverill is the southernmost of the five Deverill villages which cling to the bank of the infant river Wylye between the towns of Mere and Warminster. This stretch of water is strictly known as the 'Deverill' before becoming the Wylye at Crockerton, but what the name signifies is lost in the mists of time, although it may refer to the fact that the river 'dives' underground more than once just beyond its source near Kilmington, six miles to the west of the village.

The Deverill

At the time of the Domesday Survey in 1086, Kingston Deverill[1] was the smallest village with 34 inhabitants and Monkton Deverill the largest with a population of 285. Hill Deverill, Longbridge Deverill,

---

1 Throughout the book future references to these villages will be designated KD, MD, HD, LD and BD respectively

and Brixton Deverill came somewhere in between. This situation had changed radically by the mid- 17th century when Longbridge was by far the largest community with Kingston in second place – and this remains the same today.

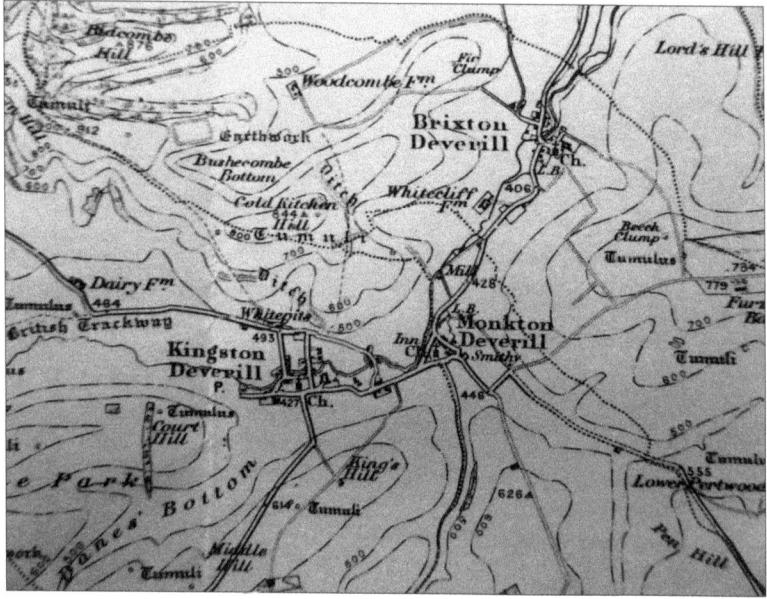

The Deverill Valley in 1897

The village is dominated to the north by the West Wiltshire Downs in their final thrust westwards towards the Somerset border. There are effectively four summits – Cold Kitchen Hill, Brimsdown, Little Knoll and Long Knoll- and if you walk by the river past the duckpond to the end of the village in order to view the sunset, it is Little Knoll which captures the scene with its Mohican haircut – bald to the south and thickly forested to the north. But it is the easternmost of these downs, Cold Kitchen Hill, which is the most significant, since it encapsulates virtually the entire ancient history of the valley.

The name of the hill is both strange and evocative, and no one knows for certain how it originated. John Aubrey, the Wiltshire antiquarian (1626-1697) fails to mention it in his *Natural History of Wiltshire* which he completed in 1691, although he lists other local hills: 'in this county are Clay-hill, near Warminster; the Castle-hill at

Little Knoll

Cold Kitchen Hill

Mere, and Knoll- hill near Kilmanton [*Kilmington*], which is half in Wilts, and half in Somersetshire'.[1] The name does appear, however, on

---

1 This latter statement is no longer true since the Wiltshire border is now a mile to the west of Long Knoll on the edge of the Selwood Forest at Yarnfield Gate. Christopher Saxton's map of 1576 also confirms that Long Knoll was at an earlier time in Somerset. The boundary change took place in the late 19th century.

John Aubrey (1626-1697) by Michael Vandergucht, after William Faithorne. Line engraving, published 1719

Andrews and Dury's map of Wiltshire published in 1773, so perhaps in the intervening years someone had noticed a collection of broken Roman culinary receptacles in a declivity on the open down and – not knowing what it was called - had come up with an imaginative name. Alternatively, the discovery that in Celtic times the hill was known as 'Col Cruachan', may have led to a subtle transliteration to 'Cold Kitchen'; in fact, a strict translation of the Celtic would be 'Hill of the Wizard'.

However named, the hill is an archaeological treasure-trove – and one which has still not been fully explored. The most ancient of the many

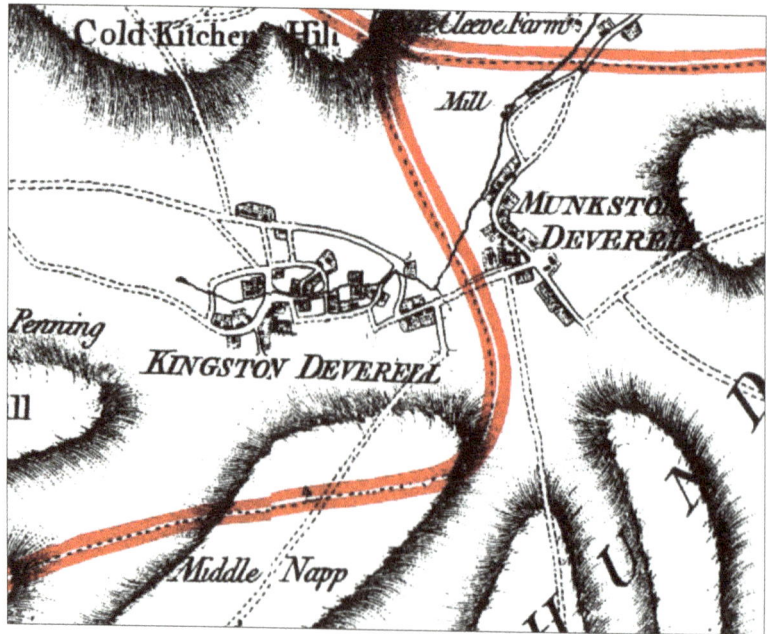

Andrews & Dury's map 1773

archaeological sites are two Neolithic Long Barrows, the larger of which is situated on the summit at the Brixton end of the hill, and the smaller lower down on the Kingston side. There are also Bronze Age tumuli, Iron Age ditches, traces of Celtic field systems, a Roman Temple and two Roman roads, one running north and the other to the west. The presence of these antiquities was pointed out for the first time in print in a book entitled *Ancient History of North and South Wiltshire* by Sir Richard Colt Hoare (1758 – 1838), antiquarian, archaeologist, artist

left: Sir Richard Colt Hoare (1758-1838); right: Sir William Cunnington (1754-1810) by James Basire, after Samuel Woodforde. Line engraving, (1808)

and traveller – and owner of the nearby Stourhead Estate which he had inherited from his grandfather in 1785. Colt Hoare, did not, however, conduct any excavations himself on the hill, concentrating instead on Stonehenge and on barrows on Salisbury Plain. In this latter exercise he was assisted by a local amateur archaeologist from Heytesbury, William Cunnington (1754 – 1810), whose work Hoare decided to assist financially. Cunnington had earlier (in 1803) excavated the Roman Temple on Whitecliffe Down at the junction of Brimsdown and Cold Kitchen Hill and had unearthed painted stucco walls and various votive offerings. However, archaeology as a technical science was in its infancy at this time, and the researches of both Hoare and

Colt-Hoare and Cunnington overseeing excavation, c1810 by P. Crocker

Cunnington were more valuable as an historical exercise than they were as a means of dating sites and artefacts to a precise era, unless- as in the case of the Roman Temple- the provenance was obvious.

Hoare's *Ancient History* was published in 1819, and Cold Kitchen had to wait in frigid isolation for more than a hundred years before the first professionally organised excavations took place. These were undertaken by the exotically named Rex de Charembac Nan Kivell who arrived on the hill in 1924 and returned again for further searches in 1925. Nan Kivell was a New Zealander who had enlisted in the New Zealand Expeditionary Force in 1916 and who was posted later to one of the many camps set up during the First World War at Codford, just below the southern edge of Salisbury Plain. He thus knew the area, and once he had completed his antiquarian studies, he arrived in the Deverill valley to see what he could find. The results of his careful investigation were

Rex de Charembac Nan Kivell (1898-1977)

astonishing, and form the basis of everything that is known about the early history of the area. He established from the presence of flint tools, that a Neolithic farming community had existed on the then heavily forested hills, and was able to follow the progress of their descendants through the discovery of bronze brooches,(one, in the shape of a blue and red-enamelled horse and rider, being a notable example), bangles, rings and pins, glass beads, iron utensils and weapons (including a rare socketed axe), pottery from the 6th and 7th century BC and early British coins – the last of these dating from the end of the 4th century and thus indicating the probable demise of the community on the hill.

All these artefacts, including those found from the Roman period (notably a figurine of Mercury, and a red and green glass bead

above: Bronze Age enamelled horse & rider brooch; right and below: Early Roman blue glass bead necklace

necklace) - together with a magnificent bronze age necklace made of faience, jet and amber beads discovered in a disc barrow near Keysley Farm – found their way to the Devizes Museum (now known as 'the Wiltshire Museum, Devizes'). Most of them were donated by Kivell, and are now on display in the museum's newly reconstructed galleries.

The discovery of the amber necklace is of particular importance since it indicates the existence of very early trade between Britain and the continent. This is confirmed by an analysis of the amber beads which shows that they came from the same Baltic source as those discovered by Heinrich Schliemann in his excavation of Agamemnon's tomb in Mycenae in 1876. It would appear, however, that foreign influences and contacts gradually lapsed in the centuries that followed, and that after 400 BC the Cold Kitchen scene was virtually empty, apart from a few lonely farmers cultivating their Celtic fields, until the sudden appearance of the Romans under the leadership of Vespasian in 42 AD.

The task of Titus Flavius Vespasian (09 -79), commander of the Legio 11 Augusta, was to subdue the local tribes – the Durotriges and the Dubonni – which he achieved after a major struggle with a determined enemy, notably in engagements to the west at Cadbury Castle and - if the discovery by Sir Mortimer Wheeler of the skeleton of a British soldier with a Roman arrowhead in his spine is indicative - also to the south at Maiden Castle. These were highly fortified Iron Age enclosures, with a complex system of defensive ditches and earth ramparts, and the Roman legionnaires were fiercely opposed. Vespasian triumphed, however, and with the establishment of the

The Emperor Vespasian (AD09-79)

Fosse Way in 47 AD as a defensive barrier against the tribes further to the west, the local inhabitants of the valley settled down to a peaceful co-existence with their conquerors – the needle straight Roman road forming the north-west boundary of Wiltshire to this day.

The existence of two local Roman roads has already been mentioned. One of these ran from south to north - from Poole via Vindocladia (Badbury) to Aquae Sulis (Bath); the other –known as the Lead Road and following an ancient trackway - east to west from

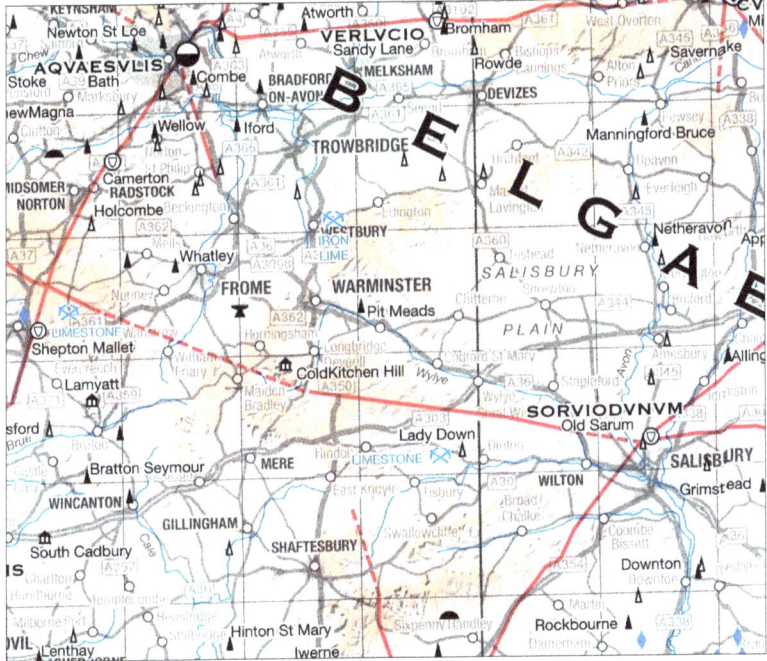

Roman roads (in red)

Venta Belgarum (Winchester) via Sorviodunum (Salisbury) to the Mendip Hills at Iscalis (Charterhouse). It was thought until recently that both these roads met at the ford on the river at Kingston, but excavations in the 1980s have indicated that the road which runs north at the eastern edge of Cold Kitchen crossed the river at a ford nearer Monkton. There is, however, a close convergence of the two roads on Cold Kitchen Hill, and travellers on both must have made use of the Temple and doubtless some hostelry by the river between the villages.

The Ford

During the Roman period arable farming continued to thrive in the valley, and there is vivid evidence of this in the existence of vertical strip fields on the north side of Court Hill, dating from around 60 AD, and still visible in the late spring when the difference in the appearance of the growing grass in the previously cultivated and uncultivated areas comes into focus. These strips were still being cultivated in the 1780s and the names of the tenant farmers who worked on them at that time are recorded. Initially farming was undertaken in the valley itself and on the lower slopes of the downs rather than on the upper reaches as had been the case in earlier times, but by the end of the Roman occupation large numbers of sheep appeared, and their flocks grazed the downs as they do still.

After the gradual departure of the Romans in the late 4th and early 5th centuries, the area reverted to what might be described as British rule and was initially unaffected by the Saxon tribes who took over most of eastern England between 450 and 500 AD. The proximity of Cadbury Hill to the west and Amesbury to the east gives a frisson of credence to the possibility that King Arthur was around at Camelot during this period, prior to his demise in the Vale of Avalon, and that

Guinevere, his one-time Queen, was also visibly involved before her retirement to the Amesbury monastery. Myths return to facts, however, when the west of the country was overrun by the Saxons in the 6th century, the first king of Wessex being Cerdic who reigned from 519 to 534. Just how much influence these early rulers had on the area of the Deverill valley is unknown, and no fewer than 21 kings followed Cerdic before any referential evidence can be established. However, with the reign of Egbert (802 – 839), Alfred the Great's grandfather, we reach a definite connection with the mention of 'Ecgbryhtesstan' (Egbert's Stone) in the entry in the Anglo-Saxon Chronicle for the year 878. The chronicle states that Alfred gathered his forces - 'men of Wiltshire, Somerset and Hampshire' at a place 'east of Selwood' – before defeating the Danish King Guthrum at the battle of Ethandun near Westbury.

left: King Egbert (802-839); right: Statue of King Alfred in Winchester by Hamo Thornycroft 1901

Extract from the Anglo-Saxon Chronicle for the year AD878-Alfred's arrival in Selwood

Tradition has it that Egbert held regular councils on Court Hill, just south-west of Kingston Deverill, at a place marked or commemorated by the presence of two standing Sarsen stones joined by a lintel. These stones, forming a kind of 'chamber', stood for centuries on the hill, cared for or ignored by generations of farmers until in the 1790s the Rev. Millington Massey, Rector of Kingston Deverill from 1770 to 1808, ordered the stones to be brought down and placed in the ford, near the crossing of the two Roman roads. There they remained until around 1875 when the Rev. David Clerk (Rector 1845-1879 and living in the new rectory built in 1858) had them transferred to the rectory garden (a labour in which the father of one of the recent residents of the village, Jack Carpenter, who died aged 100 in 2003, was involved). At some point, possibly during the second world war when American forces were resident in the property, or earlier, the lintel went missing, but two stones still stand leaning against each other in the garden of Kingston House, formerly the Rectory. A

Egbert's Stones

suggestion that they should be removed to the downs above Westbury in 2000 as part of a memorial to King Alfred's victory was voted down by the villagers.

Alfred's Tower

So Alfred passed this way, emerging from his hideout in Athelney in the Somerset levels, gathering his forces in Selwood Forest where the county boundaries of Wiltshire, Somerset and Dorset meet (but strangely not including a contingent from the latter county, but rather men from Hampshire whose nearest border was some forty miles away), and marching them via Egbert's Stones to a triumphant victory which marked the beginnings of England as a nation.

Today Alfred's passage is commemorated by the magnificent 160 ft high Alfred's Tower, erected in 1772 on Kingsettle Hill above the Stourhead estate near the Somerset village of Brewham. The tower was conceived by Henry Hoare II (1705 – 1785) and constructed by Henry Flitcroft as a memorial marking the end of the Seven Years War and the accession of George III as well as a tribute to King Alfred- although it is only the latter dedicatee who is remembered today. Until 1970 when it became a private house, the church at Monkton Deverill (originally under the aegis of Glastonbury Abbey) was also in later years dedicated to King Alfred, but the only relevant reminder of that dedication today is a processional banner depicting the King which now resides in Kingston Church.

Despite these associations, it is almost certain that Kingston Deverill does not owe its name to King Alfred, but to a closer relationship with the crown which emerged 200 years later during the reign of the last Saxon King of Wessex, Edward the Confessor (1042 – 1066) whose wife Edith, whom he married in 1045, was given lands in the area. Edith retained her property until her death in 1075, at which point the Normans, following their conquest of the country nine years earlier, divided the Kingston property into two, reserving the newly constituted 'hundred' of Mere for the Crown and granting the remainder- now known as the 'hundred' of Amesbury- to the canons of Lisieux. The 'crown' portion of the village subsequently became part of the Earl of Cornwall's property, and it is probably during this period that the name of the village was firmly established.

Queen Edith (c.1025-1075) – wife of Edward the Confessor (detail)

In the meantime, Christianity had become well established in the valley, and it is even possible that a place of worship existed in the village prior to the arrival of King Alfred. What is certain is that at an unknown point in the Saxon period a church was erected on the site of the present medieval building, since a Saxon font was unearthed in the churchyard during renovation of the church in 1847, and now stands under the window at the west end. The history of Kingston Deverill Church and its clergy belongs to a later chapter, but it is relevant to mention here that the mid-nineteenth century excavations also brought to light the sculptured effigy of a nobleman who is thought to be a descendant of the Vernon family who came over from Normandy with the Conqueror in 1066, and became, together with the Stanters, important landlords in the vicinity of the village.

At some point, probably in the middle of the 12th Century, the Vernon and Stanter families (connected to each other by marriage) acquired tenancies in both Kingston and Horningsham from the canons of Lisieux. Sir Robert de Vernon founded the church in

14th-century effigy, reputed to be of Robert Vernon, sheriff of Wiltshire

Horningsham in the early years of the 13th century, and his son John is reputed to have established the Priory for Black Canons at nearby Longleat at about the same time. Both John and his son Robert became Sheriffs of Wiltshire, and it is possible that the effigy mentioned earlier represents this younger Robert who was appointed patron of the church in 1302.

It is to be presumed that the medieval church was constructed around this date, replacing the Saxon building which had formed the focus of the village for some three hundred years. The Vernon/Stanter family continued their patronage, together with that of the Augustinian Priory at Longleat, throughout the 14th and 15th centuries, until a new regime arose following the dissolution of the monasteries in 1537. At this point the two long-standing landlords were replaced by two others – the Thynnes and the Ludlows. The Thynne family came into the picture with the purchase in 1541 of the old priory and surrounding estate. The buyer was John Thynne (1515 – 1580) who paid £53 for the site, and proceeded to build a substantial house. John (who was later knighted for his valour in a Scottish war) had connections at the court of Henry VIII, and caught the eye of Edward Seymour, (brother in law to the king, and subsequently Duke of Somerset), who appointed him as his steward. The Seymour family who had extensive estates in the Deverill valley and the villages of Maiden Bradley[1] and

---

1 Bradley House in Maiden Bradley is still in the ownership of the Dukes of Somerset, their other property being at Berry Pomeroy near Totnes in Devon. The former mansion was originally constructed in 1710 by Edward Seymour, 4th Baronet and replaced by a much smaller building in 1820. The Seymour connection makes the presence of the Somerset family in Wiltshire understandable – but it is still rather confusing that neither of the family seats is in the 'right' county.

left: Sir John Thynne (1515-1580); right: Edward Seymour, Duke of Somerset (c.1500-1552)

East Knoyle, became increasingly powerful following the marriage of the king to Jane Seymour, and even more so on the king's death and during the minority of his successor Edward VI, when as 'Protector' the Duke of Somerset virtually ruled the country.

In 1549 the Duke was forced out of office and subsequently executed on trumped up charges in 1552. His disgrace inevitably affected John Thynne by association, and the new owner of Longleat was briefly imprisoned. With the accession of Queen Elizabeth his fortunes revived, however, and he was able to continue the construction of his impressive mansion. A serious fire caused major damage in 1567, but at the time of his death in 1580, Longleat House, as we know it today, was virtually complete.

Despite the imposing presence of Longleat and its powerful owners, the patronage and ownership of the village of Kingston Deverill did not come into the hands of the Thynne family until the 18th century, although they had acquired the immediately neighbouring manors of Longbridge and Monkton in the 1540s. There were, however, two rival landlords in the valley, both of whom had powerful dynasties and connections. The first of these were the Ludlows who had moved to Wiltshire from their native Shropshire at some point in the

A View of Longleat, 1675

13th century. William Ludlow, who held important offices under no fewer than three King Henrys – IV, V and VI, acquired the manor of Hill Deverill in around 1430, and one of his descendants, George Ludlow – who was appointed High Sheriff of Wiltshire in 1567 – bought the manor of Kingston Deverill from Roger de Stanter a few years later.

George Ludlow died in 1580- the same year as his rival Sir John Thynne- but the influence of both families on the lives of the villagers in the Deverill valley continued under their descendants. George's son Edmund became MP for Hindon in 1604, and passed on his anti-monarchical views to his son Henry who sat in the Long Parliament (1640).

Lieut. General Edmund Ludlow (c.1617-1692)

In turn, Henry's son, Lieutenant-General Edmund Ludlow, joined the Parliamentary Army and was made governor of Wardour Castle following Lady Arundell's surrender of the royalist fortress in 1643, later adding his name to the signatories of Charles 1st's death warrant. It is possible, therefore, that some of the inhabitants of Kingston Deverill were involved in the Civil War on the side of Cromwell, but there is no definite evidence to substantiate this. Meanwhile Sir James Thynne (1605 – 1670) was sitting relatively quietly at Longleat, keeping his royalist sympathies to himself.

The second rival family to the Thynnes were the Mervyns (or Marvins) who had established themselves in the 1470s at Fonthill Gifford. Since they had arrived in Wiltshire very much earlier than the owners of Longleat, they regarded themselves as infinitely superior, and a member of the family – described as 'Mr Mervyn' but nonetheless a prominent figure as Sheriff of Wiltshire - had been responsible for conveying the first Sir John Thynne to the Tower in 1552. Unsurprisingly, hostility between the two families continued up to the time of Sir John's death in 1580, but increased in menace immediately thereafter when Sir James Mervyn attempted to entrap Sir John's elder son into marriage with his daughter Lucy. If this had come about, the Mervyn family would have effectively taken over Longleat, but Lucy's promised dowry of a number of Mervyn properties turned out to be fraudulent, as the estates concerned were already entailed. The advisors of the new owner of Longleat – another Sir John (1550 – 1604) – recognised Sir James's criminal intentions in the nick of time and the marriage did not go ahead. Sadly, however, this was not the end of the story, since the Mervyn family, through their spurned daughter Lucy, was intent on revenge. Time had moved on and Lucy had married a member of the notoriously crazed Touchet family, Lord Audley, by whom she had a daughter, Maria. By means of a clever ruse, the Mervyn family persuaded Sir John's son, Thomas- then a sixteen-year-old undergraduate at Oxford - to attend a party at the Bell Inn, Beaconsfield, where he was introduced to the stunningly beautiful Maria. It was a drink-filled evening and with astonishing speed, the two fell immediately in love. Thomas signed a promise of marriage and the betrothal was marked in time-honoured fashion by the couple entering a bedroom together in full public view. Needless to say, Thomas's father

Sir John, and his mother Joan were aghast at the news and took every possible legal recourse to annul the marriage. In this they failed, and on Sir John's death in 1604, Maria and Thomas moved into Longleat. At this point it appeared that the Mervyn family had triumphed and that they would be the leading family in the area. Their success was short-lived, however. When Sir James died leaving no direct heir, his estates passed to a nephew who immediately started selling them off, the last Wiltshire property passing out of the family in 1660. By the time the Mervyn's most valuable estate at Fonthill was purchased by Alderman Beckford in 1744, the Thynne family had moved up the social scale and the owner of Longleat was a Viscount. We shall meet them again in the mid-18th century just before their patronage and ownership extends to the whole valley. Meanwhile the only reminder of their great rival's name is enshrined in Marvin's Farm, a substantial and historic house in the centre of the village.

Sir John Thynne, junior (1550-1604)

Maria Touchet (1575-1611)

2 The Church and the Clergy

Early maps of the Kingston Deverill area show that travellers arriving from Mere, some four miles to the south-west of the village, descended towards it on a track which reached the valley half way between Kingston and Monkton. This remains the case with Andrews and Dury's map of 1773, but by the time of the first Ordnance Survey map of 1811, there is a fork in the road below Kings Hill, and a new track runs straight down the hill towards the church.

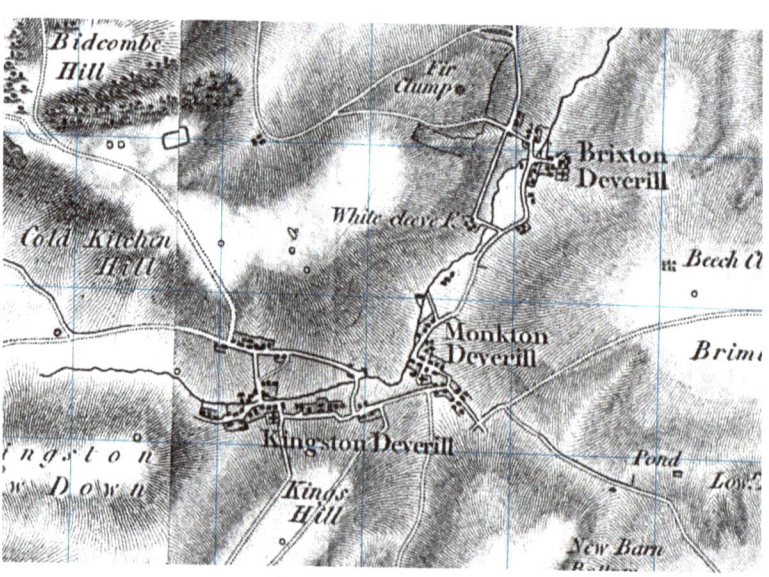

Ordnance Survey Map, 1811

The fork is effectively a right-angle bend and as a result the church appears suddenly and surprisingly as a vivid focal point amongst its enclosure of trees, beneath Cold Kitchen Hill which rises behind. Since the installation of floodlighting at the millennium, this view is enhanced at night, and the sight is so breathtaking that one is tempted to stop and admire, rather than proceeding downwards until the spire on the tower has risen above the horizon formed by the summit of the down.

According to Bishop Osmund's Church Register, dating from 1099, the church was known, at this early point in its history, as the Chapel of St. Andrew, and its patrons were probably members of the Vernon family. Any earlier or pre-14th century information about the building is sadly lacking, possibly due to the destruction by fire of records held at Glastonbury Abbey.

The first registered rector of Kingston Deverill was John Cockerill, who held the post from 1302 until 1334. It might well have been during his incumbency, or that of his successor, William Aldebourne (1334 – 1361) that the medieval church was constructed and dedicated to St. Mary the Virgin – but the dating of either event is uncertain.

The external appearance of this church viewed from the South East, as depicted by J.Buckler in an etching contributed to the edition of the *Gentleman's Magazine* for November 1815 and in two further etchings which appeared in the same paper in 1835, differs surprisingly

The Church in 1835 – south side

The Church in 1835 – north side

little from its appearance today, despite the renovation which was completed in 1847. The 14th century tower with its windows on the middle, upper and lower floors, the buttresses at the four corners, and the short, but delicately tapering spire, is unchanged. The chancel shows minor changes in that a second window has been added, and the roof reshaped, but the central buttress is still there and the medieval stonework is also still in place, matching that of the tower. The main alteration was to the nave, and this involved the partial demolition of the south aisle, the eastern end of which was retained as a side chapel to accommodate the organ and extra pews. This action meant that the entrance porch required to be moved inwards, the slant of the roof adjusted and a narrow parapet inserted above the windows and continued beyond the tower and along the lower edge of the chancel roof to give a homogeneous aspect to the south side of the church. Two windows, one on either side of the porch, were also added, - the porch itself, although moved, retaining its medieval stonework. The nave buttresses were preserved and the only other external alteration was to the two windows whose upper level was now surmounted by arches. In addition, many of the gargoyles and other decorative features of the medieval church were re-distributed around the lower part of the roof of the reconstituted nave, and left where they were on the tower.

For a description of the interior of the church prior to its renovation we are dependent on just one source, the previously mentioned Richard Colt Hoare in his *History of Modern Wiltshire* (1822):

> The church is dedicated to St.Mary. It is a plain edifice built of stone & measures 92 feet L & 16 feet W. In the S side is an aisle or chapel, separated from the nave by 2 pointed arches. There are 6 grotesque heads near the ceiling. The remains of a very rich screen, carved in wood, painted, gilded and ornamented, principally with roses, in 8 square compartments, separates the nave from the chancel. In the chancel on the pavement is inscribed the following record near the altar: 'Brune Berjew 1718, aetat 74; Jane Berjew his w. 18 Jan 1699, aetat 44" [This memorial tablet is still in situ.] On a tablet fixed to the wall on the S side of the altar: - Here underneath resteth the body of Mr.Ludlow Coker, 2nd son of Edmund Coker, rector of this place, d 8 July, age 3, 1704; Elizabeth Obourne, w of Wm Obourne gent, eldest daughter of Edm. Ludlow Coker, rector d. 20 March 1765, aged 73.The font – a simple circular form, of one block of stone, supported by one large central pillar & 4 others of smaller dimensions at the angles.

The incumbency of the 4th rector of St.Mary's, Roger Typell (1375 -1390) coincided with the career of John Wycliffe (c.1330 – 1384) who has been described as 'The Morning Star of the Reformation' as a result of his disputes with the established church and the translation of the Bible from the Latin Vulgate which he and his collaborators completed in 1382. It is unlikely, however, that any hint of the activities of Wycliffe and his followers, the Lollards, would have penetrated to remotest south-west Wiltshire, and certainly neither Roger nor his congregation would have been aware of the existence of a bible in English, since it was immediately proscribed by the authorities.

The earliest definite information about the mediaeval church occurs 150 years later in a 1533 report which mentions that four new bells were hung in the tower. The years which followed were very different from those which encompassed the earlier putative and failed 'reformation' and were probably the most chaotic that the church has ever experienced, involving a multitude of liturgical changes, many of which must have appeared impenetrable to both clergy and laity. In the same year that the new bells were provided for KD church by a Salisbury foundry, Henry VIII defied Pope Clement VII by divorcing his wife Catherine of Aragon, marrying Anne Boleyn and taking on the leadership of the English Church. In these decisions he was opposed by Thomas More (who had been deposed as Lord Chancellor in the previous year) and supported by Archbishop Cranmer and Thomas Cromwell, Henry's new Chancellor. In this capacity and that of Vicar General, Cromwell in 1535 organised visitations of all the country's churches, monasteries and clergy in order to establish the value of their properties and to extract appropriate tax.

Richard Roe, the local Rector from 1516, died on 29th December 1534, and it was his successor Richard Dudd (1534 – 1549) who was present for the KD Visitation of 1536, after which the inspectors reported back as follows:

> Richard Dudd – rector ... the rectory to be of the annual value in land, tithes, oblations and all profits each year, as it appears by the bill of accounts £15. 4s. 4d, out of which the archdeaconry of Wilts at the synod procures 10s 9d. Total £14.14s. 9d. 1 tenth tax: 29s 51/4d'

The most important of the various reformatory changes which took place during this period was undoubtedly the introduction of the Bible in English. The first version, known as the 'Matthew Bible' was printed by John Rogers in 1537, but was immediately supplanted by the 'Great Bible' produced by Miles Coverdale under the auspices of Thomas Cromwell in 1538. Both these works were almost entirely based on the translations accomplished by William Tyndale (c.1494 – 1536) in the 1520s and 1530s. Tyndale had been forced to work abroad, in

THE CHURCH AND THE CLERGY

William Tyndale (1494-1536) by unknown artist oil on canvas, late 17th or early 18th century

Germany and the Netherlands, as a result of determined opposition to the idea of a vernacular version of the Biblical text by senior clergy, and more particularly by Thomas More and the King. He nonetheless completed his translation of the New Testament in 1526 (with a revision in 1529) and it was published in Germany. Any attempt at importing it to England was, however, as fiercely opposed as had been the case with John Wycliffe's 1391 translation, and Tyndale had to keep himself carefully concealed both from Henry's agents operating under the control of Thomas More, and from those employed by the Holy Roman Emperor. Tyndale moved on to the translation of the Old Testament, latterly in cooperation with Miles Coverdale, but failed to complete the work before the authorities caught up with him and he was strangled and his body burnt at the stake in the village of Vilvoorde near Antwerp in 1536. By 1537 Coverdale had completed the translation of the few books of the Old Testament left unfinished as a result of Tyndale's murder, and his name is commemorated in particular by his magnificent version of the Psalms. The fact that Tyndale was responsible for most of the translation had, however, at this point to be concealed from the King, so it was probably for this reason that the first version was given the otherwise curious title of the 'Matthew Bible'. Tyndale's name must surely have been out in the open by the time the Great Bible was produced and nothing was going to prevent Cromwell from distributing this version throughout the country. A copy would, therefore, be duly delivered to Richard Dudd, under the instruction that he should provide ' one book of the Bible of the largest volume in English, and the same set up in some convenient place within the said church that ye have care of, whereas your parishioners may most commodiously resort to the same and read it'.

Just when the 'book' arrived in the village is unknown – it probably took some time – and also unknown, but can be guessed at, is the number of parishioners who – with due respect – were able to read it. There might also have been some opposition to its introduction, both by Richard and his flock, and we can only surmise the problems which arose from an attempt to combine the continuing existence of the Latin Mass with readings from an English bible. Opposition, however, was distinctly muted in southern parts of the country, as compared with the north where violent riots took place in Lincolnshire and Yorkshire in a movement which became known as 'The Pilgrimage of Grace'. The participants took exception to the possible sequestration of their church treasures and to Cranmer's '10 Articles' which were seen as a forewarning of creeping Protestantism and a veering towards Lutheran beliefs. The rioters were brutally put down, and more than 200 executed. The position of the clergy became temporarily more comfortable however in 1539 when the king published his 'Six Articles' which indicated his support of a return to the major tenets of the Catholic faith, especially in regard to a belief in transubstantiation, clerical celibacy and the importance of confession. Whatever the confusion caused by the myriad injunctions descending from London concerning religious observance, there is no doubt that Richard Dudd, in common with members of the clergy throughout the country would have complied with Cromwell's 1537 edict that he should ' keep one book or register, wherein ye shall write the day and year of every wedding, christening and burying, made within your parish for your time'. The continued existence of the Parish Registers, an invaluable historical source, is perhaps the greatest legacy of Cromwell's tenure of the post of Vicar General.

But the rector would have been up against it once again with the death of Henry VIII in 1547, and the succession of his young son Edward VI who was very much under the intense protestant influence of his chief advisor Protector Somerset (who we have met earlier) and of Archbishop Cranmer. Within a few years – give or take the time which

THE CHURCH AND THE CLERGY

would elapse before the book arrived – the KD congregation would be faced with the acceptance or otherwise of the first edition of Cranmer's 'Book of Common Prayer' (1549) which aimed to replace all aspects of the Latin Mass with services in English for all occasions – Morning and Evening Prayer, Holy Communion and the Litany, together with orders for baptisms, marriages and funerals, specified readings from the Old and New Testament, Collects to be read before the Gospel and Psalms to be sung or read on a daily basis throughout the year. Inspections for compliance inevitably followed, and for the first of these, in 1550, we actually have a manuscript record: '1550. Thomas Tryncelle, rector. John Batte, curate. Cuthbert Michell, John Barnard, William Hurle, Cuthbert Michaell, John Freestone, John Lokyer, parishioners which presented all things to be well in that parish'. Following a revision of the Prayer Book in 1552, another inspection took place: '1553, Dom Thomas Tryngull, rector, dom William Nettulton, curate, William Clove, Henry Batt, churchwardens; Robert Rose, Robert French, parishioners. They present the chancel to be in decay; the quarter sermons be not kept or else all is well; the church stock is 26s 8d; 8 sheep remain in the hands of Richard Barnard'. Liturgical considerations apart we have here the names of lay people living in the village in the mid 16th century (many of whose families continued here, as will be seen, in later centuries) together with named churchwardens, upon whom the present incumbents can look back over a period of 460 years. Also around this time an inventory of church treasures was drawn up on the basis of instructions received from the Privy Council, and KD church revealed that it possessed '16 cups or chalices, 4 bells – 16 (in plate for the King's use)'. Since this information pre-dates the installation of 4 bells in the tower in 1555, it is evident that the church had the wherewithal to replace bells which had been hung only 22 years earlier.

But the vicissitudes which accompanied Thomas Drinkell's tenure of office as Rector (1549-62) were not yet over, though we lack the details. Suffice it to say that the month of July 1553 must represent one of the two most confused and fearful periods in the history of the church, the other being the Civil War. On the 6th of that month the dedicated protestant King Edward VI died at the tragically early age of

15, to be succeeded for a mere nine days by the equally unfortunate Lady Jane Grey, who in turn was succeeded on 24th July by the virulently Catholic 'Bloody Mary'. Once these various items of news had filtered down from the capital to remotest south-west Wiltshire, what exactly happened at the church up the road? Did Thomas immediately restore the full Latin Mass, and what were his thoughts when he heard that Cranmer, the author of the recently promulgated services in English, was martyred in Oxford on 21st March 1556? We shall never know the answers, but what we do know is that Thomas survived all these tribulations and came out the other side into the Elizabethan era, dying in 1562.

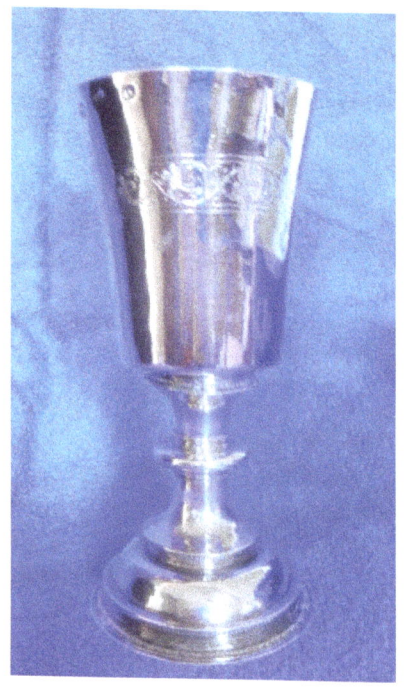

The 1578 Chalice

Apart from the names of the rectors – and the fact that a beautiful chalice with the monogram 'KD' on its base and still in existence, was donated in 1578 - few details about the church have come down to us for the following 70 years, although it is worth noting that one of the incumbents, Edmund Lillie, who was in charge of the parish between 1576 and 1589, went on to higher things. He was already a fellow of Magdalen College, Oxford before he arrived at KD, and then became Chancellor of Oxford University between 1585 and 1593 and Master of Balliol College from 1580 until his death in 1610.

During the incumbency of Edmund Lillie's successor, Guy Clinton (1589 – 1616), KD church would have been presented with copies of the Authorised Version of the Bible which appeared during the reign of James 1st in 1611. This bible was conceived in 1604 and the translation was undertaken by 47 scholars divided into 3 'companies' and 6 'committees', the companies being made up of divines from

THE CHURCH AND THE CLERGY

Westminster, Cambridge and Oxford. Thus there was a 1st and 2nd 'Westminster Committee' etc. each led by an eminent theologian -the most prominent of whom was Lancelot Andrewes, Bishop of Winchester- and these committees were given specific parts of the bible to translate, the results of each translator being compared and analysed. Their main sources were the earlier Matthews, Geneva, Great and Bishops Bibles (the latter published in 1568) and the differences between the Greek, Hebrew, Aramaic and Latin versions of the texts were minutely studied. Despite –or perhaps because of – the extreme diligence of the translators, modern scholars have established that the 1611 Authorised Version is- given minor changes and corrections and a modernisation of some spellings- very largely derived from the work of William Tyndale, to the extent that 83% of the New Testament and 76% of the Old Testament is effectively his. So in so far as Thomas Newland and his parishioners made use of it – and there was no mandate for this – they would be unaware of many differences from the bible translation that had been in their hands for the past 50 years.

Thomas Newland (1617-1647), found himself in a spot of bother in 1636 when the Archdeacon of Sarum, Thomas Marler -under instruction from the Bishop of Salisbury, John Davenant (1621-1641)- took action against the KD churchwardens for failing to report that their parishioners had taken part in a football match on a specific 'holy day', and brought them to court. The Archdeacon of Sarum Act Book reference dated 12th November 1636 indicates that the action taken against them was

> for neglecting to present a football match upon Ascension Day before morning prayer about 4 years since in the time of their churchwardenship. [*Court told*] that true it is there was a football match played at that time in their parish, and Peter Hurle one of the churchwardens confessed that he was at it himself, but John Watts the other churchwarden affirmed that he was not there but was at home at morning prayer. And they farther confessed that they neglected to present it, but they say they informed Mr Newland their minister thereof and desired him to join with them in that presentment which he refused.

The churchwardens were then required to produce a list of the names of all the villagers who had 'profaned' Ascension Day and to bring this information to the next court. Unfortunately the records of this subsequent court make no mention of the KD football drama, with the result that we are unable to name the team or teams involved or the numbers of the participants- 11- a- side, 6-a-side or simply an indeterminate rabble. It is interesting that the churchwardens attempted to exonerate themselves by accusing the minister of not being prepared to go along with them when they suggested that the footballing misdemeanour should be reported to the authorities. Perhaps this indicates that Newland was a free-thinker as far as downland leisure pursuits were concerned, and was prepared to turn his back on diktats from the diocese. In any event he retained his job for another 11 years and it may have been because of an unrecorded intervention which he made with the court that no further action was taken. (Incidentally, the churchwarden Peter Hurle was the father-in-law of Eleanor Hurle whose generous bequest to the parish is described later).

During the Civil War the KD incumbent was Thomas Aylesbury. He was appointed in 1643, but when the royalist forces were defeated he was deposed from the living and was forced into retirement at Cloford in Somerset. He returned with the Restoration in 1660, but died the following year. Apart from his deposition and the inevitable interruption to services at the church, the only notable event which we are aware of at this time is the mooted amalgamation of the three parish churches of KD, BD and MD in 1649. This idea was shortly afterwards discarded and was not revived until 1939 when the parishes were duly combined.

The incumbency of Thomas Aylesbury's successor, John Berjew, coincided with the introduction of the revised version of the Book of Common Prayer in 1662. This revision was undertaken as a result of the Savoy Conference of 1661 when chosen members of both the Anglican and the Nonconformist churches met in order to establish an agreed liturgy. Suggestions for major alterations to the 1552 Prayer Book by the Nonconformists were brusquely rejected, and when the 'revision' was published, virtually the whole of Cranmer's wording

THE CHURCH AND THE CLERGY

was retained, with the exception of the Psalms which now appeared in the translation by Miles Coverdale. The immediate result of this decision and the subsequent 'Clarendon Code' (so-called because it was instituted by Edward Hyde, Duke of Clarendon, Charles 11's Chancellor of the Exchequer) was the resignation of upwards of 2000 members of the clergy and a permanent breakaway of those who lent towards 'non-conformity'. In fact the term 'nonconformist' derived from the tenets of the Code which incorporated four separate 'acts', and which determined the effects of non-compliance on the opponents of the liturgy. The first of these was the 'Corporation Act' (1661) which forbade such opponents from holding any significant civil office; the second was the Act of Uniformity (1662) which attempted to confine worship of any kind to the strict use of the Book of Common Prayer; the third was the 'Conventicle Act' which aimed to reduce the numbers of dissenting worshippers to no more than 5 in any one place, and the fourth was the 'Five-Mile Act' which effectively exiled nonconformist clergy to that distance from any town or their former place of ministry. The problems which arose as a result of these injunctions were disastrous for the majority of nonconformists at this time, but from the point of view of posterity the attendant imprisonment of John Bunyan in Bedford brought about the production of 'Pilgrim's Progress'- as shining an example of English prose and as vivid a projection of the Christian message as it is possible to imagine.

John Berjew MA, was obviously unaffected by any of these machinations – and it is fairly certain that few of his parishioners were either, if one is to judge by the future lack of success of nonconformity in the immediate area, (although it was later a very different matter in Horningsham and in the west Wiltshire towns to the north.) The rector died in 1688, but resigned his living in 1682 when Edmund Ludlow Coker took over, having been previously a curate at Hill Deverill, where he was born. Edmund was presumably a scion of the Ludlow family who owned HD and KD manors, and the splendidly carved Bishop's Chair which is still in situ and which is dated 1682 in Roman numerals was probably donated by the Ludlow family to mark his incumbency. Another of the church's treasures, a silver chalice, also still in existence, is dated 1681, and is marked with the monogram 'MD' on its base – indicating that it came from Monkton Deverill when the church there closed in 1970. Also in 1682 the church received a gift of a silver paten, inscribed 'ex dono MB', and probably commemorating a member of the Berjew family The beautiful carved Flemish pulpit is also of 17th century date, although the time of its acquisition is unknown.

The year 1685 marked the death of Charles 11 and the accession of the Catholic James 11, these events heralding a significant rapprochement between the Anglican and Nonconformist community in the face of the mutual 'papist enemy', encapsulated locally by the Arundel family down the road at Wardour, and more closely at Bonham in Stourton. Following the defeat of James, and the 'Glorious Revolution' which heralded the arrival on the throne of William and Mary, this better understanding of liturgical differences resulted in the Act of Toleration of 1689 which gave freedom of worship to all nonconformist communities.

The Bishop's Chair, 1682

The previous year, 1688, marked an event which has had continued reverberations for the KD community down the centuries. This was a bequest of a sum of money by a wealthy resident, Eleanor Hurle, for the benefit in perpetuity of the poor of the parish. The Hurle family had lived in the village since at least the mid-16th century (a William Hurle appears, as has been seen, as a signatory to an Inspection document in 1550, and is also mentioned in a tax return for 1545) and they remained in the village until well into the 19th century when they maintained a freehold property in an area otherwise almost entirely

THE CHURCH AND THE CLERGY

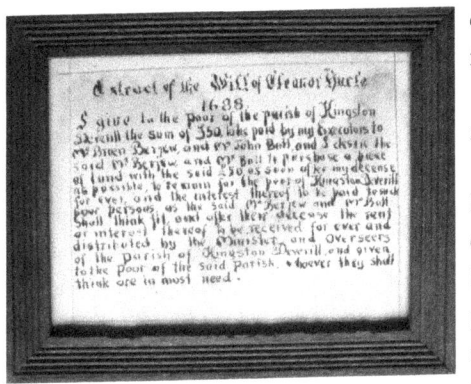

Manuscript of Eleanor Hurle Bequest, 1688

owned by the Thynne family at Longleat.

Eleanor's bequest reads as follows:

Item, I give to the poor of the Parish of Kingston Deverill the sum of fifty pounds to be paid to my Executors within six months after my decease unto Mr Bruen Berjew of Kingston Deverill aforesaid and Mr John Batt of Monkton Deverill in trust and for the only use of the poor of Kingston Deverill, and I desire the said Mr Bruen Berjew and Mr John Batt to purchase a piece of land with the said fifty pounds as soon after my decease as possible to remain for the poor of Kingston Deverill for ever and in the meantime the said fifty pounds to be putt out to use and the interest thereof to be paid to such poor persons as the said Mr Berjew and Mr Batt shall think fit and after their decease the rent or interest thereof to be received for ever and distributed by the Minister and Overseers of the poor of the parish of Kingston Deverill amongst the Poor of the said parish where they shall think most fit.

The subsequent history of the Hurle Bequest is best related in the words of Richard Stratton, who was treasurer of the charity when he wrote the following brief essay in 1982:

In the event, the two gentlemen purchased two separate fields in Mere Parish, three acres altogether. The £50 would still have bought them in 1931. In 1886 the land was in the tenancy of Mr. Chas Lander at a rent of £4 per annum. From that date the rent was raised to £5 per annum until 1879 when the trustees endeavoured to negotiate a sale of property and £270 was offered for it, but subsequently withdrawn.

And the trustees leased the property to Mr. Lander for the term of 10 years at a rental of £7 per annum, tenant to pay all charges. Mr. Lander continued the tenancy until Sep. 29th 1893 when Mr. Edward Gatehouse of Burton, Mere, was accepted as yearly tenant at £7 per annum paying all charges as before.

The rent continued at this figure for years and by the end of the Second World War had only reached £9 a year. Until 1920 cash was distributed. In 1868 12 men over 60 years received 3/- each, 29 over 30 received 2/- each. Names are faithfully recorded over the years. The change to coal was made in 1921 when 32 people shared 68 cwt. at a cost of £18, 8/3 in all. In 1926 a note of my father says 'Coal very dear as a result of coal strike' and only 3 ½ tons was bought (at 57/6 per ton). By 1927 the same money bought 5 ½ tons for 32 recipients. The price of coal delivered in 1939 was £2 per ton and £4 at the end of the war.

In 1975, with the annual rent as a result of much pressure at £17, the Trustees were authorised by the Charity Commissioners to sell the two fields to the tenants for £1700. With the proceeds invested in Government Stock, income increased overnight to £238 a year where it remains. Surely there is food for thought in these figures over the years. Nowadays the charity money is used to reduce the electricity bills during the winter months of those residents over 70 years old or those prevented by disability from doing a full day's work. The Trustees are the Rector [Michael Hinton], Miss Maitland-Makgill-Crichton and myself.

At the time of writing, 34 years after the above description and 328 years after Eleanor Hurle's original bequest, money is still distributed as required – a tribute to the efforts of the Trustees over the centuries.

In 1704 the church was given a second silver paten inscribed to the memory of 'Mary Curtis, widow'. In the following year -the penultimate of Edmund Ludlow Coker's ministry -we have the first description of the rectory building and its surrounding properties drawn up in a Glebe Terrier dated 3rd February –

A dwelling house, with hall kitchen and brewhouse, 2 butteries, 1 milkhouse, 6 chambers, 1 malt loft and 3 garrets, 1 porch with little room over it with garden adjoining on S. of the hall, and a little strip of land on S. of the house, a little garden plot at E. end of the brewhouse. A barn of 13 bays of building. A wagon house. A stable with a barton adjoining.

Arable land in the common fields: 3a. in the Churchfield abutting upon Mere way bounded lands of Hon. Henry Thynne esq., E. and W. 2a. at Kingshill 1 lying E. and W. abutting on the way to Monkton Cow down bounded 1a. of William Kiddel N. ½ a. of William Kiddel S; 1a. in the same field lying N. and S. bounded 1a. of Bodinghams farm by the way side that leads to Monkton Cow down E., 1a. of Blackhall W. 3a. in a field called Piscom lyong E. and W. bounded by ½ a. of William Phillips N., ½ a. of Mary Curtice S. 1a. at Townsend lying N. and S. bounded 1a. of Thomas Ryal E., ½ a. of William Phillips W. 1 little cottage adjoining bounded a garden of Richard Gerrat E., a garden of Peter Trimby W. and abutting against Blackhall close. 1a. under Cilden lying N. and S. abutting on Townsend way bounded with an a. of Blackhall E. and with 2a. of Bodinghams farm W. 1a. above Rowlench lying N. and s. abutting on the Broches bounded with an a. of Blackhall on e. and ½ a. of Michael Humphry W. 1a. in Longslade lying N. and S. abutting on the Broches bounded with an a. of Blackhall W. and an a. of Blachall E. 4 ½ a. in a field called Cocknell whereof 2a. lies N. and S. bounded with an a. of Mary Curtice E. and 2a. of Chas Blake W. 1a. on the top of Cocknell lying N. and S. abutting on the way from Bradley to Kingston bounded with an a. of Deborah Leversedge E. 1head ½ a. lying E. and w. bounded with an a. of Blackhall N. and the lands of Margery Hurle and Roger Curtice S. 1 ½ a. in a field called Hiscomb, the ½ a. lying E. and W. bounded with ½ a. of Brune Berjew on N. and the footpath that leads to Markham on S. 1a. in Hiscomb Field lying E. and w. abutting up against Hiscomb paddock bounded with an a. of Brune Berjew S. and with ½ a. of Thomas Ryall W. 1 little plot of coppice on the top of Bitcomb hill in Hill Deverill bounded with a sheep down of Mr. Ephraim Westly E. and with the sheepdown of Little Horningsham farm W.

Signed Edmund Ludlow Coker, rector, Brune Berjew, William Liddill, churchwardens.

The extent of the land owned by KD church as indicated by this document is quite extraordinary, as is the detailed manner in which the information is drawn up. Many of the field names mentioned are still in existence and the family surnames of a number of residents who are noted as landowners reappear well into the 20th century. It can also be readily imagined that someone skilled in the legalese of the period and with a reasonable cartographic knowledge of the area could produce a highly detailed map of the village as it stood in 1705 as a result of the information provided.

Edmund Ludlow Coker died in 1706 and was succeeded by John Drew (1706 – 1727), a local man, born in Stourton, who combined the living of KD with Stourton and Gasper. During his incumbency the church received a third silver paten, inscribed 'ex dono Rachel Berjew 1711' – Rachel being the widow of John Berjew, the earlier rector, and whose name we have already encountered on the memorial tablet on the southern exterior wall of the church, near the tower. The maker of the paten was Edward Aldridge.

During the incumbencies of Edmund Ludlow Coker and John Drew the eminent divine Thomas Ken -who had lost the bishopric of Bath and Wells as a result of his failure to sign the oath of allegiance to the new king, William of Orange- was residing nearby at Longleat, having been given shelter by Thomas

Bishop Thomas Ken (1637-1711) by F. Scheffer

Thynne, 1st Viscount Weymouth. It would be good to think that the rectors might have been able to make some sort of contact with him, but the bishop was highly reclusive and devoted himself to writing, and in particular to the production of hymns at a time when the singing of metric psalms in parish churches was all-pervasive. Perhaps it would be not too long before the KD congregation were raising the roof with 'Awake my soul, and with the sun' or 'Glory to Thee, my God, this night' –hymns which are universally current today.

    Edmund was followed in the ministry by Benjamin Coker (1728 – 1742) who was responsible for replacing the 1555 bells with 6 new ones in 1731.

These bells were forged at the bell foundry of William Cockey in Frome, and their specification as to diameter measurement, weight and tuning, together with the inscription on each is as follows:

> Tenor 43 in 13 ¾ cwt. F# 'Wm. Cockey , Bell Founder 1731'
> Fifth 39 in 11 cwt. G# 'God Preseve the Church 1731'
> Fourth 36 in 8 ½ cwt. A# 'Wm. Cockey, Bell Founder 1731'
> Third 34 in 7 ½ cwt. B 'Mr Robert HURLE 7 Mr Robert
>   RYALL 1731'
> Second 32 in 6 ¾ cwt. C# 'Peace and Good Neighbourhood 1731'
> Treble 29 in 5 ½ cwt. D# 'the Rev. Mr Benjamin Coker A.M. Rector
>   Mr Robert Hurle & Mr Robert Ryall
>   Churchwardens 1731'

Sadly the state of the bell-chamber in the tower and the condition of the bells themselves means that they can no longer by 'swung', although the provision of small clappers enables them to be chimed, given that someone is prepared for a climb in order to put this into effect. In 1997 the PCC decided to ask Nicholson Engineering of Bridport to assess the damage to the bells and to prepare an estimate for their repair and whatever was required by way of reconstruction of the bell chamber, but the resulting request for £35,336 was unsurprisingly too steep to be considered. Today the asking price would be considerably more, unless – as is a possibility – the estimated cost of strengthening the tower was exaggerated.

The Third Bell (1731)

The Bell Mechanism

Whilst on the subject of bells, a schoolchildren's rhyme has come down to us, doubtless from a much later date, and it runs as follows:

Kingston says: 'which bells ring the best?'
Monkton says: 'we do, we do!'
Brixton says: 'liar, liar!'

Benjamin Coker died in 1742 and was succeeded by Thomas Howe, who rather surprisingly had acquired an MA from Aberdeen University, before moving on to obtain a further degree at Christ's College, Cambridge. He was not Scottish, but was the third son of Baron Chedworth who lived in Gloucestershire. Perhaps his presence in KD could be accounted for by a connection between the Chedworths and the Ludlows. He married Frances White of Tattington Place, Suffolk and combined the living of KD with that of Great Wishford, where he died in 1770. During part of his ministry he was assisted by a curate, Edward Burnett, who later became rector of Walton Chapel, Street.

Of much greater fame as far as the history of KD church is concerned is the incumbency of the next rector, the splendidly named Millington Massey (1770 -1808). Massey was born in Cheshire and was remotely related to the owners of Dunham Massey, a 17th century house near Altrincham, now run by the National Trust - the Massey family being the original owners in the 14th century. He graduated from St John's College, Cambridge with an MA and BD, and possibly as a result of his aristocratic connections, was appointed Chaplain to Viscount Weymouth at Longleat in 1768, a post which he held until 1783. His first job as rector was at Corsley (1768 -1774), combining this post with KD from 1770 and with Warminster from 1773. He obviously needed some help and this was provided by two successive curates - William Slade (a BA of Queen's College, Oxford who held the curacy of both KD and BD), and John Davis. As previously indicated, the most notable action which Massey undertook during his period of office was the removal of the standing stones from Court Hill to the ford in the Deverill river. This arduous task - the stones were very heavy - was undertaken at some point in the 1790s, but its purpose is unclear, unless Massey felt that the stones stood in the way of cultivation on a part of the Church property. The idea that they were somehow less likely to be damaged down by the ford can be discounted since they were used in that position for many years as stepping stones, and there was a threat at one time that they might be broken up for use in road making.

Another 'Glebe Terrier' document was drawn up on 29th July 1783, the wording of which is as follows:

> The Parsonage is built of stone and tiled. It contains a cellar, 6 rooms on the first floor, all of which are ceiled except one; 5 rooms on the second floor all ceiled. 2 dark garrets not ceiled. The walls are mostly plastered and white washed. A small brewhouse, a stable for 7 horses, a large barn containing two threshing floors, 1 for wheat, the other for spring corn. A carthouse and a pigsty. The glebe is undefinable at present. An Act of Parliament past last year by virtue of which the estates in this parish are to be exonerated from tithes by an allotment of glebe land. The award is not yet made, when it is made and a plan annexed, there will be a perfect terrier of the glebe. The tithes will be extinct. There are no pensions to or from the minister. There is no church impropriate in this parish. There is a pulpit cloth and cushion, 6 bells, a silver cup for the communion containing a pint, 2 small silver dishes, or plates, the one with the inscription 'Ex dono Rachel Berjew 1711' the other 'Mary Curtis wid. 1704' and a pewter chalice containing 3 pints.
>
> There are no lands or money in stock for repairs of the Church or writings concerning the same. The parishioners repair the church, the rector repairs the chancel, the parishioners repair 3 sides of the churchyard fence viz. E.S.and W. sides and the owner of land on N. has usually repaired the n. fence. Whether the land on the N. will be charged with the fence will depend upon the commissioners' award. The clerk is sexton. His wages are 40s p.a. paid by the churchwardens besides Easter offerings. He is paid likewise for graves and knells. He is appointed by the minister.
>
> Signed: Millington Massey, rector, William Slade, John Knight, churchwardens.

THE CHURCH AND THE CLERGY

There are three names in this document which are worthy of note. Rachel Berjew may or may not be the lady who is commemorated on a tablet which is now attached to the exterior wall at the eastern end of the south aisle next to the tower, the only question being that she died in 1699 and the paten was donated in 1711. What is certain is that the Rachel Berjew who is commemorated was the daughter of John Berjew, the rector who died in 1682. William Slade is here a churchwarden and becomes a curate several years later in 1797 – perhaps an unusual progression. Mary Curtis is mentioned in the earlier Glebe Terrier of 1705 as an owner of land and may be considered as one of the wealthier parishioners.

Just who was occupying 'the Parsonage' in the latter years of the 18th century and the early 19th century is unknown since Millington Massey took himself off to Warminster where he died in 1808 and was given a memorial tablet in the Minster. During his ministry the Bishop of Salisbury, Shute Barrington, issued in 1783 a questionnaire to all the parishes in the diocese asking for comprehensive details of how each church was run. The 'Visitation Returns' which resulted sadly do not include a response from KD, since Massey was either too preoccupied with his duties at Warminster and at MD (he also held the curacy of 'the chapel of ease' there), or perhaps too idle to complete the 20 answers required.

The history of KD church does not reveal anything of particular interest during the incumbencies of the next three rectors - Charles Philott (1808-1813), Josiah Thomas (1813 – 1820) or Henry Bridgeman (1820 – 1823) although in 1817, in Josiah's time, the beautifully carved chair which sits next to the organ opposite

Bishop Shute Barrington (1734-1826)

Lord John Thynne (1798-1881)

the 1682 chair was installed by an unknown donor. (In that same year it is interestingly recorded that Thomas Heathcote, the curate, received 'a stipend of £60 and all surplice fees' and that he requested that he be 'permitted to reside at LD, as the Kingston parsonage house is unfit'. Whether Henry Bridgeman later shared this view of his local accommodation is unknown, but since he combined the rectorship with the archdeaconry of Bath, perhaps he had more comfortable quarters elsewhere. In any event, there is a memorial to him and his wife Louisa in the church).

A new era dawned with the arrival of Lord John Thynne as rector

Thomas Thynne 3rd Viscount Weymouth/1st Marquess of Bath (1739-1796)

in 1823, and at this point it is relevant to explain what had happened to the Thynne family since we last met them. Thomas Thynne (1640 – 1714) had gone up in the world after the Restoration and was appointed 1st Viscount Weymouth in 1682. He was succeeded by his great nephew, whose son Thomas became the 3rd Viscount (1734 – 1796). In 1747 the Thynne family took over the Manor of KD from the Ludlows, and from that date the village came under the patronage of Longleat. The 3rd Viscount was further elevated as 1st Marquis of Bath in 1789.

John Thynne was officially the rector of KD from 1823 to 1837, but just how much time he spent in the parish is an open question. In the same year as his appointment to the incumbency he became sub-dean of Lincoln Cathedral and in 1836 he rose to a similar position at Westminster Abbey, retiring in 1881 and subsequently receiving the honour of burial in the Abbey Cloisters in 1888. No fewer than four curates looked after the village church during his absence – James Downe in 1824, Joseph Griffith in 1825, John Brigstock in 1831 and William Gale in the following year.

What is particularly relevant to the history of the church in this period is the development of the 'Oxford' or 'Tractarian' movement which began with the publication of a series of tracts at Oxford University in 1833 and blossomed over the next few years into a fully-blown Anglo- Catholicism which, despite widespread opposition, revitalised the Anglican Church. Its primary movers were John Keble, Edward Pusey and John Henry Newman and these eloquent and influential high churchmen recommended that the church should employ a more 'catholic' or formal adherence to the liturgy, that services should be less 'plain' and more 'ceremonial' and that much of the 'colour' of pre-Reformation Catholic practices such as the use of vestments and incense should be restored. These new ideas appealed to many – and in particular to the more conservative aristocratic patrons of country churches. It is therefore significant that on Lord John Thynne's retirement as rector, his successor should be his brother Lord Charles (8th son of the 2nd Marquess) and that the opportunity arose for his family to support the revitalisation of KD church in common with a countrywide view that now was the moment for the Anglican communion to step forward with renewed confidence.

This was exemplified in KD by the action taken by the Marchioness of Bath,[1] once she had taken account of a presumed complaint put forward by her brother-in-law to the effect that he took exception to holding services and preaching in a church with crumbling walls, no heating and a leaking roof. Contact was made with the architects Manners and Gill of Bath, and work started on the rebuilding

---

1 It should be explained that the Marchioness was now running the Longleat Estate during the minority of her son, John Alexander, the 4th Marquess, who was only six when both his grandfather and his father died in the same year, 1837.

The Hon. Harriet Baring, 3rd Marchioness of Bath (1804-1892)

of the church in the spring of 1845. The contractual details for the reconstruction were summarised later by Harriet Bath as follows:

> Agreement with regard to the rebuilding of the Parish Church of Kingston Deverill in the County of Wilts
>
> We the undersigned do hereby guarantee and promise to the Parish of Kingston Deverill in the County of Wilts or their officers the Church

Wardens for the time being (of the said Parish) that on their paying or causing to be paid to us or to our bankers Messrs.Stuckey & Co. of Frome in the County of Somerset, on account of the Kingston Deverill Church Building fund – the sum of One Hundred and fifty pounds sterling (150£). We will & do hereby undertake to pay and discharge, all and every expense which shall be incurred, in the alterations, restorations and repairs, now about to be undertaken & engaged in at and upon the Parish Church of Kingston Deverill aforesaid (including the Bounds and Church yard of the said Church) – according to the plans and specifications of Messrs. Manners and Gill, architects Bath - & contracted for by Mr. Brown, Builder, Frome- up to the time of the completion of the said works as specified in the said contract – viz June 24 1847.

And we in case of our deaths do hereby bind our Executors, Adminstrators & Appointees to complete the said works out of monies which may be lying in Messrs. Stuckley's hands –to account of Kingston Church building fund- or if there be no such monies or fund remaining – then out of our private estate and effects, so that the Parish of Kingston Deverill shall be at no further charge than the above sum of one hundred and fifty pounds, on account of the above-named works. Witness our hands this 29 day of June in the year of our Lord 1846. Harriet Bath. D.M Clerk, Rector Kingston Deverill.

However, it is evident from a 'Proclamation' sent to the rector from the Vicar General of the Diocese on 20th November 1846, that both David Clerk and the Marchioness had jumped the gun in an embarrassing manner for failing to seek in advance the permission for the demolition and reconstruction of the church from the Bishop of Salisbury. Effectively the proclamation gives retrospective permission for the work, but it is perhaps fortunate for the parish that the highly influential patronage of Longleat was involved. Before writing his letter, the Vicar General must have pointed out to the rector the error of his ways, as the preceding 'Petition' (in arrears) indicates:

> To the Right Reverend Father in God Edward [*Edward Denison – Bishop 1837 – 1854*] by Divine Permission Lord Bishop of Sarum his

Vicar General and Official Principal Surrogate or any other persons having or to have sufficient authority in this behalf, The Humble Petition of the Rector Churchwardens and other Inhabitants of the Parish of Kingston Deverill and your Lordship's Diocese of Sarum Humbly Sheweth: that the parish church of Kingston Deverill aforesaid having been ascertained by the Survey and from the report of an experienced Architect (with the exception of the Tower) in a dangerous and insecure state, and the said Church having been also found to be inadequate to the accommodation of the present population of the said Parish, a Vestry Meeting was on the 16th day of April last (One thousand eight hundred and forty-six) duly holden in and for the said parish for the purpose of considering what measures should be taken in respect of the said Church. That at such meeting it was by the persons there assembled resolved that the sum of one hundred and fifty pounds should be raised by Church Rates within the parish towards rebuilding of the said Church as far as might be found necessary, and your Petitioner the said Rector thereupon undertook to indemnify the parishioners from all further cost therein and to provide from other sources the amount which should be required. That in pursuance of such resolution the said church has been wholly taken down and removed and in lieu thereof a durable and substantial church is being erected and fitted on the same site and upon adjacent portions of the Churchyard according to the plans and elevations hereunto annexed marked respectively A, B and C. That the total estimated cost of the said work is One thousand, nine hundred pounds or thereabouts, of which sum One hundred pounds have been granted by the Diocesan Church Building Society, One hundred and fifty pounds will be raised by Church Rates and fifteen pounds have been raised by voluntary contributions – that your Petitioner the said Rector has undertaken to defray the expenses attending the erection of the Chancel and the remainder will be provided by the family of the Marquis of Bath, (the Patron) aided by an expectant grant from the Incorporated Society of Building Churches, and other sources. The said church is to be furnished with seats and sittings capable of accommodating one hundred and thirty persons, of which number one hundred and ten are to be free and unappropriated for ever, and

eighty-eight appropriated to children attending the Sunday School. Your Petitioners having omitted to obtain as in duty bound your Lordship's Licence and Faculty in the premises – your Petitioners therefore humbly pray that your Lorsdhip will be pleased to grant your Licence or Faculty confirming the taking down the said church (with the exception of the Tower) and the rebuilding the same in manner hereintofore set forth and according to the said plans and drawings.
D.M Clerk, Rector. James Compton, William Weaver, Churchwardens.
13 November 1846.

As well as admitting an 'omission' in failing to approach the diocese and indicating that the demolition of the church was a fait accompli, the 'Petition' gives chapter and verse as to the source of funds, the estimated total cost, the reasons for the need for reconstruction, and provides detailed architectural plans. (See Appendix C) . The answering 'Proclamation' received from the Vicar General, Robert Phillimore, one week later simply repeats the means and aims set out in the Petition by David Clerk and grants the licence whilst emphasizing that 'the said Rector, and the Churchwardens and other Inhabitants of the said Parish omitted to obtain, as in duty bound, our License and Faculty in the premises'. Phillimore also goes on to state that he is granting the licence on the condition that 'our so doing would not be in the least detrimental, prejudicial or inconvenient to the inhabitants of the said parish' – a bit difficult to accomplish, one would imagine, in the circumstance of the church having already been demolished. The Rector is then enjoined to 'affix a true and authentic copy of the licence on or near the principal door of the church aforesaid' – again rather tricky in the door's absence – 'and a further true and authentic copy on or near to the principal door of the School Room ... before the time of divine service in the forenoon of Sunday the twenty-second day of this present month of November-' (where was the service to be held? Hardly in the open air at this time of year)- 'and admonish James Compton and William Weaver, Churchwardens of this same parish.... to appear before us ... in the Cathedral Church of Sarum between the hours of nine and twelve on the twenty-fifth day of the month... in order to witness the granting of the licence.'

Perhaps because he felt that he had behaved irresponsibly, or more likely because he was acting out of pure generosity, one of the 'admonished' churchwardens, William Weaver (a wealthy farmer who had arrived in the village to take

Gargoyle on church tower

on the tenancy of Manor Farm in the 1840s) donated no less than half the figure requested by the Marchioness as an initial payment for the rebuilding of the church – as is attested by a receipt signed by David Clerk on 30th January 1847. All the other expected donations were received in due time and the reconstruction was completed by the end of the same year.

Although the outward appearance of the restored church had changed very little from its mediaeval antecedent, closer inspection would reveal that the quality of the replacement stonework was inferior to

The 17th-century Pulpit

that of the tower, whilst retaining a similarity of colour. The changes to the interior were considerable, however, as can be noted from the 1822 description of the church by Richard Colt Hoare given earlier, although the two chairs and the 17th century pulpit already mentioned were retained, as was much of the mediaeval flooring, including a number of 'coffin lids' dedicated to past rectors, and a very

Altar Coffin Lid – with list of clergy

much earlier incised cross at the entrance to the church. There is no doubting the quality of the replacement furnishing, since the pews and the roof indicate that expert carpenters were involved (one of them being a local man, James Maxfield, who in 1845 sent a bill for £6 1s 11d to the churchwardens in which he lists, amongst other things, work on window and bell frames and the replacement of the 'wicket gate'). Similarly, the loss of the mediaeval glass is amply compensated for by the splendid stained-glass windows in the chancel, designed and installed in 1847 by the firm of William Wailes of Newcastle. Wailes (1808-1881) had learnt his trade in Germany and his work received widespread recognition as he was employed to produce windows for

THE CHURCH AND THE CLERGY

The East window

restored churches throughout the country, amongst the most notable of which are the West Window of Gloucester Cathedral and the Rose Window at St. Matthias Church, Richmond.

The glass of the west window is clear, with the exception of a 'roundel' at the top in which has been inserted an imported panel

The West window – late 15th-century glass

of German origin, dating from *c*.1450. This depicts Christ washing the feet of St. Peter, with the other eleven disciples gathered around him. The decorative elements surrounding the grisaille depiction of the disciples are 19th century and are based on 14th-century designs which also appear in the 20th-century porch lantern. Almost invisible from below is an inscription which reads 'Peter Kanengisser', and it has only recently been established just who this gentleman was, and whether or not he was the 'patron' who commissioned the glass. It turns out that he was one of the leading textile merchants in Cologne in the 15th century, and that he and his family were particularly associated with the Benedictine monastery of St Agatha in Cologne whence the panel originated, with the name inscribed below. Along

THE CHURCH AND THE CLERGY

with other churches in the Rhineland, the monastery was suppressed following the Peace of Amiens in 1802, and many artefacts appeared thereafter at various auctions in London and elsewhere. It is possible that an agent of the 2nd Marquess of Bath attended one of these sales, and as a result the 'Kanengisser panel' was conveyed to Longleat and subsequently to the restored KD church.

The rediscovered Saxon font and recumbent effigy were added to the internal furnishings. There was also a new organ, purchased prior to the rebuilding, as the following receipt indicates:

The Saxon Font

Chancel, Altar Cross and effigy

Received of the churchwardens of Kingston Deverill the sum of £42, as the remaining payment for the organ erected by me in the church, having received £20 for the whole contract, being £62. Signed

Sam Hayter Nov 25 1842. (At the same time I do agree with the Churchwardens to tune and keep up the Organ in repairs for seven years, free from any expenses to the Parish if called upon to do so).

The Parish Register confirms the appearance of the new organ as follows: 'A new organ installed in the church in the year of our Lord 1842. Signed – Hon the Rev C Thynne, Rector, Rev.John Perkins Clerk, Curate'. This new instrument must have been safely housed elsewhere during the reconstruction of the church. At least its maintenance was undertaken free of charge, and it did good service to the congregation and choir for nearly 40 years.

Charles Thynne did not see the restoration of his church through to completion, since he left the parish in 1845 to become sub-dean of Canterbury – following in the footsteps of his brother in the way of preferment. He was, however, present in the village when his sister-in-law, the Marchioness of Bath founded the local school in 1840, and it may be that he was able to start a church choir by virtue of his status as the school's manager. His subsequent history is interesting, given the

Kingston Deverill Church (after completion of restoration in 1847)

influence of the current wave of Anglo-Catholicism. Charles seceded to Rome, both theologically and geographically, in 1852 after only a few years in Canterbury. He 'recanted' once again, however, returning to England and the C of E in 1886, and remaining in the bosom of his original church until his death eight years later.

Meanwhile, in 1825 a Wesleyan Methodist Chapel was built on the south side of the road between KD and Monkton on land which was leased from the interestingly named Mr & Mrs Rabbits. A fine building was erected (costing £98.3.5) but, for whatever reason, it never attracted a sizeable congregation. The numbers gathered together during the ministry of Brother George Moore between 1851 and 1871 never rose above 17 (in 1859) but the average attendance was around 8. In 1903 the chapel was taken over by the Primitive Methodists based in Mere, under their minister Francis Leadley. Again the attendance tailed off until by 1907 just one person turned up each Sunday, and a letter was sent to the local Methodist circuit headquarters in Trowbridge requesting that the chapel should be closed. The building then remained derelict until 1926 when the KD Rector, William Henderson, who had walked out of his overwhelmingly large rectory the previous year, decided to offer £10 for the lease through his Warminster solicitor. There was then a considerable delay whilst the lawyer searched in vain for any descendants of the Rabbits (who most unusually were less than prolific) and in the meanwhile Henderson solved any immediate problem by dropping dead in the street. The future of the chapel is a later story.

Back up the road, Charles Thynne's successor in 1846 was David Clerk who was educated at St. John's College Cambridge and who combined the position of rector of KD with that of Prebendary of Wells Cathedral. Having overseen the completed reconstruction of his church, he very shortly turned his attention to the total replacement of the existing rectory – thus initiating one of the most remarkable stories in the history of the parish, since the end result could only be viewed as the equivalent of a rural Bishop's Palace.

Just who was immediately responsible for the decision that the old rectory should be replaced is uncertain, but it was probably made jointly by David Clerk and the Marchioness of Bath in the light of

THE CHURCH AND THE CLERGY

what might well have been the legitimate complaints about their accommodation made by successive rectors, who included in their number the Hon Rev John and the Hon Rev Charles Thynne. However, neither of these noble gentlemen was at any point obliged to live in a rat-infested, crumbling hovel if only for the reason that they were rarely present in the village – in fact, Lord Charles had a vicarage especially constructed for him in Longbridge Deverill in 1838. The go-ahead did not happen immediately on the appointment of David Clerk, and it is probable that the plans took some time to mature, since the building work did not start until 1855 at the earliest.

David Clerk was fairly wealthy on his own account, but he and the Marchioness decided that in order to erect a suitably palatial rectory, they needed to obtain additional finance from another source. As it happened, they knew of a certain Henry Festing, a resident of Maiden Bradley, who was very knowledgeable on the subject of ecclesiastical law, and the various charities which came under its jurisdiction. One of these was entitled 'The Bounty of Queen Anne for the Augmentation of the Poor Clergy', and Festing's view was that this could be put to good use, and that the obvious absence of impoverishment in the case of Rev.Clerk could be ignored. What happened next was that the Treasurer of the Diocese of Salisbury, with the agreement of the Bishop, Walter Kerr, offered Clerk the sum of £750 from the 'Queen Anne' fund -on the basis that it was 'mortgaged' against the 'rents, tithes etc.' of the Kingston Deverill glebe, 'for the purpose of rebuilding in part, enlarging and altering the Parsonage House and the neighbouring offices'. The offer was duly accepted, Henry Festing signed the contract as the 'guarantor', and the architects Manners and Gill -who had earlier renovated the church- were employed to put the construction in hand.

The History Centre at Chippenham holds a fascinating and comprehensive collection of receipts and invoices sent out by the various builders, carpenters, metalworkers etc. involved in the work, and in addition the archive includes the original architect's drawings, illustrating the north and south outside elevations and the interior layout of rooms on both floors, not only of the new Rectory but also of the 'Parsonage House' which it was about to replace. A selection of these can be seen in Appendix K.

At this point it is worth mentioning that the above story replaces the myth handed down to or invented by the current owner of Kingston House to the effect that the Rectory was constructed, lock, stock, pinnacle and turret from a demolished manor house in the village of Camerton in Somerset. It is, however, interesting that the name of the previous owner of that particular manor, Rev. John Skinner (1772 – 1839) is engraved, together with the date 1835, on a windowsill of one of the rooms in the new rectory, and just how it got there is a mystery. In a way it is sad that Skinner, who was a remarkable gentleman, noted for his archaeological research and a fascinating diary, cannot be more closely associated with Kingston Deverill, not least because he had many other Wiltshire connections, including a close friendship with the Bremhill poet, William Bowles, to whom he left a substantial sum of money in his will. As his diary reveals, he was a forceful and opinionated character and this is notably exemplified by his decision to sack the male-voice choir of Camerton Church in 1833 and replace it with a choir consisting entirely of girls- a foretaste, perhaps, of the introduction of the first girls cathedral choir in the adjacent diocese 158 years later.

When David Clerk took on the incumbency of KD following the departure of the Hon Charles Thynne, he moved into an unoccupied rectory, since his predecessor did not reside there but on his brother's estate at Longleat. The 1851 census reveals that the Rev Clerk (aged 42) was living at the old 'parsonage' and that the other occupants were his wife (aged 49) his son Allan (12) his brother Edmund (aged 34 - described as a 'visitor' and a 'landed proprietor') together with the local schoolmistress, Emma Cozner (22) and two house servants, Eliza Hale (36) and Elizabeth Eames (21). (The census is also interesting in that it indicates against the name of the Rector that he is 'from Somerset' – doubtless referring to his additional job at Wells, but also possibly to a past connection with John Skinner.)

The move into the new Rectory was accomplished around 1858 when the building was completed, and it appears from the 1861 census that the family would have been rattling around in the enormous pile, since the number of registered occupants totalled 10 (only three more than 10 years earlier), and that most of them were in any case visitors. Apart from David and his wife there's a brother-in-law and a nephew, a sister-in-law and two nieces, Eliza Hale (now elevated to 'cook') Elizabeth Eames (10 years older but still a 'servant') and a new housemaid Ann Burdon (21). The son, Allan, has left home. The massive new Rectory is curiously described as a 'Parsonage', despite the contrast with its 1851 equivalent. (Incidentally expenditure in relation to the church during this period was dwarfed by the amount of money spent on the rectory – the only record to payments involving the former indicates that at Easter 1873 'new churchyard gates were installed for £14.16.10.')

In 1874, during David Clerk's ministry, Harriet, Dowager Marchioness of Bath (who earlier drew up the financial agreement concerning the renovation of the church) donated a silver flagon, inscribed 'Glory of God on High' and made by E. J and W. Bannard of London. David Clerk remained in office until 1879, but his retirement was preceded by one of the most important acts in the history of the village, namely the rescue of the sarsen stones from the ford. Clerk had received information from the villagers that the stones which had been lying in the ford for the past 100 years, were very probably 'Egbert's Stones' and that their

Flagon – donated by Harriet, Marchioness of Bath in 1874

significance merited their being placed in a position where they could be viewed by the public, and where they were less likely to receive permanent damage. The rector accordingly ordered them to be brought up to his garden by a team of horse-drawn wagons, where, in 1877, they received official recognition on the occasion of a visit by the Wiltshire Archaeological Society.

In November of the following year Messrs. Harding & Sons of Warminster, auctioneers, state in an advertisement that

> they have been favoured with instruction from Rev. D.M. Clerk who is leaving the neighbourhood, to sell by auction ... the whole of the valuable contents of the Rectory ... handsome antique oak cabinets, chairs, tables etc, Dresden, Worcester and other china, an elegant inlaid drawing-room suite a library (- a rare collection of valuable books, consisting over about 1600 vols), bedrooms, domestic offices etc. 2 Alderney cows, Nag horse, Carriage, hay, with various other effects.

The rector was obviously a man of means, and was determined that his successor would arrive at a substantially stripped-down 'parsonage'. He died in 1893 at the age of 84 and there is a memorial to him in the church.

The next in line was Thomas Kingsbury, an MA from Trinity College, Cambridge and a canon of Salisbury Cathedral. He was reaching the end of his career when he arrived, and was already a widower. In the 1881 census his age is given as 58, and he is living in the rectory with his daughter, Helen (23) and three servants, William Reid (40) 'a Chelsea Pensioner', his wife Elizabeth (34) and a housemaid Emily Holt (29). Down the road is James Newbury (46) who is described as the 'Rectory Coachman'. Thomas's incumbency was short, but on his retirement he and his sister Martha gave the church a magnificent organ, built by Forster and Andrews of Hull – an instrument which is still in regular use. (This was an astonishingly generous gift, although the rumoured cost of £500 is likely to be an exaggeration).

In 1892, during the ministry of William Moore (1885-1898), the benefice of KD was combined with that of Monkton Deverill, and

THE CHURCH AND THE CLERGY

Organ, by Forster and Andrews of Hull, 1885

the Rector thus had two churches to run. It was during his time that the sarsen stones which for the past 20 years had been leaning against the churchyard wall in the rectory garden were moved by steam tractor to the nearby paddock and arranged as a 'mini-henge' or trilithon. The reason for the removal was apparently connected with the safety of the younger members of his family and their friends from the village school. The 1891 census reveals that the Moore family comprised the rector (40), his wife Alice (39) and four children – Dorothea (11), Eleanor (9), Katherine (7) and Edmund (5), together with a cook, Elizabeth Carpenter (21) a housemaid, Rose Carpenter (19) and a nurse, Martha Hallett (23). There is also – for the first time – the mention of an organist, Catherine Kneller, aged 39, who combined that job with that of 'Elementary Certificate Mistress' at the village school. She also resided at the rectory.

In August 1887 the church received the gift of an altar cross in memory of the Rector's eldest son, Philip Urban Moore, who died in that year at the age of 9. The cross is still in use, and the rector also commemorated his son with the installation of a beautiful stained glass window which greets the visitor on the opposite wall as he enters the church. Coincidentally in the same year the other stained-glass window in the nave was installed, and this is dedicated to the memory of Amy Stratton, (nee Flower) who was the second wife of William

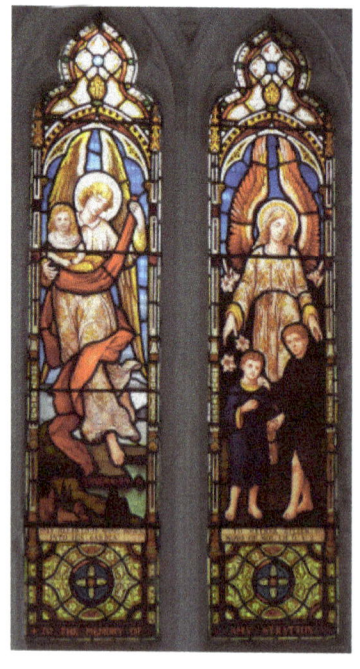

Philip Urban Moore window, 1887   *Amy Stratton window, 1887*

THE CHURCH AND THE CLERGY

Stratton (1834 -1919). William had moved from North Wiltshire in 1865 and took on the tenancy of KD Manor Farm in that year. Amy bore him 7 children and died when she was only 32, the family having experienced a previous tragedy, since their eldest son and heir William (1874 – 1883) was killed by a rolling barrel when he was nine years old – his age matching that of the Rector's commemorated son. Amy was responsible for planting the magnificent copper-beech trees which line the road outside the manor house – a very visible alternative memorial.

Amy Stratton's copper beeches – June 2016

The churchwarden's accounts for the period also hold some information of interest – namely that in 1889 insurance of the organ cost £1 and its annual tuning £3; that at Easter 1896 Mrs Curtis received £2. 18.1 for oil and candles, Mr Wilson £1.7.0 for Communion wine and Mr Locke £1.3.11 for coal - and that at Easter 1897 the Sexton's salary was £8.9.7.

In 1895, we have – also for the first time - photographic evidence of the existence of St.Mary's choir – or at least the 20 treble and alto members of it – the adult males being strangely absent from the picture (perhaps they were 'working' or at the pub?) And from

Kingston Deverill Church choir, 1895

1898, the year of William Moore's retirement, there exists the School Logbook, with its detailed account of events at the school and its close association with the church.

The next rector to confront the daunting immensity of his 'parsonage' was Edmund Caudwell (BD St.Mary Hall, Oxford) who arrived with his wife Ethel but apparently no children in 1898. In the 1901 census they are living (aged 35 and 36 respectively) with an elderly couple Robert Mather (84) and his wife Jane (68) – presumably Ethel's parents – and three servants, Kate Reeves (22), cook, and two housemaids Alice ? (17 -surname illegible) and Agnes Baker (15). Rev. Caudwell stayed for only a short time and moved to the Bristol parish of Backwell in 1903. The only record of church activity in his period of office refers to a restoration of the bells and the provision of a 'chiming cord' (for which Mr.Hooper received £5.13.1), and a payment of £7.7.0 to Novello's for Church Music, indicating that the choir was in reasonably active fettle.

Caudwell's successor as occupant of the Rectory was William Henderson who took up his post in 1903 and remained in office until his death in 1926. He was aged 47 and unmarried when he arrived,

THE CHURCH AND THE CLERGY

and the 1911 census reveals that he lived in the Rectory with only a gardener Henry Helps, (44), Henry's wife Eliza (42) who acted as a Housekeeper, and a lad, (oddly described as a 'page'), Arthur Sollis (16).

At some point in this period the lintel which formed the 'roof' of the trilithon which had been transferred to the rectory grounds by David Clerk, was dismantled and laid by the side of the two upright stones. The decision to 'topple' the stone was made by the smallholder who was at the time renting a part of the paddock for grazing his cows, since he was concerned that they might be injured if it fell. Whether or not William Henderson concurred with this action is not recorded.

The Stones in 1924

For the years that cover Rev Henderson's ministry and after that until 1941, we are fortunate in having a record of the Vestry and subsequently the PCC minutes for their annual meetings. These meetings took place at Easter and, as ever, discussions were often, but not exclusively, about matters of finance. The following entries are of some interest:

'1905: F Carey, Sexton, asks for a supply of wood. Agreed.
1907: Mr Stratton senior produces his annual accounts. Mr R

Stratton promises to make up the deficit.

1908: estimate for new heating in the church by means of hot water pipes £44.2.9. Contributions: Lord Bath £12, The Rector £5, Mr Pullin £5, Mr W Stratton £5, Messrs R & J Stratton £5, Mr John Walton £2 & Mr H Gilpin 5/-.' Obviously the winter comfort of the parishioners could only be secured by means of individual subsidy from members of the Vestry Committee. (Mr Gilpin's official title was 'People's churchwarden').

'*1910: the present state of the choir was discussed, and the Rector at the suggestion of the Churchwardens promised to write to Mr Fred Maxfield, intimating that it was desirable for him to resign his position as a member of the choir.*' This is a fascinating entry and one wonders just what Mr Maxfield had been up to in order to cause offence. Was it simply that his voice was regarded as in some way inadequate, or too raucous for the sensitive ear of Arthur Daintree, the organist, or was it that he regularly turned up in a drunk and disorderly state – an eminently feasible possibility since his family ran the New Inn at Monkton.

'*1911: a special fund was raised towards the restoration of the church bells, raising £39.10, (estimate £30.) KD Trust donated £10; KD Glee Society £1.*' (At last the members of the Vestry Committee are getting some outside financial help). '*Year's expenses included £6.50 to Mr Daintree, organist, organ blower 15/-, Mrs Carpenter (washing surplices) 16/6, John Carpenter (churchyard) £1.10.*' (John was aged 65 in 1911, and lived at the Post Office; the Mrs Carpenter mentioned was not his wife - she had died many years earlier).

'*1912: Organist's annual salary now £10. New cassocks required. Expenses incl. Mrs. Pearce (cleaning church) £.2.12; ringers £1.00. Vowles organ tuning £1.10. W. Mabbitt organ blowing 15/-.*' It is notable that many of these salaried jobs are now, 100 years later, undertaken on a voluntary unpaid basis- and indeed at the time of writing (February 2015) the current churchwardens have been busily engaged in pumping the organ by hand, following a breakdown of the motor, and the likelihood of their receiving any money for this exercise (I use the word advisedly) is remote in the extreme.

'*1913: Organist now Mr Elliott.*' His predecessor Arthur

Daintree was 62 in 1913 and had presumably retired. He is described in the 1911 census return as 'a widower from Islington'.

'1914: New cassocks supplied – used first on Christmas Day 1913. Church gate repaired and Psalter and Hymnbooks rebound. Gift of £10 from Lord Bath.

1915: Mr Brashier now organist (also headmaster at school).' Walter Ernest Brashier had taken over the headteacher's job from Augusta Elliott in March 1913, and remained at the school until 1920. *'Gift of white brocaded alms bag from Miss Griffith. Music 7/-.'* The choir was obviously very active during this first year of the war – the organist having very conveniently the pick of the boys at the school.

'1916: the church gate had been broken during the year by the military and they now offer £4.6.4 this being the amount estimated for the repair.' The army must have been on manoeuvres since there was no military camp in the immediate vicinity. Given the expense incurred, one of their vehicles completely destroyed the gates. There are no other minuted references to the effect of the war on the local community.

'1917: Mr Alfred Trimby now People's Churchwarden on retirement of Mr. Gilpin owing to his leaving the parish.

1918: P Mills now organ-blower. It was decided on the recommendation of Mr. Stratton that the 8 o'clock bell on Sunday mornings should not be rung except for a service.' The question arises as to whether it was Mr Stratton alone who objected to being called to prayer unnecessarily on a Sunday morning when there was no service, or whether his views reflected those of other parishioners. It is unlikely at this date that KD church would lack a service of any kind on a Sunday, so the reference must be to the occasional absence of matins or early communion.

'1920: - shortage of funds. Envelopes to be sent out quarterly. Last Easter Vestry meeting. PCC formed with 11 members.' Given the date, it is not surprising that the small group which made up the Vestry Committee could no longer cope with the church finances. The 5th Marquess of Bath had lost his son John Alexander, Viscount Weymouth in the war, and was also faced with financial problems which were due to increasing Estate Duties (introduced in 1874) and to the countrywide depression of the agriculture industry, dating from well

before 1914. As a result, he was no longer in the position to dispense his patronage as he had hitherto. The expenses now had to found by the parishioners at large – a position which remains unchanged 95 years later.

At some point during this period the November 11th Armistice Day service with its 2 minute silence must have been instituted, although there is no mention of this in the PCC minutes. The first reference to the service is in the School Logbook for 1927 which indicates that the children attended the church on that day and specifically for the occasion.

'*1921: PCC to co-operate with WI. Organist now Miss Wilkins.*' Was Miss W also a member of the Women's Institute, and did she state that her undertaking the arduous task of directing the music at the church was dependent upon the PCC's co-operation with the village ladies?

'*1922: Dancing classes at the school proposed.*' The church managed the school, otherwise one might ask why the PCC was involved in this suggestion. It was probably a fund-raising exercise. '*State of organ discussed. Mr Vowles to come and examine it.*

1923: Organ repairs (by Mr Siminson) to cost £10, but this would not cover bent and broken pipes. Annual tuning proposed @ £3.00. Mrs Carey now organist.

1924: Mrs Carey resigns.' None of the organists during this period lasts very long in the job. '*Lord Bath to be asked for extra land for graves.*

1925: Mrs Bush appointed organist. New bell ropes £3.5.10. Garden Party suggested for funds; whist drive idea rejected.'

It was in this year that William Henderson decided he'd had enough of the cavernous spaces of the Rectory and informed the Diocesan Board and the Marquess of Bath that he deemed the Rectory too large for the purpose of accommodating the incumbent of a small village. The diocesan authorities agreed, and the Marquess accepted the idea that the building should at some appropriate juncture be sold. Henderson then moved to Warminster for what proved to be the last year of his ministry.

'*1926: Bellringers to be re-organised. Mr Stratton says how nice

THE CHURCH AND THE CLERGY 77

it will be to hear the bells again.' The son has changed his father's tune and obviously prefers to hear several bells rather than one (cf.1918). *'New heating apparatus proposed – also that the door leading to the belfry be closed. Rev Henderson has died: Lord Bath looking for a replacement.'*

Shortly after Henderson's death, an auction of all his effects was held in the Rectory, as the following report from the Warminster Journal of 21 December 1926 reveals:

> Messrs. Hall & Sons held a sale of the whole of the contents of Kingston Deverill Rectory. A very business-like company attended, the result being highly satisfactory. Mr Dart wielded the hammer and succeeded in disposing of the whole of the 523 lots within four hours. Amongst the pieces were the following: bedroom suites £10.10s and £15.15s; chests of drawers £1 to £2; bedsteads – wooden - £3.1s, -iron - £1.5s to £2.10s; carpets £1.2s to £2. 3s; rugs 15/- to £3; washstands 15/- to £2.10s; barometers £2.2s.6d and 30/-; gate-legged table £4.5s; chairs 10/-- to 25/-; corner cupboard 26/-; occasional tables from 15/- to 32.10s; ecclesiastical books from 1/- to 27/- per set; couches 30/- to £4; easy chairs £1.10s to 33.10s; 'Welbeck' piano £26 [This is more likely to have been a 'Welmar'. The firm had begun manufacturing pianos based on the upright version of the Bechstein in 1925, and Henderson had obviously invested in a fine instrument.] Sideboards £3.10s to £4.10s; Sheffield tray £2.2s; cutlery 6/-, 8/- & 14/- per dozen; blankets 10/- to £1.7s per pair; sheets 10/- to 21/-; tea and dinner services £1.8s to £2.16s; hens 2/6 to 4/3 each. Keen competition ensued for the 1925 Morris Oxford car which started at £100 and quickly rose to £185. [It is recorded elsewhere that as early as 1914 Rev. Henderson had invested in a 20hp dark blue open Ford touring car, and presumably he was still in ownership of this vehicle immediately after the war when he would have been competing on the local road system with

Model T Open Ford Touring car 1914

Richard Stratton who bought a grey version of the same model in 1919.]

Rumour has it that William Henderson died of a heart attack in the street in Warminster following an argument with his cook, but there is no way of establishing whether this assertion is true. What is unarguable is that he was a highly popular figure in the village, and a greatly respected pastor, as is attested by the emotional obituary which appeared in the Warminster Journal on 7th January 1927, written by his friend Rev K D B Dobbs, Curate of Mere- extracts from which read as follows:

> the deep sorrow felt by the parishioners of Kingston and Monkton Deverill at the tragically sudden death of their beloved Rector I share in full measure ....He had an extraordinarily lovable nature will long be remembered, as will his genial personality, his keen sense of humour, his love of merriment and his jovial spirit at social functions which was no way diminished by his habitual deafness... When I last saw him at the funeral of Mr.Brocklebank in Warminster on November 17th he remarked on his comparatively sudden death, little knowing that his own death three weeks later would be even more tragically sudden... In the December Parish Magazine he wished his parishioners a happy Christmas ... how vividly then must his Christmas message have gone home on Christmas morning, which would have proclaimed it afresh from the pulpit, was stilled in death.... The tragic suddenness of his end was a great shock to us all, but with it comes the realisation that it was a beautiful homecoming. All unconscious of the fact, the journey he took on the last afternoon to Warminster was to be the final journey of all. For him, to borrow the language of the hymn, the golden evening was already brightening in the west.

So, very sadly, William Henderson was not able to enjoy his immediately impending retirement, in anticipation of which he had bought a new car and a new piano.

It is interesting that even at this late date the local patron of the church had the responsibility of finding a successor for the departed rector.

'*1927 Lord Bath has consented to give land for the churchyard. PCC now has 14 members. New Psalm board proposed: flowers to be put on grave of previous rector. New prayer book discussed. Sunday School to start at 3 pm on Oct 2nd.*'

Following William Henderson's death there was an interregnum of about a year before the next rector, Robert Cooper Fugard, was appointed. Fugard (1868-1942) was of Irish extraction. His family had moved earlier to America where he was brought up, and he received his ordination to the ministry in Duluth, Minnesota. He was a published author of religious books before his arrival in the village – 'The New Birth' dates from 1907 – and he wrote 'Drops of Dew and other Essays' in 1931 while living in the valley. He took up residence at the KD Rectory, with his wife Margaret, apparently happy with the space it afforded (unlike his predecessor) and remained there until 1937, shortly before the diocese contracted a sale for the building. At this point he moved to the rectory at Brixton Deverill, and this became the home of successive rectors until 1975.

'*1928: Church fete on rectory grounds on 16th June.*

1929: Yew tree to be cut back. Choirboys surplices need replacing. Memorial tablet to Rev. Henderson proposed.' This latter suggestion was carried through and William Henderson's memorial is to be found on the south wall of the chancel.

'*1930: PCC members: Mesdames Cooper-Fugard, Stratton, Hayes, Harrington, Trimby, F Carpenter, Cooke, Legge, Larksworthy Lemon, Pullman, Hayes, Gibbs, Newbury, S Pearce, Matthews & Miss Garland; Messrs G Trimby, F Haynes, F Legge, W Harrington, Capt. Hayes, E Haynes, Cooke, Legge – total 25,*' ladies well outnumbering the gentlemen – 17 to 8. '*Arrangement for visit of Bishop of Sherborne on Sep 13- confirmation at 2 pm, consecration of new burial ground 3 pm; tea at rectory; entertainment at Manor Farm; dance at school. Altar back given by Mrs Stratton in memory of her mother, the late Mrs Stratton.*' Worry about condition of church tower. The manor farm was now in private ownership, having been sold to the Stratton family in 1920. (One wonders what is meant by an 'altar back' – a frontal being the more usual gift – and whether it still exists.)

The War Memorial

For 1931 there are no extant minutes, which is strange in that it was a particularly significant year in the history of the church. On 31st July of that year the churchyard War Memorial for the fallen of World War 1 was dedicated by the Dean of Salisbury (Very Rev John Randolph) and unveiled by Percy Seymour, 18th Duke of Somerset. There are seven names on the Memorial, and the details of the men who lost their lives are given at Appendix B.

'*1932: Money to be found for Tower fund.*

1933: Flagpole removed as unsafe.' Presumably this was on the tower and it is sad that it has never been replaced.

'*1934: repairs to church gate and enquiry into cost of matting to cover the gratings in the nave. 1938: new boiler required.*' Neither the gratings nor the boiler any longer exist, since the church is now warmed by overhead electric heaters.

'*1939: first combined meeting of KD and MD PCCs. At MD combined salary of organist and sexton @ £6 considered unsatisfactory. It was suggested that it was no longer necessary to heat the churches every Sunday if services were held in each church on alternate Sundays.*'

This is the first mention of any diminution in the number of services being held in individual churches in the Deverill valley on any given Sunday. Since the MD and KD churches were so close and employed the same rector, it made sense for the modern practice of sharing to start here.

'*Cleaning rota organised.*' This still exists, as does a flower rota. '*Induction of Rev Cecil Heath Caldwell (Rector of BD) to the living of KD and MD. Rector suggests* Songs of Praise *as the hymnbook.*'

With the arrival of Cecil Caldwell the idea, dating back to the mid-17th century, that the livings of KD, MD and BD should be combined in one incumbent was at last realised. The PCC minutes for this event could be construed as implying that the new rector had hitherto also been the incumbent at BD, but this is not the case – he was taken on for the three parishes at the same time (fortunately for his predecessor Robert Fugard, since otherwise they would be residing together in the same rectory). The hymnbook 'Songs of Praise' had been published in 1925 (with a revision in 1931) as a slightly less 'up-market' version of the 'English Hymnal' which had been in use since 1908. Both hymnbooks had as their editors Percy Dearmer and Ralph Vaughan Williams, and 'Songs of Praise' employed the additional expertise of Martin Shaw. As might be expected with RVW involved, both books have a wonderful selection of hymns both old and new, and it would be interesting to know with what other music the KD choir was involved at this, and earlier stages, of its history.

'*Emergency meeting Aug 4: Letter to Salisbury Diocese Dilapidations Board stating that an offer of £500 had been received for KD Rectory and garden – this valuation coming from Messrs Rawlence and Squarey. Sale to be concluded at an early date. The Rector explained that the house was not likely to be required by an Incumbent by reason of its size and the cost of upkeep, and that Lord Bath had given his consent through the SDDB for it to be sold some years ago. Organ at MD 'past repairing' and needs replacement.*

1940: the rector said that owing to the 'Black Out' the evening service would be in the afternoon at 3.pm. Organ at MD to be replaced by one from Swindon for £40.' It would be interesting to know what happened to this instrument when MD church closed and became a private property in 1970. *'Impossible to black out KD but possible at MD.*

1941: Mr G Carpenter, sexton, wishes to resign. Insurance against war damage to organ and pews discussed. Sandbags also to be provided in porch. Question of closure of one of the churches –either to the end of the war or permanently. Vote was 7 against closing either church, 1 for closing MD temporarily and one for closing KD temporarily.'

The writing was already on the wall for one of the churches – the villages were simply too close to each other to command sufficiently numerous separate congregations.

Whatever their difficulties, however, BD, MD and KD churches continued to provide a spiritual resource both to the parishioners and to KD school throughout the war, under the leadership of Rev. Caldwell. Meanwhile, the rectory had become a private house, but from 1943 it was used as a billet for American servicemen prior to the D-Day landings of the following year. Their accommodation also extended to huts in the paddock and it is thought that the capstone from the Saxon trilithon was used as some sort of foundation or as a

Lantern in Church porch

THE CHURCH AND THE CLERGY

The King Alfred banner. *Madonna and Child (14th century)*

covering for stored ammunition and then concreted over. Whatever the cause, the stone has sadly disappeared – but perhaps not for ever. Next door, the church remains today much as it has been described earlier in this narrative, but lacking the music of swung bells and a choir. However, the post-war period saw three notable embellishments to the interior, and these comprised the highly imaginative lantern in the porch, constructed in the 1950s by Arthur Fear; the processional 'King Alfred' banner which came from MD church when it closed in 1970; and – most significant of all – the beautiful carved Madonna and Child, which was added to the church furnishings in 1968.

The history of the latter acquisition is particularly interesting in that the donor was Herbert Leigh Holman of Woodlands Manor in Mere, the first husband of Vivien Leigh. Holman (1900-82) met Vivien Hartley (1913-67) in 1932 and they married in December of that year. During the 1930s they were often to be seen together in Mere when

Vivien Leigh (she had taken her husband's middle name for professional reasons) came home from her travels in pursuit of an acting career. The marriage was dissolved after Vivien's meeting with Laurence Olivier, whom she married in 1940, but she remained on amicable terms with Herbert, who was given initial responsibility for the upbringing of their daughter Suzanne (1933-2015).

The connection with KD came about following the arrival of Giles Martin Spinney

Baptism Shell – donated by Canon Richard Askew

as rector in 1954, at which point a friendly relationship developed between the two families, culminating in the rector being asked to officiate on the occasion of Suzanne's marriage to Robin Farrington at St Margaret's, Westminster, in December 1957. The mutual friendship continued, with the ultimate result that the Madonna and Child statue was offered by way of a gift of gratitude to Martin Spinney – and duly collected and conveyed to the church in 1968 by his son Tim. The wooden statue is Flemish, very finely carved, and dates from *c.*1360. It is particularly notable for the fact that the Child is standing rather than sitting on his Mother's knee, and has this attribute in common with carvings of similar date in churches throughout northern Europe and particularly Scandinavia. It also has distinct traces of original paint – a remarkable surviving feature over such a long period of time. Rumours to the effect that it might have been 'acquired' from Malines Cathedral by a soldier involved in a war in the Spanish Netherlands or that it hails from Strasbourg are conjectural – but it may be that at some point the true provenance of this highly evocative image will be established. Also around this time the churchyard was – for some unrecorded reason – cleared of the majority of its 19th century and earlier gravestones and tombs. The clearance has resulted in greater ease

THE CHURCH AND THE CLERGY

Brixton Deverill Church

of access in respect of mowing and general tidying up, but otherwise represents a sad historical loss.

The later history of KD church and its clergy is dependent upon the discovery of more recent PCC minutes and on living memories. However, details of the various changes which took place in the organisation of the ministry in the Deverill valley area towards the end of the 20th century and the beginning of the 21st, together with the personnel involved, are included in the list of clergy which appears at Appendix A.

3 Kingston Deverill School

The first mention of any educational activity in Kingston Deverill occurs in a document entitled 'The Education of the Poor Digest' published in 1818. Apparently there were 'Two Dames Schools, usually attended by 24 children' and 'A Sunday School, containing about 50 children, supported by voluntary contributions, which are both small and uncertain'.

In far off Scotland, John Knox had proclaimed the ideal of 'Universal Education' in the 1570s, and although his ambition was not realised in his lifetime, the Scottish Education Act of 1633 stated that a school should be founded in every rural community, and by the end of the 17th century this aim had been accomplished throughout the lowland areas of the country. England was a little behind - 178 years in fact - since it was not until 1811 that the Church of England set up what became known as 'The National Society' to promote the education of the rural poor in our part of the world. It took some time. 'Dames Schools' and 'Sunday Schools' had existed in some villages for many years, but the former were usually no more than day care establishments for infants, and the latter were primarily set up to offer religious instruction, although many also included basic teaching of the 3Rs.

At the time of the 1818 report, the Rector of KD was Josiah Thomas (1782-1820), but it is evident that he was non-resident and probably ill when the report was published, since the details of the educational establishment in the village were given to the commissioners by a stipendiary curate, John Offer.

The next mention of education in the area comes from a report entitled 'The Abstract of Education Returns' which was published in 1835. According to this, the Dames Schools and the Sunday School at KD no longer existed, although there were thriving Sunday Schools at

MD and LD, and it is possible that children from KD attended one of these. However, by this stage the connection between the church at KD and the 2nd Marquess of Bath at Longleat was more firmly cemented by the appointment in 1831 of the Marquess's third son, Lord John Thynne, as Rector, with the result that there was an obvious opening for increased patronage of the C of E — and by inference the National Society - by the Thynne family.

That this was indeed the case has been proved by a recent discovery in the Longleat archives of a document which states that a carpenter's cottage tenanted by a Mr Young on the site of the present School House was taken back into ownership by the Marquess of Bath in 1840, and set up as a school. That was the beginning.

At the time of the establishment of the school in the carpenter's cottage the Rector of KD was Lord Charles Thynne, who took over the benefice from his elder brother in 1837. Despite the departure of Rev. Charles for Canterbury Cathedral in 1845, the patronage of the school by Longleat continued, as is proved by an entry in Kelly's Directory of 1848 which reads: 'Here is a National School supported by the Marquis of Bath and a Wesleyan Chapel. Miss Elizabeth Earl, Mistress of National School.'

The next mention of the school is from the 1851 Census which lists the occupants of the Rector's house, as including 'Emma Cozner, 22, Mistress at Parochial School' and 'Sophie Sturgess, 20, assistant teacher'. These young ladies were teaching in a tiny cottage, possibly with an ex-carpenter's workshop attached, and were living in the home of the new Rector, Rev. D.M Clerk who was effectively their manager. Sometime during this year, the Marquess of Bath realised that the school premises were completely inadequate for the purpose and drew up plans for a new building. The new school was completed in 1853 and is essentially the building as we see it today. It is likely that the whole structure was financed entirely by the Marquess, although, as a National School, the establishment was also eligible for a small government grant under an Act of 1833.

The first mention of the school building as we know it (later alterations apart) appears in 'Rev Warburton's Census of Wiltshire Schools, 1859'. His report concerning schools in the locality is fascinating and is worth quoting in full:

> KD pop. 402. 50 - 60 scholars, mixed, are taught by a mistress, untrained, in an excellent school-room with brick floor and wall desks. At MD 30-40 scholars, mixed, are taught by a mistress in a lean-to with brick floor and wall desks. Mistress well-informed but inexperienced. At LD 60-70 children taught by a certified master and pupil teacher in a school-room 48x17 and classroom 14x10 with boarded floor and parallel desks. Mr Hughes (Feb 1858) reports that the discipline is very good and the instruction sound and judicious, though elementary. The LD School is the only one of this group under a master, and is consequently attended by several of the elder children from the Deverills and Crockerton. Crockerton has 40-50 children, mixed, who are taught by an unqualified mistress in a good school-room recently erected, with boarded floor and parallel desks. Mr Hughes (Mar 1857) reports unfavourably of the discipline and doubtfully of the instruction.

It might appear that Rev Warburton is a shade sexist in his criticism of the women teachers, but it has to be remembered that certified teacher training was not available to them at this date, and it is for this reason that the master at LD School attracts a following amongst the parents of older children.

For information about the school over the next 40 years we are solely dependent upon the Census Returns and Kelly's Directory, the relevant entries being as follows: 1861 Census: 'Leah Pressley 20 - teacher'; 1871 Census: 'Georgina Callaghan 29 -teacher (Board School).' 1881 Census: 'Anne Gilbert 18-National School Mistress; Elizabeth Ford 26 - assistant school teacher.' Kelly's Directory 1889: National School (mixed), built in 1853 for 60 children; average attendance 30; Mrs C. Wheeler, Mistress'.

During this time, the Government had passed the Elementary Education Act of 1870, which aimed to make the provision of education compulsory for all children between the ages of 5 and 13. In order to achieve this, it set up School Boards in areas where a number of children were not in fact attending school, and instructed these Boards to obtain funds in order to provide school places where there was a shortfall. Most parents were still required to pay a small fee for their children's education, and the receipt of municipal or government funding for individual schools was to an extent dependent on the children's attendance. The Act also made provision for the institution of 6 'Standards' by which the children could be judged on their abilities in Reading, Writing and Arithmetic, and school classes were set up on this basis, with Standard 1 being at the lowest, or Infant level.

School Photo from c.1878

The Act took a long time to implement, and it was not until 1880 that the ideal of compulsory attendance was achieved. School Boards were abolished in 1902 and replaced by Local Education Authorities.

We now reach a period when we are fortunate in being able to give a far more detailed and intimate view of the school and its daily life, by virtue of the existence of the Headteachers' Logbook which dates from 1898 and continues right up to the closure of the school in 1969. The following entries give some idea of the aims and activities of the children and their teachers over a period of seventy years, encompassing two World Wars and substantial social change. Quotations from the Logbook are given in italics.

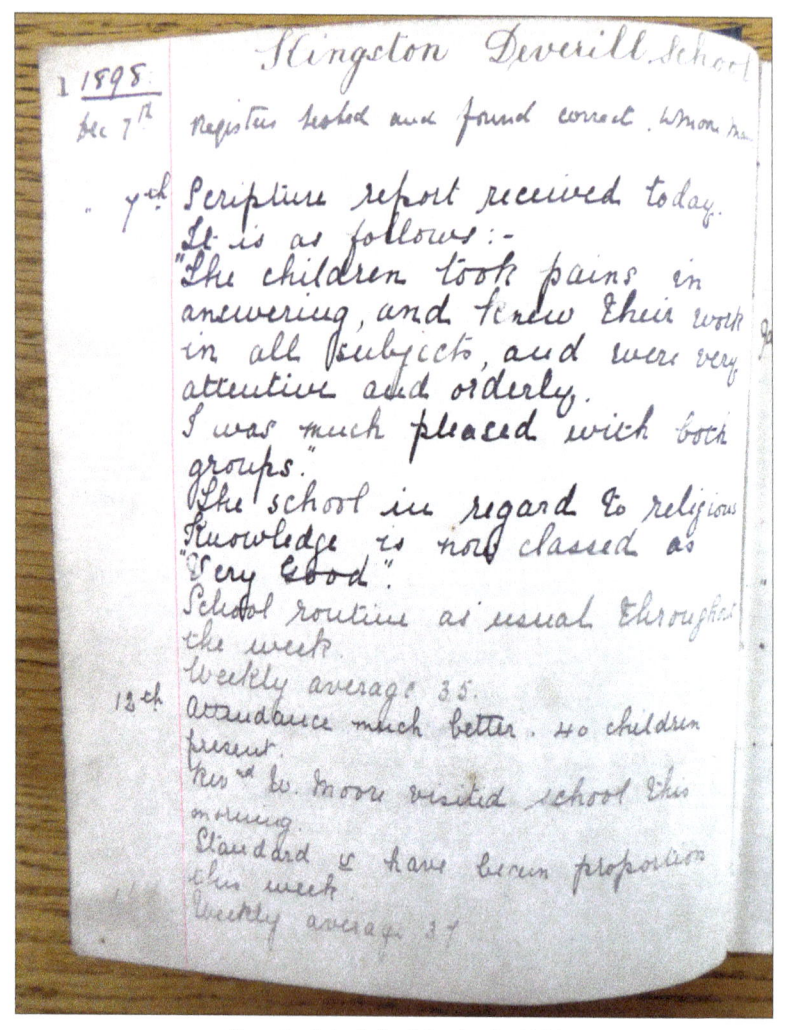

Page 1 of the School Logbook, 1898

1898 - Dec 7: weekly average 35. Dec 12: 40 children present. Rev. Moore visited school this morning. Since the school was a Church of England foundation, the local Rector was the school manager and paid regular visits. William Moore was appointed to the KD benefice in 1885.

1899 - Mar 23: Standard 111 were very careless in Arithmetic, and Standard 11 in Geography. At this point in the school's history, the children were divided up into five 'Standards'. Standard 111 refers to the 8-9 year-olds, and Standard 11 to those aged 6-7. *Jun 16: attendance very poor indeed - 20 children absent with bad colds and sore throats. Sep 4: Rose Draper began duties today.* Rose Draper lived with her parents and elder brother and was only 17 when she took up her post at the school. Presumably she would have helped with the infants. *Sep 28: several boys away potato picking. Nov 1: am disappointed in all the infants' work. Nov 6: Rev Moore is leaving the parish. The vacancy will be filled by Rev. Edmund Caudwell.* Rev. Caudwell remained as Rector until 1903.

1900 - Jan 23: School closed today for the childrens Xmas tree given by Mr. Stratton. Feb 14: school closed today on account of very deep fall of snow. Mar 28: Rose Draper 7 minutes late this morning. The infants' teacher is obviously suffering from the perennial teenage problem of not being able to get up in the morning. *Apr 9: Inspection by George Gordon - 'the Upper Deverills infants' Arithmetic was very poor indeed. Only one child got anything at all right. In the lower division, 2 children who have been in the school over 12 months do not yet know their letters.' Jul 2: It's a nice little county school. The teaching is bright and effective.'* Obviously the standard of teaching and learning had shot up in the three months between the two inspections. *Oct 29: Rev & Mrs Caudwell heard the children sing.*

1901- Apr 30 I give up charge of the school today - B. Perrin. May 1:1, Annie Penny, take charge of KD School today. Oct 18 - school closed today by medical officer through an outbreak of Scarlet Fever.

1902 - Jun 11: During the hay-making season school commenced at 1.30, dismissed at 3.45. This is an interesting indication of the continuing dependence on the help of young children in the fields in the early Edwardian era. *Nov 3: Thomas Marshall 3 years old left during winter months.* Tom Marshall lived with his parents, a younger brother and two older sisters. His father was a Cattleman and perhaps needed the help of his very small son in his cowsheds. Either that or it was simply too cold for the lad to walk to school.

1903- Jun: Rev.Henderson now manager. The late Rector Rev.

Caudwell and Mrs Caudwell brought presents of sweets for the children. It would have been difficult for the Rev. Caudwell to have brought sweets to the school if he had indeed been 'the late', and presumably what Annie Penny means is that he has retired. His successor, William Henderson, had a long stint as Rector, retiring in 1926. *Sep 30:1 give up charge of the school today - A.Penny. Oct 30: The Tudgays have left the village.*

This statement can only refer to one branch of the Tudgay family, since the 1911 census reveals that Eliza Tudgay (69) and Moses Tudgay (77) were still around, as was Emma Tudgay (60) who ran the village shop. There were still Tudgays in the village in the 1960s. *Nov 9: commenced duties today as Headmistress - Minnie Newson.*

1904 - Jan 22: Mistress absent to be married. Mar 31: I Minnie Walters (nee Newson) give up charge of the school. Apr 11:1, Beatrice Alice Maxfield have taken charge of school. Jun 10: Ida Maxfield (probationer) 12 minutes late this morning. No excuse given. Since Ida was the Headmistress's daughter, this stricture seems rather harsh. Why didn't she wake her up? Perhaps an excuse was elicited back at home. *Jun 29: the stove should be protected by a high fixed iron surround.*

1905 - May 23: There is a brook flowing beside the playground. During the past year 8 children have fallen into it, in two cases with near fatal results. Some steps should be taken , either to erect a fence, or otherwise to remove the danger. The stove and brook questions develop into an ongoing saga. *Nov 27: Emma Louise Dunford begins duties today as a supplementary teacher.* Emma was the daughter of Charles and Amelia Dunford, and lived at Manor Farm Monkton Deverill, where her father was the tenant farmer. She had five brothers and three sisters, and the family name lives on in the Deverill Valley every Remembrance Sunday, since her elder brother Walter died of wounds on 1st September 1915 during the battle of the Somme, and is commemorated both at the service, and in perpetuity with six others on the War Memorial in KD churchyard.

Walter Dunford

(Walter's great –niece Karen Dunford often visits MD and is a mine of information about the Dunford family.)

1906 - Jan 1: Emma Dunford is taking the infants, Ida Maxfield Standard 1 and Mistress Standards 111- VI1. Jan 16: A terribly wet morning. I was obliged to send four children home as I could not possibly dry their clothes. Mar 30: Need for guard for stove reiterated. Jul I: Emma Dunford has left. She came back later. *Sep 16: Amy Dunford has left, being 14 years of age. Oct 12: stove guard fixed.*

1907- School closed 15-21 Jan as mistress has influenza. May 10: Gertrude May Harding from Swindon started duties today. It was obviously difficult to recruit local assistant staff.

1908 - Feb 4: Several children caned today for disobedience. Jack Mills, a boy in Standard 1V refusing to hold out his hand received 3 stripes on the legs with a cane and remained until 5. 15 pm. Sep 21: Miss Harding 10 minutes late. Sep 24: Miss Harding 12 minutes late.

The School House

It might seem reasonable for Miss Harding to arrive late if she were travelling from the extreme north-east of the county to the extreme south-west, with the only route available skirting the Plain to the north and the west, but in 1908 she would in any case be unable to accomplish this journey in less than a day, and she certainly lived nearby. What is more evident is that Beatrice Maxfield is a hard taskmistress both to her pupils and to members of her staff.

1909- Mar 14: weekly average attendance 54.6. Jun 21: School closed for the afternoon as children taken to Longleat to welcome the Prince and Princess of Wales. Sep 3: Three of the older boys have been harvesting all week. Oct 20: Lily Mabbitt punished for independence.

The School House Bell

Throwing herself on the floor when told to hold out her hand she received several stripes on her legs which would not have happened had she held out her hand. Lily lived with her parents and elder brother and was nine years old at the time of this incident. It is interesting that at this date 'independence' was regarded as a crime, and physical violence against young children wasn't.

1910 - Apr 5: 67 on books. Jul 1: During the haymaking play has on several occasions been dispensed with and the school closed to enable the children to carry parents tea in the fields. Aug 10: C of E Manager's report: 'English and Arithmetic deplorable. The teacher of the infants suffers from the proximity of the noisy Standard children, and they are backward with their work.' Dec 21:I give up charge of this school today - Beatrice A Maxfield. It appears that Mrs Maxfield's autocratic regime failed to lift the academic standards of the school, and it would be unsurprising to learn - though we have no evidence - that for a combination of reasons (including her harshness to the children) she had been sacked.

1911 - Jan 1: Mrs A Elliott ACP takes over duties as Headmistress. Jan9: Lily and Gladys Marshall away this afternoon having gone home to

The Headteacher's house

dinner 2 and a quarter miles. *Jan 16: I punished Stanley Marshall this morning for rude behaviour to Ethel Marshall (one each hand). Feb 3: Attendance 64.5 (96.8%). Jun 1: I sent Eva Feltham and Percy Mills home in the afternoon because Bert Wilson had saturated them with water. 2 Jun: Bert Wilson had a fit this afternoon. 20 Jun: School closed for coronation – 26 June.* This was the coronation of George V. *Bert Wilson further fits – exempted school. Jul 20: I was obliged to be absent from lessons from 11 – 12 to be present while the tuner was at the organ.* Presumably the rector, who was the manager of the school, had asked the headmistress to deputise for him for this particular task. *Sep 15: Mrs Stratton visits the school this afternoon to present coronation mugs to each child. Oct 17: Bert Wilson leaves – mentally deficient.* Such a harsh description of Bert's state would hardly be acceptable today.

1912 Jan 4: As Mr Stratton gave the children a Christmas tree there was no school in the afternoon. Jan 17: I found it necessary to caution the pupils about speaking untruths. Jan 19: Snowy weather. 4 Rixons, 8 Marshalls, 2 Ruddicks, 2 Gibbs, 1 Carpenter, Lily Mabbitt and M Day present. Jan 27: I punished B Gibbs, P Gibbs and Tony Marshall for interfering with Muriel Maxfield on way home. These lads would seem to have been getting their own back on the previous Headmistress by bullying her daughter. *Feb 20: owing to visit of Bishop of Salisbury, no school this afternoon.* Jack Carpenter who lived in KD all his life and died in 2003 aged 100, remembered this visit, and spoke of seeing the Bishop (Frederick Ridgway) being driven up to the Rectory in a coach and four. *Apr 1: numbers: Standard V – 1 girl; Standard IV – 6 girls; Standard III – 6 boys, 2 girls; Standard II – 6 boys, 2 girls; Standard I – 9 boys, 5 girls; Infants 16. Total 53.* These statistics are interesting in that they reveal that the boys left the school when they were 11/12 presumably to help their fathers in their work. *Oct 28: As I cannot light the fire owing to no pipe having been fixed to the stove, the walls are in a very damp and unhealthy state.*

1913 - Mar 19: I Augusta Eliott, give up charge of the school. Mar 31:I Walter Ernest Brashier take charge of this school. Apr 1: Miss E Dunford commences duties as asst. teacher on supply. Apr 7:I have cautioned the children against playing near the river. Apr24: Several boys have a habit of laughing when corrected. As a second warning had no effect, I punished William Mills (2), Alan Marshall (8) and Fred Rixon (3) today. Were William and Fred really aged 2 and 3 respectively and would they fully appreciate that they shouldn't laugh when corrected? *Jul 23: Some of the boys took part in a cricket match at Brixton Deverill. Dec 11: Garden tools received today from Semley School - 3 spades, 5 rakes, 5 hoes, 2 Dutch hoes, 6 forks.* Apparently the Headmaster had managed to persuade the authorities to rent a small piece of ground from the Strattons, and later reports indicate that the gardening efforts of the students were a great success.

1914 - Mar 10: a very snowy morning - only 25 children present. Jun 23: Eugenie Lander refused to hold out her hand at first and afterwards closed it up so that the cane struck her knuckles, this being, of course, entirely her fault. What exactly the original fault was that resulted in Eugenie having to hold out an initially open and subsequently closed hand is not recorded, but it could be argued that the damage to her knuckles was not exclusively down to her. *Nov 6: New stove pipe not yet arrived - very cold in the morning. Dec 4: the new stove has arrived.* Only a month late: plus ca change.........

Dec 4: The new stove gives a good heat (!) But no mention of the First World War – there are more important matters.

1915 - Jan 27: Report by Mr G Pardoe: ' Important defects in the premises - the offices of the boys and girls are in the same part of the playground; the entrance to the boys' offices [i.e. loos] *should have a screen put in front of them. The schoolroom is undivided - there are 3 classes with 2 teachers and an infants class of 26 children taught in one room. A partition should be provided. The pails in the offices should be more frequently emptied,'* The conditions of work for the teachers and pupils in the school building as described must have been chaotic, and it is extraordinary that, as later reports will reveal, the situation remained much the same until the early 1960s. It was only mitigated when the leaving age for the children was reduced to 11 in 1924, with the result that there were fewer pupils on the premises. *Apr 12: Miss Dunford leaves.* Emma Dunford was aged 28 when she left the school, and given that her brother Walter was killed later in the year, it was quite a possibility that there could have been an additional misfortune - as happened to so many families over the next few years -namely yet another daughter left on the shelf. Happily, as has been revealed by Emma's great-niece, she married at the end of 1915 and lived on into the 1950s. *Jul 2: numbers on books 75; present 43.*

1916 - Mar 31: Attendance has been wretched -17 away with trivial pretexts e.g. John Marshall (5) wooding with his mother; Annie Marshall gone to Warminster to mind horse; Dorothy Pullinger - no reason at all; Laura Newby and Dorothy Carpenter - minding baby. Given the appalling academic conditions at the school and the lack of hygiene, these children were probably better off tending babies and horses elsewhere.

1917 - Jul 3: In religious instruction some children held up their hands without being able to answer. There have always been small people who have raised a hand without any connection between their so doing and their ability to give an answer. *Oct 10: John Coward refused to hold out his hand and he received several stripes on his back and seat. During the dinner hour I was visited by the boy's father who made a number of offensive remarks in front of the boys and took his part - saying that he would also do so on any further occasion.* John's dad must have been under the impression that he was living in the 21st century. *Oct 22 -prize for the best garden plot given by Mr R Stratton to Ernest Wiltshire.*

1918 - Oct 31: 280 lbs of blackberries and 255 lbs of elderberries gathered by children for jam making. No mention of the end of the war.

1919 – Feb 18: deep snow this morning. May 17: I have removed the name of James Marshall from the Infants Register as he is dead. This stroke of the pen by the Headmaster might seem unnecessarily conclusive.

1920 - Jan 28: I left the school to play the organ at a funeral at MD. It is recorded elsewhere that Mr Brashier combined the posts of Headmaster and Organist of the local churches - hence a connection with the next logbook entry. *Aug 4: Children on choir outing. Sep 11: I Walter Brashier give up Headmastership of this school. Oct 8: two boys misbehaved - the elder Alan Jack expelled for insubordination - he snatched at the cane and broke it - boys sent home.* Another Lily Mabbitt - but what can you expect when the school has no headteacher?

1921 – 6 children taken to Bruton New Hall to see scenes from A Midsummer Night's Dream. Mar 22: School divided into two 'houses' Red and Blue. The Blue House wins a shield (homemade) at end of Feb. Netball now instituted for girls. Football already in existence. Mar 24: Mr Stratton addressed the school on the subject of 'The Empire.' Jul 19: Outing to Bournemouth.

1922 - No headmistress yet appointed - Miss Sly and Miss Williams are now on their own. Apr 12: Miss Sly and Miss Williams resign. The school now has no teachers. However, later in the summer we have the following entry: *Jun 16: A. Tanswell resigns as headteacher* ...although there is no previous record of her/his appointment. 3 days later all is well ...*Jun 19: Miss Phoebe Garland commences duties as headteacher.*

1923- Apr 26: A holiday given at the King's wish in honour of the wedding of his son the Duke of York. Jun 26: 4 children late after walking 2 and a half miles from Keysley. Keysley Farm is right on the outer edge of the Kingston/Monkton parish and it must have been the case that the children were usually transported in some way to and from the school. *Jun 19: holiday outing to Portsmouth. Jun 24: The children assemble at the top of the village to see the Prince of Wales pass on his way to Mere.*

1924 - Jan 25: attendance poor - heavy snow. May 20: Diocesan inspection 'hymns sung well and reverently, but the enunciation lacks clearness. The infants have bible stories read to them, but the lack of pictures prevents them from having a clear idea of the meaning.' We now take for granted colourful displays of pictures in both primary and secondary schools. No doubt good quality coloured prints were less easy to obtain in the 1920s.

1925 - School room still undivided. This statement is extraordinary, given that the Inspector's report of 1915 stated that there were very obvious disadvantages for both teachers and children in a situation where there was just one room to accommodate all, and yet nothing had been done 10 years later. *Mar 5: holiday for point-to-point races. Jun 21: holiday to Weymouth. Jul 23: outing to Bournemouth.*

1926 - All children who are 10 or who reach that age by 31 July to be transferred to Maiden Bradley school after the Easter holidays. This major change in the history of the school was brought about by the report of the Hadow Committee on the subject of 'The Education of the Adolescent', which decided that there should be a break between the primary and secondary phases of education at the age of 11. For reasons unknown, the local authorities took it into their heads to transfer ail the children aged 10 or over from KD school, although perhaps the new Act was unclear at this point. At least the transfer of the children eased the chaotic conditions of the undivided classroom. *Jun 28 - report: ' The school has suffered recently from devastating changes ...the singing was homely but hearty. The children were very happy in their work. The infants as last year were charming. They answered capitally in OT (David) and NT (the parable of the talents -not easy), and they recited without fault Ps 100. Altogether they made an excellent impression. Jul 20: to Bournemouth. Jul 27: to Weston-super- Mare.* Two separate outings to the sea within a week!

1927 - Jul 19: outing to Weymouth. Nov II: The children attended divine service to observe the two-minute silence, being Armistice Day. This is the first mention of the children having attended this particular service which was instituted in 1919. Matters concerning Remembrance were, however, severely delayed in remote villages, and the War memorial in KD churchyard was not erected until 1931.

1928 - Jul 2: outing to Weymouth. Report: 'since April 1925 the school has been a Junior School for children under 10 years of age. Headteacher absent in November and assistant is also absent. But these interruptions are not only accountable for the weaknesses that exist. Classes are conveniently small with 17 children in 1st class (Standards I to III) and 15 in 2nd class (infants). Need for higher standard of attainment in written English and arithmetic and for the teaching of History and Geography to be more realistic.'

1929 -Sep 9: 11 children transferred to Maiden Bradley School. Sep 19: the 11 children who were transferred return to the school today, the age of transference being raised by one year. What the children or their parents made of this 10-day wonder is unrecorded, although many of the families would have exchanged a 300 yard walk for a journey of 4 miles. It is also a strange situation anyway, since the 1926 report definitely states that the transfer age is for the over 11s. *Nov 28: admitted Amey, Harry and Robert Watts being boarded out children for the waifs.* These so-called 'waifs' were in fact young children who were being boarded out in a rural area under a scheme instituted by Dr.Barnardo (1845-1905). Later, unless the children found adoptive parents, they would be transferred to one of the Barnardo 'homes'.

1930 - Nov 17: 'waifs' left the village.

1931- Mar 17: 7 Emma May Higgins arrived at the school to take charge during the time Miss Garland is away through illness.

1932-Apr 4: Arthur Garrett is very ill with meningitis. Apr 20: Arthur Garrett has passed away. This entry is yet another example of the way in which the School logbook encapsulates the day-to-day history of the village, including its most tragic events.

1933 - May 24: Empire Day - the children spent the last hour in the school field when they sang patriotic songs and saluted the flag. The Rector gave a short speech in explanation of the Empire. This scene would be unimaginable in a school now, or indeed at any time after the Second World War. The children would have to attend the Last Night of the Proms in order to participate in a similar experience.

1934 - Jun 10: Diocesan report - 'on the whole the children are not of the brightest'.

From 1932 until the closure of the school in 1969 we have an

'Admissions Register' which details the birth, parentage and address of each child. As a result it would be possible to name and shame every student who is so disparagingly described as above - but it would be invidious to do so. *Jul 24: outing to Weymouth.*

1935 – Apr 17: Mrs Phoebe Garland gives up the post of Head Teacher at this school. Apr 29: Mrs Doris Ivy Richards commences duties as Head teacher today. The current owner of the School House (this being the cottage next to the school itself) received a letter from Mrs Richards in February 1981 from her address in Welshpool, expressing a wish to visit the school and her old home. Sadly, however, she fell ill before she could come. She was 25 when she was appointed as Headmistress, and 71 when she wrote. It is possible that she came at a later date and visited the Cammels when they were in residence at 'Bell House' – the original school building. Meanwhile Phoebe Garland had moved in her retirement to no.91 MD. *May 7: Children late because of Jubilee Festivities the previous day. I have spoken to the parents and children about punctuality and attendance.* Obviously a strict adherence

George V Silver Jubilee celebrations 1935

to the school timetable was of more importance than the celebrations which marked the 25th anniversary of King George Vs accession. *May 11: The supply of coal and wood is very inadequate and we have very little left to make fires on wet days. Jul 11: inspection -'Very good work is being done in the school under the new head teacher.* It is evident that the school had been through a very difficult time during the long periods of absence through illness of the previous headmistress, Phoebe Garland. The constant changes amongst the teaching staff had a serious effect on the childrens education. *Jul 26: a concert was given by the children. Everyone from KD, BD and MD was invited. Programmes were sold at 1d each (made by the children) and a collection raised £1. 15s and a halfpenny. During holidays a new door made into the 'Nature Room.' Oct 21: attendance 100% Nov 1-7: School closed for half-term and Duke of Gloucester's wedding (6th).*

1936 - Junior class visited 'Black Earth' excavation. We found some pots and stones of interest. We are starting a museum. A number of archaeological excavations took place on Cold Kitchen Hill, immediately to the north of the school, throughout the 1930s. One of the sites was entitled 'Black Earth Field' and the digs there yielded , artefacts from Roman times and earlier. The more important finds from this excavation are now displayed in the Salisbury Museum, and this perhaps puts in context the imaginative concept of the children setting up a museum of their own. They were fortunate indeed to be allowed on the site and to remove some of the doubtless less important 'treasures.' *Jan 28: Holiday for funeral of George V. Apr 27: 2 pictures arrive: St. Francis and St. George.* Does anyone know where these pictures are now? *Apr 30: Every child present - 28 on books.* 28 children in two classrooms – the infants separate from the others! A remarkable change from a few years earlier. *May 18: report: 'a marked improvement in the school since the new Headmistress arrived a year ago '. Jul 21: outing to Weymouth. Oct 6: 'Nature Room ' to be made into an extra classroom.*

1937- Mar 29. Rector [Robert Fugard] *warned children to be careful when walking along and crossing the roads.* Some private cars had obviously joined the farm vehicles, to the extent that crossing a road might prove occasionally hazardous. *Apr 15: Upper classes taken by head teacher for a nature walk to gather material for the aquarium and to notice birds on their nests. May - during holidays the offices were limewashed, cess-pit cleaned and rooms distempered. The piano was tuned.* Dorothy Richards is doing a great job and the school is transformed. *Jun 2: outing to Bristol Zoo. Jul 27: - village outing to Bournemouth.*

East Beach, Bournmouth 1950s

This is the first time that adult members of the community are, by implication, included in a school excursion. The departure of a vintage charabanc or two can readily be imagined as can the excitement of land-locked Wiltshire children who are on their way to what might well have been their first glimpse of the sea. *Dec 8: heavy fall - only 7 children came and they were taken home again.*

1938 - Jun 1: the children told to look both ways when crossing road. Traffic now increasing in both directions - namely from both Mere and Warminster. *Jul 1: Weymouth outing. Nov 28: Piano arrived from Duck, Son and Pinker, presented to the school by Mrs Mather. Mrs Mather has asked that the piano should always be tuned by D, S and P and not by Summerson of Warminster.* Presumably Summerson's undertook the task of tuning the piano mentioned in the logbook entry for April 15 1937 and - given the donor's insistence that the instrument should not be tuned by them - were perhaps at least partially responsible for the old piano's demise. The splendidly titled firm 'Duck, Son and Pinker' had been founded by William Duck on Pulteney Bridge in Bath in 1848, and flourished as the most famous music shop in the West Country until its closure in 2011. The instrument bought for the school by Mrs Mather was doubtless a good one and it was a most generous gift. *Dec 21: deep snow - only 4 children arrived.*

1939 - Jan 25: deep snow - only 5 children arrived Feb 3: Mrs DI Richards gave up post of Headmistress. Feb 6: Mrs June Mary Kingett commenced duties as Headmistress. Jul 14: inspection - 'plasticine modelling used to good effect' Sep 4: School would have opened today, but owing to evacuation arrangements the opening has been postponed for one week Sep 11: 27 children on register; 6 children on evacuation register. From the early summer of 1939 the government had rapidly put in place evacuation arrangements for London children should war be declared. After September 3rd small evacuees poured into the country. But effectively it was a false alarm, and when it became obvious that bombing was not imminent, parents insisted that the children came home, and most of them did. Unfortunately the 'evacuation register' for the school no longer exists, so we are not able to establish who these children were or whence they came. We know, however, that at least four of them returned almost immediately to London. *Sep 24: Mrs Jackson from HMI called concerning ARP* [Air Raid Precautions] *and evacuated children. The children invited by Mrs Stratton to tea and sports at Manor Farm. Oct 6: school closed so that 'Black Bat' screens could be made.* It was unlikely that German bombers would threaten remote 'lit-up' villages in Wessex, but in common with the all buildings throughout the country, however far from the nearest town, KD school had to be blacked out. *Dec 15: Whist Drive and Dance - funds for school and MD Church organ.*

1940 -Feb 9: number on roll 25 + 2 evacuees (both present). As it happens, we know who these two evacuees were, despite the fact that their names do not appear in the Admissions Register. Some years ago they contacted the current owner of 69 KD explaining that they had spent almost the entire war in his house, and expressed a wish to see it again, which was duly granted. It turned out that they were brother and sister, Richard and Joyce Harbud, and had been sent down from London in 1939 by their mother. Initially they were accommodated in a *'thatched cottage near the school,'* in which they awoke on their first morning *'covered in flea bites'*. A complaint to Mum resulted in a removal to the blissful comfort of 69, which happened at that time to be owned, as a holiday home, by a friend of the family, a Mrs Stephenson. They were instructed *'not to spoil any of the beautifully covered chairs and settee in William Morris design fabric in an upstairs room, nor damage the valuable ornaments'*. Eventually they were joined by their grandparents, and must have been amongst the best looked after and most comfortably housed evacuees anywhere. No wonder they stayed on. *Feb 11: School closed due to lack of coal. Jun 19: admitted 7 evacuee children from the Beckford School Dornfell St. NW6. Jun 20: admitted evacuee child. Mr Mildmay and Mr Pettit (head of the above school) called concerning these children. Admitted 4 other evacuated children and 1 other.* Given the latter information and particularly the name of the school with its intriguing local connotations, contact was made with Richard and Joyce Harbud who confirmed that it was from the Beckford School that they had been evacuated. The author thereupon phoned the school, arranged a visit and was given a fascinating guided tour. The building, a huge Victorian red-brick pile in West Hampstead, was opened in 1886 and was initially known as the Broomsleigh Street Board School. The name was changed in 1931 in recognition of the Beckford family who lived in a mansion in nearby West End Lane, and whose wealth enabled them to provide the funds for the school's construction. The family fortune derived from the sugar plantations in Jamaica owned by Alderman Beckford (1709-1770) who was twice Lord Mayor of London, and whose son William Beckford (1760-1844), novelist, art collector, musician and well-known eccentric, built the huge Gothic Folly, Fonthill Abbey, near KD. To an ex-evacuee it was an evocative experience to visit the infants class

The Beckford School, Hampstead

William Beckford (1766-1844)

Fonthill Abbey in 1823

and try to imagine what it would be like for those 21st century 4 and 5 year-olds to be suddenly transported to a remote part of the country as the Harbuds were, like the author, 75 years earlier. The two Beckford School evacuees, now aged 83 and 79, were still able to recall many aspects of their stay in KD - without, however, remembering the names of the other Beckford School pupils who were evacuated with them. They carved their initials in the belfry of the church, met Italian POWs who were working on the land, saw Mabel Carpenter pumping the organ blower whilst Mrs Carey of MD played the instrument, practised hymns from the unrevised A & M and Songs of Praise under Rev Caldwell's instruction at school on Wednesday mornings, saw Richard Stratton doing his rounds on horseback, undertook odd jobs for the owners of Hedge Cottage, and made a lifelong friend of the caretaker of no. 69, Mrs. Pearce. They were also able to confirm that the following children who appear in the Admissions Register with addresses in the London area were in fact evacuees: Betty and Joyce Matthews from Forest Gate, Philip Phillips from Childs Hill, Victor and Tony Baker from Walworth. *Jul 5: school has been closed on Fridays and Saturdays to make up for the long vacation which has been cancelled owing to the situation.* The ' situation' refers, of course, to the Battle of Britain and the imminent threat of invasion. Men who were not already in the armed forces or in 'reserved occupations' - of which farming was one - were involved in the Home Guard or in fire-watching duties. It is, however, rather surprising that a primary school's long vacation had been cancelled as a result, unless it was thought that mothers would be put under unnecessary strain if the children were at home in the absence of their fathers. It is also interesting to note that, in normal circumstances, the children would be at school on Saturdays. *Oct 7: 41 children on register.* This figure would have included about 12 evacuees. *Nov 4: Chicken pox - school closed for a week.*

1941 - Mar 7: owing to the fact that it is the local War weapons week, the school was required for a concert, so men of the 57th Royal Tank Regiment rather disorganised the school at 3 pm by erecting a stage. Jun 16: Mrs Ivy Preston took up duties as permanent Head. 20 Jun: piano tuned by Duck, Son and Pinker. Mrs Mather's injunctions are being adhered to. *10 Sep; 'blackpicking' for WI.*

1942 - May 12: the older children taken to the mobile cinema in the village. Sep 25: School holiday - potato harvest - until 12 Oct. School open on voluntary basis for attendance of children who cannot help in the fields. The latter provision obviously applies to the infants, and one wonders just how many parents offered their small offspring the choice.

1943- Jan: William Newell (aged 11) re-admitted - not allowed to go to senior school because of long absence due to paralysis. William, who lived in MD, had originally been admitted to the school in September 1935. It would appear that he had suffered from infantile paralysis, but at least had recovered sufficiently to enable him to return. There is no record against his name as to where he went after leaving KD school. *Aug 3: Inspection: ' the infants are a very happy lot of little people and had a great deal of information to impart to me'.* This does not sound like the language of a government official, and the inspector was doubtless the local Rector, Cecil Heath Caldwell, who had been appointed in 1938 and left the parish ten years later. *Nov 21:1 resigned my post as Headmistress - D Preston. Nov 29:1 Dorothy Nobbs take charge of school.*

1944 -Feb 8: Americans from Warminster call with two boxes of sweets for children. May 1:1 Barbara Hawley take post as Headmistress. This must have been a temporary appointment since Miss Nobbs still held the post and remained as Headmistress until her retirement in April 1961, three years after her marriage, when she became Mrs Newbury. *Jun 29: During the week ending June 30th admitted four more evacuees (girls). Jul 3: admitted one more evacuee (girl). Jul 26: admitted two more evacuee children. Jul 31: admitted 1 evacuee (boy)* This sudden influx of evacuees long after most of the original 1940 arrivals had returned home may seem surprising, but was entirely due to panic induced in many London homes by the arrival overhead of the terrifying flying bombs - otherwise known as doodlebugs or V1s- coinciding with the allied invasion of France. *Aug 3: Pamela Ross, an evacuee living with Mrs Joy of MD fell during playtime and caught her head on the school wall, resulting in a rather deep cut. Dr Whitby sent for. Nov 23: American Thanksgiving Day. Two officers from the American camp in the Rectory grounds came to talk to the children about America. They concentrated on their home states which were New Jersey and California.* After Rev. Henderson's departure in 1926, the Rectory was occupied by his successor Robert Cooper Fugard until his retirement in 1939 and it was not until then that the building passed into private hands. The new owners divided the interior into flats, and the occupants then experienced four years of relative peace and quiet before the Americans requisitioned part of the Rectory and its grounds for one of their camps, in preparation for the allied invasion of France in 1944. *Dec 5: Mr Michael Stratton came to the school to talk to the children about Burma.* Michael, Richard's brother, fought with the Chindits in the earlier part of the campaign against the Japanese. Family tradition has it that he was 'in charge of the mules'. *Dec 14: the children gave a concert of carols in the evening at 6.30. Parents and friends were invited. Certain carols were requested at the evening service at church the following Sunday when the lessons were read by two children - Norman Hobbs and Anne Brand.* (Anne Brand was an evacuee and after the war her family joined her and lived in the village for some years.) *During the morning, five children took the Intelligence Tests in the Wiltshire County exam -Anne Brand, Patricia Farr, Philip Phillips, Brian*

Fear and John Farr.

1945 - Jan 23: heavy snowfall. May 8: VE Day - school closed May 8,9 & 10. No mention of any celebrations, but doubtless the children and their parents danced excitedly around numerous bonfires as happened in every village and town throughout the country. (The author, earlier an evacuee, was sent home from his school in north Worcestershire at the age of 10 and remembers to this day the bright flames of the celebratory bonfire and the ecstatic expressions of joy and relief on the faces of the dancers.) *Aug 2: 1 boy caned today for continued disobedience and bad behaviour. Caning witnessed by Miss Taylor.* Lucky Miss Taylor. The war has ended but life goes on. *Dec 4: Headmaster and 12 junior children went to Salisbury Cathedral for carol service.* This is confusing, since there is no mention of Miss Nobbs having resigned. In any event the 'Headmaster' is unnamed. The logbook seems to be less sure of itself than has been the case hitherto.

1946 - Jul 4: outing to Weymouth. Dec 20: School party: parents and all children from the Deverills invited for conjuror.

1947 - Jan 29: 6 children present owing to bad weather. Children sent home after phoning Education officer. Feb 3: - no children turned up. Reference is made here to the famously severe winter of 1946/47 when there was huge disruption throughout the country as a result of massively heavy snowfall. Many villages were cut off for days - in some cases weeks and in many areas, notably the west Midlands, the drifts were so deep that the telephone wires on the top of their poles were only inches above the level of the snow. *Mar 5: very icy conditions - no milk. May 10: Brixton and Monkton children sent home at 3 pm as floods are out and they may not be able to get home otherwise. Jun 16 - ration books changed.* The end of the war brought no immediate reduction in the rationing of food, clothing or petrol. Indeed the reverse happened, since the harvest of 1946 was so poor that bread rationing was introduced in that year, and in 1947 the severe winter ruined the potato crop so that potato rationing was also added. It is doubtless as a result of these two events that the children's ration books were changed. It is also worth mentioning that bread remained rationed until 1948 , clothing until 1949 and meat until 1953, making the feeding and clothing of children at school and at home a nightmare post-war problem. It should also be remembered that mains electricity did not reach the Upper Deverills till well after the end of the war. Of more significance to the children themselves was the fact that sweets were not removed from the ration books until 1953 - although many of them were probably inured to existing on one square of chocolate a week, as opposed to the current customary intake of at least five bars. *Nov 20: School closed for Royal Wedding. Party for children from 3 villages held 2-5. Tea paid for by Mr Stratton.* The wedding of Princess Elizabeth and the Duke of Edinburgh must have seemed a welcome bright spot in these bleak years.

1948 - Jan 26: school to pantomime. Feb 4: this has become a Voluntary Controlled School from Dec-31, 1947. Under the Education Act of 1944, 'Voluntary Schools', that is to say those schools - mostly primary - who were governed and run by religious groups, were offered the option of 'aid' or 'control' by the state, the object being to improve the school facilities by means of finance derived from the taxpayer. KD School chose the Voluntary Control option which meant that the Local Education Authority would in future appoint all members of the staff and finance any necessary maintenance, although the Church of England would continue to own the building and retain a presence on the governing body. *Apr 14: county architect came to consult about the future of the field behind the school. Apr 26: School closed this afternoon for the Silver Wedding of the King and Queen. Jun 14: Children go to Mr Stratton for a short visit to see the sheep-shearing. Jun 17: Standards I - IV go to the brickyards in Crockerton to see the processes of brickmaking, tile making and pottery.* Successive generations of KD children would have been aware of sheep-farming from time immemorial, since that was what the downland which rose above them was all about. A springtime

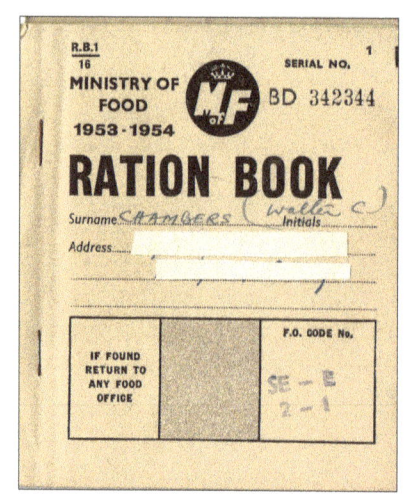

Ration Book

visit to the lambing sheds whence the incessant bleating spread throughout the village, was a special treat, as was a later introduction to sheep-shearing. Pottery had been made at Crockerton - hence the name - since the 13th century, but had been largely replaced in the early 19th century by brick and tile making. One of the clay pits was on the site now occupied by the ornamental lake at the Lakeside Garden Centre at LD. *Jul 20: annual outing to Weymouth. Nov 1: chimney and ceiling repairs in holidays. Fire in main classroom smoking too badly to continue fire. Report sent to Rector.* It appears that the Rector is still the local 'manager' of the school, but doubtless he would pass on this reported problem to the LEA who would in any case have paid for the chimney and ceiling repairs. *Nov 11: Mr Stratton gives a talk on the dairy, Nov 18: Mr Stratton gives talk on nitrogen in soil and plant food. Dec 2: Mr Stratton gives talk on birds.* The LEA's 'control' of the school has certainly not affected the continued input of the Stratton family. *Dec 20: - new tortoise stove installed in holiday.* Considering how long the school had to wait, the new stove is well-named.

1949 -Jan 25: infants from Maiden Bradley join KD infants class because of Mrs Newbury's illness. Apr 3: Miss Stratton gives a talk on her trip to Gibraltar. The Miss Stratton mentioned was one of Richard's two sisters Jean and Ruth, but which of them had recently visited Gibraltar is unknown. *Jul 23: 3 children transferred to Mere, 1 to Trowbridge.* The Admissions Register reveals that most children went on to Senior School at Mere, and that there was otherwise an almost equal spread between those going on to Warminster or Trowbridge, together with the very occasional scholarship entry to Dauntseys School at West Lavington.

1950-Apr 25: Standards 11-IV visit Warminster Station in afternoon. Shown round by Stationmaster. Sep 4: 24 on roll. I regret to record the loss of Mr R Stratton during the holiday. Mr R Stratton is the new correspondent. The elder Richard Stratton was the son of the original member of the Stratton family who took over the tenancy of KD Manor Farm in 1865. His son, a second Richard and father of the current owner of the farm, kept up, as did his family, the 'correspondent' interest in the school until its closure in 1969. This 'younger' Richard died in 2011. *Oct 31: Mrs Stratton gave a talk on her holiday in France.* The lecturer was Richard's wife, Pamela.

Kingston Deverill School, 1950s

1951 -27 on roll. May 20: Mr Stratton gave picture of Bluebell Woods to school. Jun 6: Stoolball match with Maiden Bradley. This mention of 'Stoolball' is fascinating in that the game - a variation of cricket - died out as an activity in schools during the course of the later 1950s. It was invented in Sussex in the 15th century and there are still adult Stoolball leagues in that county. *Dec 7: children to Warminster for carol festival.*

1952 - 29 on roll. May 5: Mr Kelly gave talk on Australia. Jul 3: School goes to Mere to see the Queen. The Queen had acceded to the throne on February 6th 1952 and she was in Mere on one of her many perambulations round the country prior to her Coronation the following year. *Nov 10: 3 dinner plates sent to Kilmington [!] Dec 11: Miss Basard talks to children about China.*

1953 -26 on roll. Apr 16 - cabinet for radiogram bought. Jun 2: Television and tea in school on the day of the Coronation of Her Majesty Queen Elizabeth. This may have been the second view of the Queen for many of the children, but for all of them, as for the adults, it would probably be the first time that they had sat in front of a television - black and white and lots of 'snow'. *Jun 12: outing to Stonehenge.*

1954 - Miss C J Burton appointed as infant teacher. Jan 21: heavy snowfall. Feb 22 - the school weighing machine is overhauled. Mar 2 Miss Burton absent - weather. Mar 8: Mrs Stratton on supply in infants class. Apr 14: Miss Burton resigns. Apr 21: Mrs Stratton takes over infants. Jun

30: Mrs Stratton leaves. Jul 5: Miss Dufosee begins as Infants mistress. This is an amazingly disruptive year for the infants. Was it the LEA who appointed Miss Burton, unaware of how her tenure would be interrupted by the weather and the weighing machine? It is interesting to read how local people immediately take on responsibilities at the school, presumably with the LEA's approval.

1955 -Apr 6: Plays etc. performed this afternoon. 10 shillings given to MD church roof. Apr 20: milk now delivered in bottles supplied by C.H Smith, Warminster. Jun 28: Major Miles came to give a talk on Germany after his service there. Jul 7: Mr Stratton gave a talk on Spain after his holiday. Sep 5: Scripture report: ' the atmosphere of the church permeates this school. Great pains are taken to provide freshness in its devotional life. It may be said that the school is a good power source for the church.' The school's recently acquired 'voluntarily controlled' status does not seem to have affected its close attachment to the C of E, and it may well be that the extremely popular local Rector, Giles Martin Spinney, who was appointed in 1954 and remained in the post until 1982, had much

Giles Martin Spinney, Rector 1954-1982, Miss Dufosee and Miss Nobbs with school group, 1955

to do with religious instruction at the school. He must have been very pleased with this highly complimentary diocesan report. Meanwhile it is notable that the children have been all round the world in the last few years - to Burma, France, Spain, France, Gibraltar, China, USA and Germany - with the result that their appreciation of Geography must have been right up there with RE.

1956 - Jul 27: annual leavers service in church.

1957 - Mar 12: 4 chairs and 1 fireguard delivered. I had previously cancelled the order for two of these chairs. Apr 21: work on putting the screen between the two classrooms is not completed. May 2. The large classroom is now divided into two rooms and a new stove has been installed in each room. New windows have been put in. Raymond Castle won first prize in an essay on 'kindness to animals'. Forget about 'kindness to animals'; it would have been a rather more relevant 'kindness to pupils and staff' if the partitioning of the classroom had been accomplished when the idea was first mooted some 40 years earlier. *May 7: 7 children go in Mr Stratton's Landrover for polio injections at Maiden Bradley. Jul 26: Miss Dufosee leaving to get married.*

1958 - Jan 10: Trouble with smoke and sulphur fumes: Mr Hillier-Brown and Mr Deverill come for consultation. Mar 28: clock presented to me as wedding present from 3 villages. The Headmistress, Miss Nobbs, has become Mrs. Newbury.

1959 - Jan: 30 on roll. Apr 7: 35 on roll.

Given these figures it would seem a good moment to extract some statistics from the Admissions Register, if only to indicate the gradual running down of the school during the 1950s and the more precipitate fall in the intake during the following decade.

In the five years between 1950 and 1954 sixty children entered the school, and in the next five years, 1955 - 1959 forty-seven were admitted. Moving on to the 60s, in the years 1960 – 1964 thirty-two came, and in the final five years 1965 - 1969 only twenty-three.

It is also interesting to compare the numbers entering from the 'three villages' (and very occasionally elsewhere) during these last two decades of the school's existence. Of the 107 children who came to the school in the 1950s, 54 were resident in Kingston, 28 in Brixton and 22 in Monkton, the remaining three coming from Hill Deverill,

Maiden Bradley and - rather surprisingly - St.Helena (not immediately adjacent to the Deverill Valley). In the 1960s the division was: Kingston 22, Monkton 23, Brixton 9 and one from Wishford.

Thus we have a total of 107 children entering the school in the 50s and only 55 in the 60s - virtually half the number. Equally significant is the drop in the number of children coming from Kingston - 22 as against 54, indicating that a large number of families left the village when post-war employment difficulties eased elsewhere in the 1960s. The drop in numbers entering from Brixton is also considerable, perhaps for the same reason or because parents found it more convenient to send their children to Crockerton or to Sutton Veny. (Strangely neither of these considerations seemed to apply to Monkton). The average age at which the children entered the school during this period was 5 years and 9 months.

1960 -33 on roll. Jan 6: visit by HMI Lady Helen Asquith. May 6: School closed for Princess Margaret's wedding. Nov 3: much plaster down in room above school. Nov 10: Lady Helen Asquith spends day with school.

1961 - 29 on roll. Jan 19: Lady Helen Asquith's report.

Lady Helen Asquith (1908 – 2000) joined the Schools Inspectorate in 1938, and following her move to her mother's home in Mells after the war, took on the responsibility for the inspection of schools in Wiltshire. To judge by the sympathetic lucidity of her report on Kingston Deverill Primary School, it was obviously a privilege for any educational establishment to have this eminent and cultured granddaughter of a former Prime Minister as an inspector of their premises and as a judge of the children's attainments and shortcomings. (Lady Helen was the daughter of Katherine Horner and Raymond Asquith (1878-1916), Herbert Asquith's eldest son, who was killed in the war. The Horner family had lived in Mells since 1543).

Lady Helen Asquith (1980)

She begins her report by stating that the last inspection had taken place in 1943 (18 years earlier) and that the establishment which was now subject to her report had since then changed to a voluntarily controlled C of E school attended by 28 girls and boys aged between 4 and 11, taught in two classes. She goes on to describe the schoolroom as a recently partitioned area of 700 sq ft., but then immediately highlights the problems which arise, as follows: *'The two teachers greatly appreciate the convenience of the two classrooms, but the arrangement also has certain drawbacks. Although the Infants room is light and sunny, the Junior room, cut off from a south window by the partition is rather gloomy and cold .... It is also an inconvenience that the Infants' only access to the sanitary offices and playground is by passing through the Junior room'.*

She then describes the three other rooms in the property - a 170 sq. ft. lobby where coats are hung, a former classroom now used as a dining area, and a small scullery *'in which a sink, washbasin, hot cupboard and water heater have been installed. This fixed handbasin and portable basin in the scullery sink are the children's only means of washing. Most of them stay to the midday meal, and their ablutions- which are faithfully if somewhat unhygienically performed- are a hindrance to the caretakers preparations for serving.'*

Even in the 1960s she must have been concerned by some aspects of 'Health and Safety' as illustrated by the Scullery - but worse was to come:- *'Bucket type sanitary offices of the most primitive kind are reached from the playground. The closets are extremely dark and wholly lacking in privacy, but they are kept in good order by the caretaker'* [Mrs Pearce] *' who at the age of 78 continues to give devoted service to the school'*. This description is typical of the balanced nature of the report, in that a damning indictment of the facilities is immediately followed by a positive commendation. Nonetheless, Lady Helen holds nothing back when she describes the antiquated furniture and poor storage arrangements, and is particularly concerned for the infants who lack *'display space, picture books and story books of good quality, and material for the handwork and creative and dramatic play which ought to be essential elements in the teaching of young children'*. Again, however, she moves on to commend the Headmistress, Mrs Newbury, - *'a graduate of Sheffield University who was appointed in 1946 and, having given long service in the County, intends to retire next summer. She is a lively teacher and very capable organiser. Her happy combination of serenity and vigour, coupled with great kindliness are particularly effective in securing the confidence and co-operation of all pupils'.*

She then commends the infant teacher and, with some reservations, the quality of the infants' work. She is particularly impressed with their reading *'in which attainments are above average'*, but her following comments concerning learning methods point up a perennial problem: - *'the emphasis on phonetic work and the early introduction of cursive handwriting and of certain arithmetical processes usually delayed till a later stage may create difficulties for the less able children, but the abler pupils of whom there are several in the present class, do not seem to take serious harm from this forcing of the pace.'* It is then fascinating to be taken back in time by her description of the use of a radio - rather than computers and television - for instruction: *'Music and Movement broadcasts are taken in the classroom, and some unusually nimble and active Physical Training was seen with the Headmistress in the playground'*. Mrs Newbury might have been on the point of retiring, but she was clearly still more than capable of prancing around with the 5 year olds.

Lady Asquith then concerns herself with the Juniors, and both she and the school are seen in an especially admirable light in the following extract from the report: *'the Junior class contains one extremely retarded boy of 11 who is due to go to a Special School. Although he can achieve very little in school work, he is treated with the greatest patience and kindness and is never allowed to feel out of it, either by his teacher or his fellow pupils.'* She is impressed by the pupils' progress in History and Geography and *'particularly Religious Instruction'*, but is critical about the provision of appropriate books: *'the supply of books is quite generous in quantity but rather disappointing in quality. Textbooks are old-fashioned and there are rather too many cheap editions and abridged or simplified versions of story books which would be more profitably studied in their complete form ... in particular the children need more opportunities for reading poetry of real quality.'*

The visit ends on a high note: *'some 21 children stayed to dinner*

Kingston Deverill School, 1961

on the day of the inspection. The meal is sent from Mere and served by the Headmistress and the Caretaker, and the food on the day of the visit was plentiful and appetising. Although the dining space is extremely cramped and rather chilly, the meal was a gay and pleasant social occasion.'

The eminent, not to say aristocratic, 42-year old visitor then signs off with a final compliment: *'in spite of the limitations of material conditions, the children in this school make good progress in the skills of learning. They are happy and co-operative with their teachers, and friendly and courteous to visitors and they get admirable training here in the give and take of communal living.'*

Apr 4: 'Headmistress resigns.' *Sep 11: G Mounsden takes temporary charge. Mrs Cooper made supervisor, Mrs Jackson school cleaner.*

1962 - Mrs V Werner takes up duties as Headmistress. May 11: complaint about school meals sent to Mere: 'There was approx. a slice of egg between three children and bread buttered with a margarine-like substance'. This description of the school's culinary experience is distinctly at variance with that reported by Lady Asquith. Either matters had gone downhill or an unusually special meal had been prepared for her on the occasion of her visit. *May 19: visit to the Roman Baths in Bath. Jul 24: 7 bottles of milk were sour today. Nov 13: new building of flush toilets.* It is obvious that some heed is being taken of Lady Helen's strictures about the sanitary arrangements - but see related disasters below. *Dec 5: Mrs Coleman fainted almost at lunchtime.* It seems that the children are still conducting their ablutions whilst their food is being prepared. *Dec 13: visit to Salisbury Playhouse.* The archives of the theatre reveal that this production went under the interestingly composite title of 'Robin Hood and the Babes in the Wood' – Sherwood Forest presumably being the imaginative connecting factor.

1963 - Jan 8: snow-blocked roads; the children are bringing soup and cocoa which we had at school. Jan 11: roads to Mere and Maiden Bradley are still impossible. Jan 18: Timothy Gallup has still not attended school although the road is passable to his home. Mrs Gallup insists he uses the school bus which is not yet running. This he is not entitled to do. Presumably the Headmistress is trying to say that Timothy's usual entitlement to the non-running school bus does not mean that his mother is exonerated from sending him to school on foot. This implication would receive short shrift today. *Sep 9: waste tank full: children had to use neighbours' toilets. Request that tank be emptied weekly. Sep 16: waste tank full again. Sep 17-18: school closed: no toilet facilities.* So much for the recent provision of flush toilets. It's surprising that the school did not revert to the 19th century buckets which had provided good service up until 1961.

1964 - Jun 26: trip to Salisbury Cathedral cancelled owing to lack of transport

1965 - Jan 29: heavy snow: the Brixton children go home at 1.30. Feb 12: waste tank overflowing. Feb 18: school closed because of overflowing waste tank. Mar 25: school closed - all roads blocked to village. If it's not the toilets, it's the snow. Unless, of course, it was a combination of the two. *Apr 2: Mrs Newbury removes Elizabeth, her daughter from school to protest against a detention I set.* This is a different Mrs Newbury - not the retired Headmistress. *Jul 19: annual outing to Branksome Chine.*

1966 - Jan 6: Miss Smissen begins duties as infants teacher. More problems with sewage tank. Mar 17: visit to Wilton Carpet Factory. Mar 31: election holiday. Jul 18: This refers to the 'snap' election when the Labour Party was returned with an increased majority under the leadership of Harold Wilson, who embarked on a second term as Prime Minister. *Dec 16: Carol service at Christchurch.* The reference here is to Christ Church, Warminster.

1967 -Jan 20: Lady Helen visits. New roller towelling provided and tank emptied every other day. The Asquith magic wand is waved once again. *Mar 3: 4 children from the Gray family leave district. Roll now 22.* Perhaps this entry marks the beginning of the end for the school. *Jun 22: conference on the Plowden Report.* This report was commissioned by Sir Edward Boyle, then the Education Minister, in 1963, and the committee who published it in 1967 was chaired by Lady Plowden. It was a comprehensive review of Primary Education in the country and made a number of recommendations, very few of which, as it turned out, proved to be practicable. The major decision was that there should be a 'three tier' system, based on primary schools for children aged 5 -8, middle schools for those aged 8/9 to 11, and secondary schools for older children. This came into effect in some areas, but didn't impinge on the Deverill Valley. There was also a call for more male teachers, which went largely unheeded, but the most significant injunction, which was to be pursued immediately, was that there should be no further physical punishment for primary school children (unfortunately 22 years too late for the disobedient boy whose caning was witnessed by Miss Taylor in August 1945). Corporal punishment nonetheless continued in some preparatory and primary schools well into the 70s. What has not been forgotten is the mantra that 'Education should be child centred' - although it seems that KD School hardly needed reminding about that. *Jul 17: trip to Sandbanks - weather scorching. Nov 3: Decorators start work on the school. Nov 20: Mrs Titt - a parent visits. Dec 20: Headmistress Mrs V Werner resigns.*

1968- Poppy Smissen asst .teacher assumes responsibility for school. Feb 21: Miss Tyrer arrives as supply teacher + Mrs. Newbury. Apr 30: 20 children on roll. Jul 9: meeting of managers to discuss future development of primary school education in the area. Writing already on the wall. *Sep 9: school re-opens — 17 on roll. Sep 13: telephone installed.* It has taken a long time to replace the Bush Telegraph installed in 1840, but at least the new technology will assist the authorities in their announcement to parents (those with the wherewithal to receive calls) that their offspring will have to receive their education elsewhere. *Dec 13: notice of closure posted on school door. Dec 16: sergeant from Salisbury Police to*

Kingston Deverill School, 1968

talk on road safety. This will help on the 8 mile walk to Sutton Veny. *Dec 18: Christmas party. Dec 19: parents at the school to hear songs and carols sung by the children.* This must have been an especially nostalgic occasion. *Dec 20: I, Poppy Smissen, resign as teacher in charge of the school. 15 children on roll.*

1969- school re-opens. 13 children on roll. I have taken charge of school - M.E. Farley. Apr 2: school closes for Easter Holiday. This is the final closure of the school. Next term the 13 children from Kingston Deverill are to be transferred to Sutton Veny School.

[See Appendix D for an extract from the School Admissions Register which gives the names of those children who attended the school between 1949 and 1969].

4 Farming in the Upper Deverills

Richard Stratton (1982)

But they will maintain the fabric of the world;
And in the handiwork of their craft is their prayer.
Ecclesiasticus ch. 38, v. 34

Two thousand years ago the settled population of this country was found on the chalk hills of Southern England – the Cotswolds, west Dorset, and eastward to Kent and the Chiltern Hills. Just as Salisbury has long been a market city through being at the confluence of five rivers, so our ancestors sited their capital where the Thames drew them to the sea. At London's back door they colonised the light lands of Hertfordshire, Norfolk and Suffolk. It was only on easy working soil that the primitive scratch plough pulled by two oxen could make any penetration. The high chalk has always been a forester's nightmare, but in Iron Age times it required minimal clearance. The heavy axe and mouldboard plough which was to tackle the oak, ash and beech forests on the clay of England arrived with the Belgae only shortly before the Christian era. Chalkland may be thin of soil but it is well drained, the water being held like a sponge by the chalk beneath. Farmers have long known that corn yields excel in a wet season, and nowadays it is accepted that the amalgam of moderate summer temperatures, long days, and ample rainfall, provide almost ideal conditions for top yields of cereals. Down the centuries, from the Saxons struggling to develop the mouldboard plough, to Jethro Tull's corn drill and on to the machinery we see today, chalk farmers have at least been working on a rewarding medium. When considering the saga of farming in the Deverills over the last two centuries, it is suggested that we survey the scene at 50 year intervals, i.e. 1780, 1830, 1880, 1930 and 1980. Each date has in fact marked a turning point in the story.

> First we must learn the changeful moods of heavens,
> And all the winds, and of each several field
> The natural character, what this consents,
> What that declines to bear. Here cereals thrive,
> here grapes more gladly ripen, here again
> Green saplings flourish and unbidden grass.
> Thus on each region Nature long ago
> Her stern necessities and changeless laws imposed...
>
> *Virgil (Georgics Bk.1)*[1]

In the 18th century the difficult clays of North and West Wiltshire were given, of necessity, to permanent grass, and this was cashed in the form of milk and cheese. Farmers and herdsmen were scattered near cattle steadings and thus escaped the full rigours of the manorial system. Fifty years later they were to provide the forceful men who developed dairies and the modern corn techniques on the neighbouring uplands. By 1780, away in Norfolk, Thomas Coke was just beginning to demonstrate his four-course rotation of turnips, barley and oats, clover and grass ley, and finally wheat. The basis of farming in the Deverills, as in much of the country, was still the Open Field system, in which tractable land near the village was divided into innumerable small strips of less than one acre each, these then being allocated by the Lord of the Manor (in Kingston, Lord Bath) to leaseholders so that each had a plot in each field. When the system was first introduced from the Mediterranean seaboard the rotation would have been corn and fallow alternately to conserve moisture. In England it was soon extended to two years cereals, followed by one year fallow.

---

1   Richard Stratton has used the 1697 translation of Virgil's *Georgics* by John Dryden (1631-1700)

The villages grew up near the river for the sake of a water supply. Even in the author's childhood the river contained vastly more water than now, for the pumps at Mere had not lowered our water table and there were good hatches everywhere. There would in 1780 have been ample water to power the grist mills at Monkton and Hill Deverill. Especially in spring, flooding the water meadows for early grass presented no problem. Away from the water meadows and the Open Fields were the unenclosed Downs capped with gorse. Wood for fuel was a continuing concern and many of the woods that we see today would have then been hazel-coppice, a certain proportion being cut each year. We have recently learnt that no other method of forestry yields more timber per acre. The bound faggots were used for house-warming and bake ovens, and the better wood had innumerable uses for building, thatching spars, hurdle making and garden use.

The prosperity of our villages was linked to the Wiltshire horn ewes which were organised communally and ranged the Downs every day in charge of shepherds. The vital thing was that by night they were penned in a moveable fold of hurdles on the cultivated strips, thus manuring the soil and allowing wheat to be grown. This process however took a great deal from the Downs and put nothing back, so that after 150 years of it they had been drained of fertility. The drawback to the system was the lack of sheep food in winter, which is notoriously long and severe hereabouts. Everything, except actual breeding ewes and ewe lambs had to be sold or salted down in the autumn. Hay from the meadows was reserved until after Christmas. Salvation was provided by the water meadows which could be made to produce a flush of grass for the ewes and their lambs in March/April; when at last the Downs grew in May the meadows were shut up for hay. Sometimes vetches were grown on the fallow strips for midsummer folding.

In modern times Wiltshire is easily accessible, but in 1780 it consisted of a number of remote and largely self-contained communities. A surveyor of the time records: 'Wiltshire, as being partly a corn and partly a grass country, is capable of producing most of the articles of human sustenance, and, being in general a well-cultivated district, its produce is considerably more than its consumption. The principal products are corn, chiefly wheat and barley, cheese and butter: fat calves; fat cattle and sheep and fat pigs. The manufacturing towns within the county and in the eastern part of Somerset and the cities of Bath and Bristol furnish a constant regular demand for these products and London took no inconsiderable part of them.'[1] As far as the Deverill Valley was concerned much of its business would have been through the market at Warminster and the various local sheep fairs, through which huge numbers of store animals were sold for fattening in the Eastern counties.

There is no doubt that the local villages of the 1780's were busy, self-sufficient communities. Those men not hired to work on the land found employment in service occupations as road-makers, carriers, drowners, thatchers, builders, bakers, smiths or millers, the few unable to work being given some support on parish relief. The women too were all busy with their domestic duties, and probably organised some basic education for their children under the supervision of the parson. Dwellings were primitive and facilities non-existent, so that life must have been harsh, particularly in the winter.

By the last quarter of the 18th Century the Industrial Revolution was well under way. The manufacturing industries being established in the towns led to an increased demand both for workers and food with which to feed them, and it soon became clear that the archaic Open Field system was inadequate. Change was in the air. As it turned out then, and has so often happened since, war provided the immediate stimulus. The long-drawn-out Napoleonic wars were a true struggle for national survival and at times the threat of starvation was real. This led to rapid price rises, so that whereas in 1780 corn had been 35s.8d per quarter, by 1812 it had soared to 126s.6d and even in 1830, fifteen years after the war had ended, was still 64s.3d. This had led to furious activity in the valley. Leaseholders had been bought out to make tenanted farms, hedges planted, and buildings erected, and cows brought under cover in the winter so as to improve the milk supply. Although the local farmers had a reputation for

1   Davis, T. *General view of the Agriculture of the County of Wilts*, London, 1794. Thomas Davis was steward to the Marquis of Bath.

building good ricks, much of the harvest was stored in barns. A report says: 'their barns are indeed as well calculated as possible for the reception of corn, brick and stone walls being cautiously avoided, except for the foundations and timber and weather-board being used in their stead, and the covering usually being thatch. The general and almost the only material for barn floors in this district is two-inch oak plank laid on oak sleepers, and to prevent rats and mice from burrowing under them they are frequently laid on a bed of flints or broken cinders and sometimes raised on staddle-stones.'[1]

In the parish of Kingston Deverill an oak floor of this type which had been laid down for 34 years was, when taken up, found to be perfectly sound on the under side of the planks, while the surface had been completely worn away by the flail. Many new crops adorned the scene. Potatoes had transformed the diet of the poor, and fields of turnips, rape, sanfoin, peas and vetches along with 'artificial' grasses and clovers provided so much winter keep for the sheep that even the ewe lambs could at last be wintered at home. The nearer downlands had been ploughed, and on the extra acres barley was the favoured cereal. Yields per acre in the district – previously, wheat 22 bushels (12cwt), barley 28 bushels (14 cwt), and oats 36 bushels (13 cwt) – had been raised by a quarter. Barley perhaps increased by a third. Artificial manures were still non-existent, and all depended still on fertility brought on by sheep from the Downs. Keysley Down, being on its own, was not so treated, and the stock that grazed there slept there. This resulted in its rental value being enhanced almost to that of arable land in the locality, a clear indication of what might be achieved with manure. All this development, allied to high corn prices, made for great prosperity in the valley, and enclosure brought more benefit than drawback to the people. It is true to say that it was in this period that the mediaeval layout of our villages was changed dramatically into substantially that of the present day.

The Deverills faced the New Year of 1880 with morale at an all-time low. After the confident years of the Golden Age, 1879 had

[1] Thomas Davis, *op.cit.*

brought the worst season that anyone could remember. The winter had been one of the coldest of the Century with much snow. On 27th May, after a late spring, a great thunderstorm ushered in the wet spell. June 6.80 ins, July over 4 ins, and August 6.45 ins, tell their own story. Haymaking started on the 11th July and finished in the valley on 15th August. Harvest did not start until 4th September, and what little corn was saved was useless. Farmers were ruined in every direction, but no one else minded because corn had recently started to flood in from the fertile prairies of America at rock-bottom prices, and to cap it all the first shipload of frozen beef had just arrived from Australia. The era of cheap imported food had dawned, and British farming had begun its long decline which was to last for some sixty years. This was all the more galling because so much had been done. The downs above the valley had been fenced in, using massive oak posts dug in every three yards that were to last a century. Mechanical mowers for grass, and binders for corn, had effected a transformation, as had the new threshing machines. Superphosphate made from bones, and guano from seabird manure were joined with chalk and lime to condition the soil, while protein-rich oilcakes fed to stock also enriched the land. Cereal yields had increased and prices had held up because, in spite of all, progress had been barely enough to feed the fantastic increase in the town population. Now, however, other countries were ready to do it at less cost.

Unaware that their way of life had reached its zenith the crowded population of the valley went about its daily tasks. In the barns, wheat was bagged up from the heaps using wooden bushel scoops, weighed off at 2 1/4 cwt in each tidy sack, and loaded onto the wagons for Warminster; there were six sacks on each side and one in the middle at the back, like a priest following choirboys. The pair of Shire horses were beautifully turned out and were usually in shafts abreast. Warminster was an important market and the sacks of corn were often unloaded in the market street. Similar convoys of wagons came from the Nadder Valley through Stockton Wood and down to Boyton, and the carters had a convivial time before it was time to go to the railway station and load up Radstock coal for the return journey. The beer was strong and the potholes deep, and frequent was

Mr William Stratton (1834-1919)

the damage to life and limb, so that William Stratton was constrained to build a road at his own expense in Monkton Deverill to by-pass The New Inn! The valley road from Brixton to Hill Deverill, by then 25 years old, was a great boon.

Other carters took their team to the fields, while the shepherds turned the ewes away on the Downs, then dismantled the vacated fold into stands of four hurdles. The under-shepherd would push one post, or shore, through suitable holes in the four handles, collect up the other three shores, hold four wire hoops or raves in his hand and carry the lot forward to where the headman was pitching out the new 'Bite' with a fold bar. This routine took place seven days a week in all weathers. After dinner, taken in the portable shepherd's hut, the head shepherd would stroll out to collect the ewes from the down and, who knows, secure something for the pot, such time as his underling was collecting exposed flints from the back fold into heaps. Sometimes flints were quarried from the soil, so great was the demand for mixing with chalk quarried locally for road-making. Lambing started soon after Christmas, so that the new breed of Hampshire Down lambs had sufficient time to yield a heavy carcase in October. The lambs were always in a worm-free fold, the ewes' lot being to clean up at night the residues in the stale fold. The ration was all arable crops, first swedes and kale, then rye and temporary grasses in April/May, vetches over midsummer, then aftermath of hay until massive crops of rape and turnips were ready in August for two months fattening. Lambing had to take place adjacent to a field of swedes and kale, and most substantial pens were built in each year. The central straw yard to house the pregnant ewes at night was walled by a double row of hurdles with straw sandwiched between. From this sprung a lean-to of continuous hurdles resting on their short ends and supported at 45 degrees by timbers in front, under this being coops in which newly-born lambs and mothers could spend forty-eight hours. Beyond the central pens were hardening-off pens before the swedes and kale were re-joined. In no time at all the lambs found their way through a creep into a front pen where cake was available in troughs. No animal ever had a better start in life.

The schools in Longbridge, Kingston and Monkton Deverill were built about now and compulsory education started. They were filled to capacity as the villages were full of children. Also filled to capacity were the churches in the Deverills on Sunday evenings when the four parsons beamed down on flocks packed to the doors. Folly indeed to have jeopardised job and dwelling by non-attendance.

The year 1880 marked a watershed for our country and still more for its countryside. After a century of tremendous progress and development, farming had raised production to the highest level possible with the resources to hand. Further progress waited upon people other than farmers – plant breeders, chemists, engineers and animal geneticists – which new schools would provide in the fullness of time.

> Our stability is but balance, and conduct lies
> In masterful administration of the unforeseen.
>
> *Robert Bridges*

When the writer's grandfather William contemplated the unforeseen in 1880, his reasoning must have been thus: 'I doubt if I can ever grow corn to compete with this imported stuff.' (In fact the price of wheat dropped from a price of 45s. per qr. – about £10 per ton – to a low of 23s. per qr. – about £5 per ton – in 1894.) 'However, Cousin Arthur, at Alton Priors has several sets of steam tackle which he is anxious to hire out and we will try the effect of this on the heavy land in the Bradley Valley which ought to grow good crops if tackled this way. I was brought up to understand milking cows. The cheese dairy at Bradley Road is a success and I will start an ordinary dairy in the village. I shall push this cheap imported corn into the cows and also use it to augment the whey for the pigs at Bradley Road. At least dairy and pig products still seem to be wanted. Thank goodness Lord Bath and I have got the downs fully fenced. I will soft-pedal on the hurdle flock and buy a lot of cheap lambs from Scotland to run around for a year. If my landlord will ease back on the rent I may get through!' In the event he was one of the few that did. So impressed was he by the steam tackle that eventually he bought two engines for himself and a third, a lighter one, to drive the threshing machine. The policy of buying imported feeding stuffs was carried to such lengths that in the 1920's every barn in the valley would be chock-full in the autumn with flaked maize (cornflakes) rice meal and protein cakes all bought at about £5 per ton delivered in. The lamb venture was soon under way; the Warminster Journal of 7th October 1882 noted:

> Much interest was created at Trowbridge railway station on Saturday

by the arrival of two long special trains containing no less than 1,800 Scotch sheep – white-faced, black-faced and horned – consigned to Mr. Wm. Stratton of Kingston Deverill. They are, we understand, to be turned on to the large quantity of downland which that gentleman occupies. They appeared to be a wiry breed and on leaving the train jumped like deer. The cost of carriage alone amounted to upwards of £200. The untrucking and despatching to Warminster of flock after flock was superintended by Mr. Stratton himself.

The Great War brought a sudden call for food at any price, but motive power was still restricted to human muscle and the draught of heavy horses, and this set a limit to what could be done. There was still a full population in the valley and it took all their strength to work the farms. The war was to prove only an interruption in the remorseless decline of agriculture. The body blow came in 1922 with the sudden repeal of the Corn Production Act. The price of wheat dropped from 80s. per quarter to 40s. in a year and farm wages were cut back. This time the whole country entered into a depression which reached its nadir in 1930. Labour left the villages steadily and nothing was spent. I can remember my father buying only one new implement – an elevator made by John Wallis Titt of Warminster. Many farms could

Mr Maidment (senior) c.1920

not find a tenant, and land in the valley bought for £16 an acre in 1920 was valued at £10 in 1930. At this date mains electricity, which had come to Godalming in Surrey in 1881, was still 17 years away from the Deverills, and its absence caused no comment. Rural life was truly broken. Each day in my childhood I expected my father to announce that we were bankrupt. The repeal of the Corn Production Act put paid to corn growing, even with the help of the steam tackle which was then sold for scrap, and thousands of acres in this district tumbled down to permanent pasture which was ranched. Grassland sheep, such as Exmoors, replaced the hurdle flocks and were lambed in April. Rabbits abounded. In one year 3,000 carcases were sent out of Kingston Deverill by rail to Smithfield Market where they sold on commission. A return of 9d each brought great joy to the breakfast table.

In the 1920s the postal address of the Deverills was Bath, and the mail was delivered by horse-drawn vehicle to Maiden Bradley. A hero called Charlie Newbury then walked with it down the valley. His first drop was Kingston Deverill Post Office, so that the postmaster, Mr.John Carpenter, could deliver round the village at a salary of 5s. per week. Charlie then called at Manor Farm sharp at 8 o'clock and then delivered the post on down as far as Longbridge Deverill, where a hut was provided for him in which to spend the afternoon. At tea time he set off to walk back home up the valley, clearing boxes as he went, his last clearance at Kingston Deverill Post Office being timed for 6.45 p.m. When the writer first remembers him he had graduated to a bicycle for the trip. He never missed a day. One of the excitements of the week was the Wincanton to Warminster bus which came through the valley from Maiden Bradley. It soon gave up.

The only bright spot in the farming scene was the arrival of the natural fertiliser, nitrate of soda, mined in Chile. The nitrogen it contained did marvellous things to grass and root crops but, if applied at more than 1 cwt per acre, it caused the then varieties of corn to fall over flat with shock. It enabled a yield of one ton per acre of wheat to be grown in Kingston in 1919, which warranted a cable with the news being despatched to Hong Kong to my uncle who was travelling round the world.

What then of the much vaunted internal combustion engine? Messrs. Petter and Lister put their wonderful small-horsepower stationary paraffin engines on the market and these found a myriad of uses – water pumping, driving barn machinery and elevators in the field. Tractors were still too unreliable and feeble for this hilly country, but the famous 10/20 International Junior from America was famous 'on the belt'. The local hills proved too much for the early cars. My parents allowed an hour for the five mile journey to Charnage near Mere on Sunday afternoons. Mother had to jump out and put a block of wood behind the wheel when the engine stalled. Usually three attempts were necessary this side; to conquer Warminster Hollow on the return trip necessitated the four children being put out to walk while my father reversed the empty car up the hill under mother's direction. Certain it is that no one who lived through these times will ever forget them.

When we left the Deverill Valley farmers in 1930 they were at their wit's end to produce anything that their country needed. Seemingly all food for industrial nations could be more cheaply produced abroad and, indeed, had to be imported because it was the only way open to the new countries for their development. Incidentally, South American beef was to be halted temporarily by the German U-boats, but then more permanently because the foreign governments there eventually expropriated their British-financed railways for a pittance, interest payments ceased, and the natives could enjoy eating their own steaks at long last. The Colonies, however, were made to behave more respectfully. What saved Wiltshire at the eleventh hour was liquid milk.

Mr Richard Stratton (1875-1950)

> These seven workers on the farm of Mr. R. Stratton, Kingston Deveril, Warminster, Wilts., have been awarded R.A.S.E. long service medals. They are Messrs. E. Marshall (57-years' service), J. Pearce (55), H. Gibbs (48), L. Maidment (52), A. Trimby (55), W. Maidment (54), C. Newbury (62).

Manor Farm workers – 1930s

When town dairies became impractical after the war, and mechanical transport made collection of milk from farms dependable, large dairying businesses had built depots in the towns of North and West Wiltshire, Wootton Bassett, Chippenham, Melksham, Frome and Semley in order to process milk and rail it to London. At this time more milk left Semley each day than from any other depot in the country. In 1930 Arthur Hosier at Collingbourne Ducis and Wexcombe had ready his open-air milking bail. The sheds of six stalls, each served by a cake hopper, were on wheels and surmounted by a flat, light roof.. The cows left a collecting pen of chestnut paling, entered the stalls for milking and feed, and regained the pasture when a vertical sliding door was raised in front of them. Coupled up was a vacuum pump and engine in a portable shepherd's hut, and the milk was delivered, roughly cooled, into churns. The whole outfit could be moved around the field, to the benefit of both, and into any other field after uncoupling. A man and boy could milk 70 cows easily. Unlimited and cheap Irish heifers came over to Fishguard and were railed cheaply to Warminster Station. Most other cows were currently hand milked at an allocation of 11 per man. The dry hills around the Deverills were ideal for these outdoor bails; in the wetter valley they were often on a concrete pad near existing buildings, but it was unusual for even these herds to come indoors in winter.

While the monthly milk cheque was saving Wiltshire, a corn growing county like Hampshire lost nearly all farmers and was virtually derelict. Arable farmers had to wait until 1933 when Parliament grudgingly passed the Wheat Act. Under this a guaranteed price for a certain amount of English wheat was set at a small premium over imported, but if the pitifully small standard quantity was exceeded the deficiency payment was reduced pro rata. The Wheat Act and the advent of sugar beet crop allowed arable England to tick over until 1939.

Great developments in fertiliser production followed the fixation of nitrogen from the air earlier in the Century, the new nitrogen fertilisers being used with increased confidence and success.

Mr Grey (on right), Mr. Bletso (on ladder) – 1930s

Soil analysis pointed the way to mixtures with superphosphate and potash, and around the Deverills small plots of virgin, impoverished downland were ploughed for trial plots and sown to improved grasses. They stood out for miles, but the excited sheep and rabbits saw to it that no grass raised an ugly head! On the machinery front the eve of war in 1939 found the Deverills still well-horsed with a few tractors pulling horse-designed implements. Nothing had been done to produce improved breeds of stock or of cereals.

Mr Dennis Maidment at Keysley Farm – 1930s

The period 1939/40 saw not only an avalanche of bombs but an avalanche of machinery from the New World; combine drills, crawler tractors and combine harvesters were leased, lent or even bought by this country. Luckily farmers had little time to recriminate over the past. They quietly resolved to peep over the horizon more often in future. Over the war years local farmers accepted orders from a committee of their colleagues which organised food production for South-West Wiltshire from an office in Warminster. They struggled to grow potatoes, sugar beet and flax on top of their previous activities. They learnt to indent for gangs of Women's Land Army from their hostel in Mere and for soldiers and army lorries to help cart sheaves at harvest time. Food at any price was overnight the order of the day, but an Excess Profits Tax at 100 per cent saw to it that the fortunes of the previous war were not repeated. All worked with a will – there was nothing else to do anyway. The new P.A.Y.E. tax took some getting used to.

For some years after it was all over, food was still desperately short. During the war the downland between Lord's Hill and Mere had been stripped of internal fences and used as three huge tank training areas, cattle and sheep being allowed to roam the grass on a communal basis. By 1945 the movement of tanks had partially cleared the gorse and thorn bushes, and power was now at hand to complete the clearance and convert to arable; in this way the 'farmed' acreage of the Deverill parishes more than doubled in five years. Ample supplies of compound granulated fertilisers held the key, and Stapledon's grass mixtures were on hand to complete the transformation. Combine harvesters designed to cope with two tons of corn per acre rather than 10 cwt every other year of the prairies were at last available, and short-strawed varieties of cereals with potential to convert modern fertilisers into high yields made their appearance. The situation was also further improved by myxomatosis, which – unpleasant though it was – effectively destroyed the rabbits which had previously swarmed everywhere and allowed maximum use to be made of every acre.

All this absorbed the Deverill farmers happily until the early Seventies. The drudgery of manual work steadily eased, and technical progress drew back towards farming and its ancillary industries many of the descendants of those who had moved away into the towns. The 1947 Agriculture Act gave stable prices for two decades and farming held its head high in a world short of food. True the closing of the village primary schools at Longbridge and Kingston Deverill sapped village life, but the universal motor car softened the blows. The arrival of more and more professional and retired people added much-needed variety to the social scene. In the 1970's the climate for farming changed to the extent that farmers' net incomes halved over the decade, this being caused chiefly by the end of cheap oil and raging inflation. The value of money halved every five years, and costs increased dramatically.

IN MEMORIAM

RICHARD STRATTON, C.B.E.

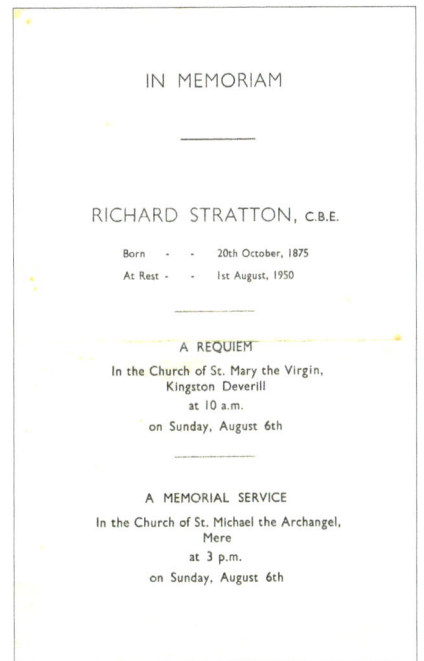

Born - - 20th October, 1875
At Rest - - 1st August, 1950

A REQUIEM
In the Church of St. Mary the Virgin,
Kingston Deverill
at 10 a.m.
on Sunday, August 6th

A MEMORIAL SERVICE
In the Church of St. Michael the Archangel,
Mere
at 3 p.m.
on Sunday, August 6th

Memorial Service for Richard Stratton, 1950

Farmers responded on the livestock side by doubling the size of their milking herds and putting their Friesians into modern buildings, where they ate silage, not hay, in winter and were in the charge of one man.

A century earlier to grow wheat after wheat was to put one's tenancy at risk. In the Seventies, with the aid of fertilisers and with power available to till the arable thoroughly, rotations steadily lengthened, so that by 1980 monoculture of cereals was both respectable and profitable. In no other way could the land here produce a higher return per acre. New varieties of wheat had a potential yield of three tons per acre and more; this needed healthy plants and the agrochemical industry was ready with herbicides, fungicides and growth regulators in profusion. The soil seemed to be merely an anchorage for potentially healthy crops and the out-turn at harvest depended only on the right blend of sunshine, temperature and rain from April until August. In order to streamline the work, fences were removed to make even larger fields.

To end our story, we can perhaps realise that, after a whole century, farming in this district has emulated the prairie farming that so nearly destroyed it in 1880. Here we grow three tons of grain per acre at high cost; in the New Countries one ton per acre at low cost. Where do we go from here? Can we flout our instincts indefinitely and farm our thin, hungry and leached soils without a proper blend of hoof and corn? Only time will tell.

Mr Richard Flower Stratton (1916-2011)

Manor Farm, Kingston Deverill 1982 -2016
David Stratton

Time has indeed moved on – in fact another 34 years – since my father wrote the above essay in 1982. Here at the Manor Farm in Kingston much has changed – and the same can be said for the other farms in the Deverill Valley.

I will start with a survey of the dairy aspect of our farm. Considerable modernisation had already taken place in the 1970s following the establishment of Kingston Dairy, with the result that the farm's 3 dairy units – Dee Barn, Bradley Road and Kingston- were each capable of dealing with 120 cows, manned by a total of three dairymen and one relief worker. By this stage also, the prime feed for the cows had changed from hay to silage, and the animals were mainly self-fed. Twenty years later, such was the technical improvement in dairy management that it was now possible to cater for a throughput of 140 cows per unit, and a decision was made to close the Kingston Dairy, following which the two remaining dairies were eventually capable of dealing with 200 cows in each establishment. By 2005, however, the profitability of dairy farming had fallen radically, with the result that the Bradley Road operation was closed,

Mr Richard David Stratton (1944-)

leaving only Dee Barn to cope with the remaining herd, which numbered 200.

In the 1990s it was decided that maize – a crop high in starch – should be grown in the fields adjacent to the Bradley Road Dairy. The idea was that this crop - turned into silage - complemented the existing grass crop, high in protein, and could be conveniently fed to the cows who were housed in the immediate area. A problem arose, however, because maize is a crop which is harvested in the autumn – at a time when conditions can be very wet – and as a result considerable damage was done to the soil, a difficulty which was exacerbated by the movement of cows, with the added snag that they often had to cross the Bradley Road. It was appreciated that the fields were better suited to the cultivation of barley and wheat, and that the maize would thrive better and be more easily harvested elsewhere. These considerations, together with that of reduced profitability, also contributed to the closure, already mentioned, of the Bradley Dairy. Continued financial difficulties face all dairy farmers at this time, and the question now is whether the possible installation of more robotics in the dairy will prove to be the way forward.

The most significant advance over the past few years has been in the development of farm machinery which is infinitely more reliable,

Manor Farm House

powerful and robust than in the past. There used to be constant problems involving bearings and clutches in particular, but the introduction of automatic transmission and a built-in computerised system which gives forewarning of any specific problem has resulted in a far greater output per machine. (Many advantages have accrued as a result, but it has to be said that whereas in my father's time most repairs could be solved with the judicious use of a hammer, it is now a question of importing a highly-skilled mechanic with advanced computer skills – at considerable expense.) The combine-harvester now has a much improved separation system, and crop-sprayers are also much more sophisticated, with the result that we can incorporate the new technology more efficiently into our farm operations. The yields of cereal production have also been increasing with the continued introduction of improved technology in the use of fertilisers and agrochemicals. However, it should be emphasized that the weather can still play a significant part in the yield of cereals in any one year.

Another change, since 1995, has been the introduction of arable break crops – linseed (a sea of blue) and oilseed (a swathe of bright yellow). This has led to a new rotation of crops, and the area of cereal growing has increased from around 800 acres to 1200 acres – 3000 being the total acreage of the farm. The growth in cereal yield necessitated the removal of the grain store from the farmyard in the village to the larger site at Bradley Road. This has resulted in a storage capacity for around 6000 tons of grain on the farm – a figure which compares with 2,500 – 3000 tons in my father's time.

This leaves the question of sheep – a feature of the Wiltshire downs since time immemorial. Downland chalk is high in calcium and is thus a healthy environment for breeding ewes. At the time my father was writing there were around 800 sheep on the down. It had long been established that cross-bred sheep improved the condition of the stock, and in the 1980s the usual practice was to put a purebred Hampshire ram to the ewes which themselves were the result of a 3-4-way cross. A high proportion of the female lambs would then have been sent for breeding to the local sheep fair at Wilton, the remainder being sold for meat production. Later, continental breeds were introduced such as the Texel, and by this stage the aim was to

David Stratton & Richard Drake with Bateman sprayer, 2016

Bateman sprayer, 2016

produce a much higher proportion of 'fat' lambs to breeding lambs. In 2005 a hardy breed of Lleyn ewes from North Wales was introduced, and this resulted in a greatly reduced shepherding requirement, and the closure of the lambing pen (or 'maternity unit') in the valley – any 'problem' ewes such as those producing triplets, being looked after at the old dairy at Kingston. Another advantage of the Lleyn breed is that they lamb very much later – in late April and May – at a time when the the grass is already growing on the downs and the lambs can take advantage of the extra source of feed. Later they can be fattened on grass in the valley and a crop of turnips which are planted after the cereal harvest. All this continues the Wiltshire tradition of sheep providing fertility on the arable land to grow greater crops of cereal. The number of ewes has now risen to 1200, and each year they will produce between 1800 and 2000 lambs.

My father was a great believer in the value of fertility supplied by animals located on the chalk farms. I have continued in this tradition by retaining a mixed farming system, a decrease in the number of cattle being balanced by an increase in the number of sheep, whilst any 'imbalance' in the production of 'homegrown' fertility can now be compensated for by 'importing' organic manure from outside the farm. Will the next generation be able to continue this tradition? To quote my father –'only time will tell'.

Receding sheep

Historical Note

The absence of any mention of wool in the above account should be perhaps explained – particularly since the county of Wiltshire was at one time as famous as East Anglia for a huge and highly profitable array of woven garments and other wool-related items sold on international markets. Vast flocks of sheep covered the downland in the north and south of the county and grazed throughout the open country of Salisbury Plain in between, and these kept the weaving looms humming for many centuries. But gradually from the 1780s and increasingly in the 19th century with the advent of the Industrial Revolution and with competition from Australia and New Zealand where the Merino sheep produced a fine, soft quality wool more suited to current fashion, sheep farmers began to look elsewhere for profitability. Today wool is a minor bi-product of local sheep, whose coarse wool is primarily employed in the production of carpets.

5 The Social Scene

With the help of the archives at Longleat, the massive collection of documents and books concerning local history held at the History Centre in Chippenham, together with an analysis of the census returns between 1841 and 1911, much information can be pieced together about individual lives and how they impacted on the village over a period of 600 years, from the mid-14th to the mid-20th century.

The patronage and ownership of the village fell under the aegis of the Thynne family of Longleat when they took over the Manor in 1747. From this date and for the next hundred years we have a more comprehensive overview of the local inhabitants and their working lives by reference to various maps and reports drawn up by the new administrators of the estate. From 1841 with the advent of the Census Returns and contemporary Directories and up to 1911 (the latest date available for census analysis) the picture is almost complete. In earlier times, for mention of individuals outside the immediate ambit of the church, we are dependent upon scholarly gleanings from local historians, most of which have been gathered together in the splendid series of books published by the Wiltshire Record Society.

A few of these records – many of them terse and inconsequential and others amusing -are assembled here as follows:

May 1305: 'John le Chapman, of Kynegston Deverel, arraigned for beating, wounding, and ill-treating Robert Reynold of Lower Leygh in Hegtredbury market of malice aforethought'. A slightly later entry is confusingly similar, although the assailant is different – 'John le Taillour, son of Thomas le Taillour, of Kyngiston Deverel, who dwells in Mere, for beating and ill-treating Robert Renard of Lye' -and it appears that Robert was beaten up twice. These gentlemen would already have been in jail for their misdemeanours and were now in court and in the process of being tried by a jury of 12 men (as set down in 1166 at the 'Assize of Clarendon', held at Henry II's palace just outside Salisbury). The jury at this period would have ascertained 'the truth' prior to the trial, and if found guilty Messrs. Chapman and/or Taillour would probably have been fined. 'Messrs' and 'le' are also appropriate since the miscreants and the jurors would at this date be speaking a mixture of French and English, the latter not coming into general use until the second half of the 14th century, in the reign of Edward 3rd. The two Johns would be respectively an itinerant peddler or salesman and – fairly obviously - a tailor, people being known by what they did or whence they came (as in the case of the author).

In 1332 Edward III instituted a new countrywide tax on 'moveable goods' (primarily livestock and agricultural produce) which meant that everyone who owned such goods which were worth more than six shillings in total, was liable to taxation of 1/10th of their value if they lived in towns or boroughs, and 1/15th if they resided in rural areas. There are two tax lists for KD which read as follows:

SEP 10 1332- KYNGESTONE
Richard le Vernon 18s 7½d
Walter le Mudewerde 17¼d
Robert de Remesholt 3s 9d
Thomas le Fisshere 12d
Simon le Kynge 2s
John Horne 16d
Nicholas Chatebane 19¼d
John Wilkenes 20d
William le Haywood 8d
Maud le Hert 2s 7¼d

Total 36s 8¼d

Reynolde de Kyngestone 10s
John Wysman 2s
Thomas Tauntor 13d
Robert Bosse 4s
John Wymond 14d
William Connival 16d
Geoffrey Haywarde 2s
Emma Badecoke 4s 6d
Walter Londdoke 2s
Thomas le Taillour 10s
Walter Os 3s
Robert le Nywe 4s
John le Haywarde 7s 3d
Richard Joye 2s
Total 54s 3d

May 1342: 'Thomas le Tailor, Walter Os, Nicholas Chatebal,

William Ebblesburne' – these four 'parishioners' are assessed for a variety of tithes in the form of wool, lambs, land values, pigs, linen, milk etc. Again their names are interesting – Chatebal being very clearly French, and Ebblesburne equally clearly English since it refers to someone who lives – or whose family has lived in the past – in the valley of the river Ebble, the southernmost of the three rivers running into Salisbury from the west.

This was also the time of the desperate plague known as the 'Black Death', which accounted for virtually half the population of the country. The immediate effect was an extreme shortage of labour in all trades but especially in agriculture, with the result that the surviving working man was able to command much higher wages and could afford to move away from his local area to secure a better future for his family. This situation was countered by the 'Statute of Labourers' instituted by Edward III in 1350, with the aim of limiting workers' pay and of preventing them from leaving their home district.

Jun 1389: 'William Remmesbury

… a virtual layman, of modest learning .. accused of preaching and teaching abominable opinions, heresies, and errors to clergy and people of diocese, openly and in secret, in churches, churchyards, taverns, and elsewhere …as…

Pope has no power to make bishops, nor bishops to make priests;
No bishop or priest has the power to make the Body of Christ;
The bread does not become the Body of Christ;
No-one should make offerings at funerals, churchings or weddings;
Anyone who has given money to a priest for a mass has been excommunicated by God;
William and his followers, alone, are in the true faith;
Nobody should confess to a priest, and no priest has the power to absolve sin;
Priests and nuns should marry;
Priests should travel the area preaching rather than saying the mass;
No-one should venerate images;
Men should have intercourse with any women, even nuns, virgins

and wives, in order to increase mankind.

William has had intercourse with virgins, wives and single women since he held these opinions. He was tonsured by Thomas Fishburn, who empowered him to preach publically and taught him to profane the mass. He confessed he had held and affirmed these heresies and errors for the last four years to the clergy and people of Longbridge Deverill, Brixton Deverill, Kingston Deverill and Boyton ... publicly in churches and churchyards, and privately in discussions over drinks in taverns, and other places. He taught all of them in some of the places, some of them in others and profaned mass and had intercourse as above ..... he abjured all his heresies..... ordered to publically renounce errors in Salisbury Cathedral, all collegiate and greater churches in diocese. And principally in the churches of the above towns where he confessed preaching, before the clergy and people assembled for that purpose.

This extreme example of 'nonconformity' some 250 years before its time, and certainly as non-puritan as can be imagined, must have been music to the ears of at least some of the KD fraternity, if not to their wives and daughters, and there could have been a measure of disappointment when the rector, Roger Typell, ordered his flock to the church for William's 'abjuration'. (At least Roger could discount any immediately local association with the offender, as his name doubtless implies that he came from the distant east Wiltshire town of Ramsbury, at this period without a 'suffragan' bishop, who might otherwise have kept William in hand.)

Perhaps William and his like were encouraged by the new attitudes to ecclesiastical and royal authority which had come to the fore eight years earlier in the 'Peasants Revolt'. This outpouring of opposition to so-called 'serfdom' and punitive taxation had been brutally put down, but in any case hardly affected the west country, apart from the area around Bridgwater to the west and Winchester to the east: resentment, however, still simmered. On a more academic reformatory level, the courageous stand taken by John Wycliffe (1331-1384) and his followers the Lollards against the established church and what they described as its authoritarian approach and luxurious living habits in the midst of abject poverty, was much admired by those in the know. This was also true of the other famously anti-clerical production of the period, the allegorical poem 'Piers Plowman' by William Langland (c.1333 –c.1386) which, in various versions, was widely disseminated and reflected in a different way the vision of Wycliffe and the participants in the 'Revolt'.

In common with the entire population of the country the villagers of Kingston Deverill were more immediately involved with one of the main causes of the 'Revolt' in the form of the three successive Poll taxes which were imposed in 1377, 1379 and 1381. The first of these was instituted by Edward 111 in the last year of his reign, and the subsequent polls were introduced by his successor Richard 11, (although he can hardly be considered as personally responsible, since he was only ten years old at the time of his accession, and fourteen when he successfully put down the rebellion at his meeting with Wat Tyler at Smithfield). The Poll taxes affected even the poorest members of the community, and the details of those who were forced to pay up in KD in 1381 are still extant – as follows:

MERE HUNDRED KYNGESTON
Johannes Shatbal agricol' [Farmer or labourer] 2s 0d
Editha Shatbal
Johannes Hodel agricol' 2s 0d
Margareta Hodel
Thomas Terry agricol' 2s 0d
Editha
Willelmus Mourcok serviens [Servant] 2s 0d
Margareta Mourcok
Elena Wylke filatrix [Spinster] 12d
Johannes Colette agricol' 2s 0d
Claricia Colette
Johannes Rochewell agricol' 2s 0d
Alicia Rochewell
Reginaldus Fadur agricol' 2s 0d
Is' Fadur

Johannes Rodde serviens 2s od
Cristina Rodde
Radulphus Bongor agricol 12d
Johannes Propter cissor [Tailor or Shearer] 2s od
Johanna Propter
Walterus Smyth famulus [family servant] 2s od
Is' Smyth
Johannes Beke serviens 2s od
Anastasia Beke
Willelmus Barun serviens 12d
Johannes Frere serviens 12d
  Summa personarum 26, inde subs. 26s od probate

(Six hundred years later when Margaret Thatcher introduced what was initially described as a 'Council Tax', it swiftly became known as 'The Poll Tax' and was just as unpopular as its predecessor- although it was by no means so indiscriminate, and in any case not many people would have appreciated the 'frisson' attached to the name.)

1415: With the 600th anniversary of the battle of Agincourt within recent memory, it would be fascinating to know whether any local people were involved, particularly since the names of even the lowliest soldiers have come down to us from preserved records of the various militias which took part. It is unlikely, however, that the KD landlords, the Stanters, had the wherewithal to gather together a local militia, comprising men-at-arms, archers and horsemen, as was required by Henry V of wealthier landowners and nobles throughout the country in preparation for his invasion of France. Nevertheless the effect of his edicts in respect of money and men came geographically close. The city of Salisbury was required to furnish the sum of £100 towards the cost of the army, but the leading citizens objected and persuaded the authorities to reduce the figure. This was not the end of the story: resentment still festered, and when some troops from the north attempted to cross the Avon by the bridge in Salisbury on their way to Southampton, they were molested and a number of citizens were killed.

Apart from the story of the church and its clergy, the whole of the 15th century is in fact a virtual blank as far as the social history of the village is concerned, as is most of the 16th century – apart from a few brief records, as follows:

1503: 'Alexander Stantor:

> ...Manor of Great Horningsham ... together with the advowson of the church of Longleat .... and the Manor of Kingston Deverill, with the advowson of the church in Kingston Deverill, 6 mesuages, 200 a. arable, 100a. pasture, 1a wood in Kingston Deverill, held of the prince of Wales ... worth £10. He died 18 March, 1503. His son Peter, is heir.... 'The Manor of Kingston Deverill, worth £8, is held of the king of his earldom of Hereford, parcel of his duchy of Lancaster.'

These extracts from research undertaken by Richard Colt Hoare are fascinating in that they indicate that 450 years after the Conquest the whole area of the Deverill valley is still under remote but ultimately royal ownership. The Prince of Wales's interest is now reduced to that of a small wood (it had earlier been a much larger holding under the Duchy of Cornwall) but the king himself (in this case Henry VIII) has ownership of the Manor. 'Advowson' refers to 'patronage' in the sense that the holder is entitled to choose the incumbent of the local church (or churches). So Thomas Aleyn, who was rector of KD from 1472 to 1511 (the longest holder of the office in the history of the church) would have been appointed by Alexander Stantor's father and continued as incumbent under his son, Peter.

1509: 'John Westley of Whitclyf in Kingston Deverill parish is pardoned.' Unfortunately we don't know what John was pardoned for, but it is interesting that the name Whitecliff is still retained in the village.

1542: In this year John Leland (1503-1552) the poet, antiquary and travel writer – described as 'the father of English local history and bibliography' – travelled through north Wiltshire in the course of a detailed survey of the West Country. He returned in 1545 and came as close to the Deverill valley as Stourton, but unfortunately no closer. While staying in the area he records that 'in its present form the bounds of Selwood Forest' (mentioned earlier in connection with the gathering of King Alfred's forces) 'extends for 30 miles; it stretches in one direction almost to Warminster and in another approaching ten miles to the Shaftesbury area'. He also states that 'the Wylye rises three or more miles above Warminster' –it's a pity he didn't explore it further, if only to establish that it springs from the ground very close to Stourton, and that he would have to walk or ride at least ten miles before reaching the town, where, he remarks, 'an important market for corn is held'.

1549: 'Kingston Deverill, Rector Richard Dudd. Value of rectory demesne £15.5.3.'

Richard's patron is described as 'Edward Stourton' in the records, but this could well be a misreading of 'Stantor' and he was probably Peter's son.

In the 1580s another eminent historian and antiquarian, William Camden (1551-1623) travelled the length and breadth of the country, visiting every county, and recorded his findings in a monumental publication entitled 'Britannia' in 1586. The book was written in Latin and was translated into English by Philemon Holland in 1610. In this translation the passage which describes Camden's visit to this part of the world reads as follows:

> By Maiden Bradley glideth Dever-rill, a prettie small Rill, so called for that ….it diveth (as it were) under the ground, and a mile off rising up here againe, hasteneth toward … a most ancient town … called Worminster … In times past it enjoyed great immunities and freedoms … Now onely for a round Corn-market it is exceeding much frequented, for hardly a man would believe waht a mightie deal of Corne is weekely brought hither and quickly sold.

Thus we have a very early interpretation of the derivation of the name 'Deverill' and one which is now considered to be the most likely.

The 17th century has rather more to offer as far extant records are concerned:

1600: '1. Edmund Ludlow, 2. Alexander Stantor esq. & Rachel his wife. Manor of Kingston Deverill & tenements, land, rent, common pasture with free fishery in Kingston Deverill, Monkton Deverill, Hill Deverill, Mere & Maiden Bradley; also advowson of Kingston Deverill church.' As previously mentioned, the Ludlows were the other dominant landowners in the valley, and this agreement effectively marked the beginning of their ownership and patronage of KD and the departure of the Stantors from the Manor House – if not from the village. (This information is taken from a manuscript detailing 'Feet of Fines' from the last years of Elizabeth's reign – a 'fine' being an agreement in duplicate, at the 'foot' of which was a third copy which was retained by the appropriate government office.)

1611: 'A note of the names of such persons as are thought fit to lend money to the King's Majestie by way of privy seales, together with their names and dwelling places and their severall summes .... Edward Poton of Kingston Deverill 10l.' The 'King's Majesty' in this case was James 1st, and this extract is taken from the 'Lieutenancy Papers' of his representative in Wiltshire, Lord Hertford. The county Lieutenant at this date was empowered to raise militias and taxes in his sovereign's cause, and Edward Poton was apparently wealthy enough to come under his hammer.

1636: We have already encountered the event which took place in this year, namely the attempted prosecution of the KD churchwardens by the Salisbury Diocesan authorities for failing to obtain permission for the villagers to play football on Ascension Day four years earlier. Whether the rector, Thomas Newland, was himself involved in these sabbatical training sessions or matches is not known, but he probably returned the diocesan ball with interest in that the court's injunction to the effect that the names of the participating footballers should be reported was not followed up.

The following five extracts concerning certain KD villagers during the period of the Civil War are taken from the Order Book for the Quarter Sessions of the Peace Court held at Warminster.

1649: The court is informed by Robert Curtis of KD that he has served in the office of tithingman by the space of one whole year ending the five and twentieth of March last .... and according to the usual custom William Hillier ought to have served next in the office but refuses to do so. Ordered that Hillier shall within one week after notice to him given of this order repair to the next justice to take his oath for the due execution of his office. (If he refuses, to be bound over).

1652: It appeared by the examination and confession of Julian Cockle that she being about four years since begotten with child by John Streete and was delivered of the child being a maid child named Elinor within the parish of Charlton Horethorne in the county of Somerset which child was afterwards illegally brought by some of the parishioners of Charlton to Kingston Deverill and there left and is now chargeable to the parish there. Ordered that Elinor be forthwith returned and carried to Charlton there to be delivered to the churchwardens and overseers of the parish to be provided for according to law. And that John Streete be bound to appear at the next Sessions of the Peace to be held for the county of Somerset to perform such order as the justices for the said county make for discharge of the parish of Charlton.

1653: The court informed by Mr Hyde of counsel with the inhabitants of Kingston Deverill that Robert Garrett having heretofore married with Edith Phillips of Kingston Deverill and is now become a covenant servant with Mr Mompesson of Corton and his wife with one child remains at Kingston Deverill and she will not live with her husband whereby she and her child are likely to be chargeable to the parish and prayed the court that the wife of Garrett with her child may be sent to her husband at Corton by him to be kept and provided for. Ordered that the overseers of the poor of Kingston Deverill shall take Garrett's wife and child and carry them to Corton and leave them with Garrett her husband there to remain and by him to be provided for according to law.

1653: The court is informed that Richard Street of Kingston Deverill gent has appeared on the behalf of the inhabitants of Kingston Deverill to an indictment against them for decay of a highway within the parish and has disbursed for fees a fine and other necessary charges the sum of seven and thirty shillings which charge ought to be borne by all the inhabitants of Kingston Deverill. Ordered that there shall be an equal rate made on all the inhabitants of Kingston Deverill for the repayment of Street the sum of seven and thirty shillings.

1653: Forasmuch as the court is informed by Mr Hyde of counsel with the inhabitants of Kingston Deverill that John Romsey and his wife of that place are both dead and left behind them four children on the charge of the parish. And that Edward Coombes grandfather to the children has taken one of them from the charge of the parish and kept him ever since. And forasmuch as it now appears to the court upon the oaths of Andrew Leversedge and Peter Hurle that Edward Coombes has an estate worth threescore pounds a year and is of ability to keep another child of the said four children. Ordered that Coombes shall take and breed up one child more of the four children and the overseers of the poor of Kingston Deverill are to carry the child to his grandfather who is hereby ordered to receive it and breed it up. And in case the grandfather shall refuse to receive it and breed it up then he is hereby ordered to pay five shillings by the month to the overseers of the poor of Kingston Deverill for the keeping thereof and to keep the first child besides. (If he refuses to obey this order he is to be bound over.)

Reference has already been made to the effect of the Civil War on the local population, and to what extent life was disrupted. The sieges of Wiltshire towns – Marlborough, Devizes, Malmesbury and Salisbury, together with the major battle of Roundway Down in 1643 hardly came close, and neither did the continuing passage of troops through the county. In addition to the Wardour Castle episode, there was the notorious occasion when the Royalist commander, Sir Francis Dodington, executed a number of parliamentary soldiers near Longleat, news of which might have filtered through – but as the above extracts reveal, meticulous legal arrangements continued to prevail, particularly after Cromwell's forces had taken a firm grip on the country.

The basis on which the Quarter Sessions Court worked in resolving local disputes such as those referred to above was an Act of 1601 by which overseers of the poor were appointed to each parish. These overseers had the power to force people to pay a local tax to help the poor, using the court if necessary. What is particularly notable is

Wardour Castle

the extent to which local taxation is administered in a remarkably fair way. It is true that in the case of Richard Street the court indicates that each villager should pay an equal rate for the repair of the highway. But given that grandfather Coombes in the last extract is means-tested on his ability to pay for his second grandchild, it is likely that this test would obtain in all the relevant court cases. Interestingly one of the most prominent local Justices of the Peace presiding at the court was Edmund Ludlow, owner of KD Manor and one of the 21 Wiltshire MPs (out of a total of 29) who supported the parliamentary cause. (Edmund had succeeded his father as the local MP- his predecessor Sir James Thynne having been deposed in 1642 for his royalist sympathies).

1655: In this year there took place what might be termed a local disruption in the shape of 'Penruddock's Rebellion'. Its royalist leader, Colonel John Penruddock, was the owner of the manor at Compton Chamberlayne, and he planned an ambitious countrywide revolt against Cromwell's rule. He succeeded in ousting the parliamentary troops briefly from Salisbury, but failed to raise an enthusiastic following elsewhere, and leaving the city to try to raise support in

Dorset and Devon he was defeated by a small troop of Cromwellian horsemen and subsequently executed. The list of names of those of Penruddock's following who were put on trial at Exeter does not include any who hailed from the Deverill valley – hardly surprising given that they were under the eagle eye of Edmund Ludlow.

1676: The 'census of Wilts' taken in this year indicates that the population of KD was 200, LD 300, BD 76 and MD 60 – and here an interesting comparison can be made with the numbers registered in 1086 when KD had 34 inhabitants and MD 285.

1680: 'Agreement between Robert Hurle of Kingston Deverill and John Oldis the elder of KD for an exchange of barns in KD farm for the storage of wheat and barley. In addition Robert is permitted to appropriate John's crop of wheat for his own use.'

1696: This was the year in which Robert Hurle- the husband of Eleanor whose generous bequest to the parish was described in Chapter 2- died. The probate inventory of his effects was drawn up on 25th September, and apart from the fascinating detail of its content, it provides ample evidence of the family's wealth.

Total wealth £841 12s 8d
Four hundred of chees £3 0s 0d
Eighteen bushels of old Barley £1 13s 0d
In the Buttery 9 Barrells and 3 horses £1 12s 0d
Three long Zifters,[Sieves] 1 Trendle [a low carriage bed on wheels],
    9 pailes, one Butter Churn, one powdering tub £1 4s 0d
In the same Buttery 2 Tubs, 8 cheses vates, 2 Virkines [firkins]and
    other Lumber 6s 0d
In the same Room one Table Board and Frame 3 Joynt Stooles, 1
    forme, 2 Brass pans, 3 milk pailes and other Earthern wear £1 5s 0d
The Wooll in the hous with the Beame Waites and Scales £1 0s 0d
One Peas Rick £4 0s 0d
One Rick of Oates £10 0s 0d
One Wheat Rick £10 0s 0d
Two Rick Stavells [staddle stones, on which ricks stood to keep rats
    from the grain] £2 0s 0d
The Wheat in the Barne £40 0s 0d

The Barley in the Barne and field £100 0s 0d

Oates and Pease in the Barne £1 0s 0d

Two Waggons, 4 Shullows [ploughs], 3 Ayes and other plow Tacklen £15 0s 0d

Two Waggon Lines and 3 Wood Strapes 12s 0d

Eight Picks, 6 Rakes, 1 Fork and 1 Ladder 8s 0d

The Reck in the Stale 3s 0d

One Roler, draughts, sheep reeks and beast Recks £1 10s 0d

The dust in the dust coop 10s 0d

Five Horses and Harness £15 0s 0d

The boardes about the dust coop, the tallet [loft], the little reck, 8 mangers, picks and shovels, 4 hand barrows and 1 Willon 15s 0d

One van and half Bushell seaves and mill, 150 sacks and shovel £1 10s 0d

Five and twenty pigs, great and smalle £8 0s 0d

Three acres of vatches [vetches] and a half £2 0s 0d

One gley [hay] Rick at Bitley, 3 load of hey in the hous ther, 6 other hey ricks at severall places £100 0s 0d

Two yoke of Working Oxen with ther Harness £20 0s 0d

Four Steeres £10 0s 0d

Two barren Heifers £4. 0s 0d

Nine Milch Cows £22 0s 0d

Five Calves £3 0s 0d

A hundred of fat Sheep £102 0s 0d

Three Hundred and 10 Ewes £108 0s 0d

Two Hundred and 40 Hogs £88 0s 0d

Three Hundred and Sixty Wheathers in both flocks £147 10s 0d

Four Quarters and half of Wheat Sown in the ground £9 0s 0d

12 dozen of Hurdles old and new £1 0s 0d

Things omitted and things forgot £1 0s 0d

1700: 'I, William Hurle, bequeath to my 'now', wife Anne, £20.'

It is to be imagined that 'Anne' is by no means to be confused with any previous wives who may still be alive, but in any case – given his father's astonishing wealth, at least some of which William must have inherited – his bequest to his current spouse appears to be relatively stingy.

1715: 'James Oldis, son of John, sent as apprentice to Henry Nash, distiller, Bristol. John Oldis, also son of John, yeoman, apprenticed to William Moore, clothier, Wincanton.'

It is interesting that John Oldis the elder, a presumably prosperous farmer (see the entry for 1680) is happy for his sons to leave the land and take up apprenticeships in totally unrelated businesses.

1715: 'Inventory of Charles Blake of KD late deceased: 3 horses £9; 3 cows £6; wood; waggon £5; other plows; one pigg £1; pewter dishes 15/-; 2 pots and skillet and 2 bottles £2; 2 spits and dragon pan and 3 candlesticks 8/-. In the middle chamber one feather bed and feather bolster and 2 feather pillows £3.10. Things omitted and things forgot 5/-: total £86.11 -.'

Note that at this period a lawyer would allow a reasonably well-found yeoman to put a price on 'things omitted and things forgot'!

1722/23. During these years Daniel Defoe (1660 – 1731) visited the West Country, including Wiltshire, and recorded his findings in his 'Tour through the Whole Island of Great Britain' published in 1726. He is highly complimentary about the county, stating that 'it is important to the public wealth of the kingdom. The bare product is in itself prodigious great; the downs are an inexhausted storehouse of wool and of corn, and the valley, or low part of it, is the like for cheese and bacon'. His journey coincided with the high point of the wool industry, just before its rapid decline, and in our area of chalk, rather than cheese, he mentions the

Daniel Defoe (1660-1731) by Michael Vandergucht, after Jeremiah Taverner line engraving, 1706

importance of the woollen mills at both Mere and Warminster, the latter doubtless including Bull Mill at Crockerton which had been in continuous action since medieval times. Many of the villagers in the Deverill valley would be supplied with wool which they wove into garments at home, in exchange for payment by the local millowners.

1724; 'I, Henry Garrett of Kingston Deverill bequeath to father Richard (Kilmington) £2, brother Richard of Wilton 5/-, ditto to Margaret Moore of Gillingham and sister Sarah. To kinsman Philip all my iron-shop tools and other items belonging to the trade of a blacksmith. All other goods to my dear beloved wife, Deborah.'

1739: 'This is to certify to the public that on 7th June last a fire broke out at Kingston Deverill in the County of Wilts which in two hours consumed the dwelling- houses, outhouses and barns of William Hurle, Charles Blake and James Bond, the loss of which amounted to the sum of six hundred pounds, and upwards'. This extract from the Salisbury Journal is the first of many over the years which mention various newsworthy happenings in the Deverill valley. The Journal was first published 10 years earlier, in 1729, and is one of the oldest extant provincial newspapers in the country.

1747: In this year we have the first recorded mention of a public house in KD – the 'Buck's Head' whose 'licensed victualler' was John Holmes. It is likely that this inn occupied the same site as the later 'Rose and Crown', namely at the ford.

In this same year the Thynne family of Longleat became the owners of Kingston Deverill Manor, and thus began the gradual process of taking under their wing virtually all the land and property in the valley. In 1748 the first detailed map of the parish of Kingston Deverill was drawn up (see Appendix J), and this indicates the acreage, and in some cases, the names of the fields, the adjacent downs, the road system through the village and the parish boundary. The map was probably drawn up by the Longleat steward, John Ladd, who in the next year conducted a meticulous survey of the tenancy and freehold holdings in the village, including the names of the various owners and tenants - of which the following record is a summary.

1749: 'Survey of the manor of Kingston Deverill by John Ladd
The Farm: Church Field, Brook Furlong, Kingsale,

Walbury, Forerudge, Church Close, Peascomb, Court Hill, Down Leze, Dean Bottom, Broad Mead, Dean Layes, Little Mead, Aishley Close, Fox Linch, Hescomb Field, Hescomb Coppice, Red Mead, Kilton, Home Field, Frampton, Billey, Marcombe Copse, Tonguecomb Wood, Wheeler's Close.' These fields all came under the immediate ownership of the Manor and totalled 1022 acres. The names which follow are all tenants of parts of the manor estate.

John Marvin - holding not specified. 'Sarah Lambert' – holding of 100 acres including small areas in the fields mentioned above and also in 'Rod Mead Field, Short Furlong, Lower Furlong and Upper Furlong. William Philips - 10 acres. William Toakes – 63 acres' in small holdings in the fields mentioned under 'The Farm.' 'Margaret Dib - 7 acres. George Townsend – 88 acres' including strips on the Farm property, and also on 'Court Hill, Mullen's Croft & Sheep-pen Field. Philip Gerrett – 9a. Richard Humphrey - 32a. William Hurle – 58a. John Blake 11a. Mr Oborn 19a. Henry Sturgis 16a. William Turner 1a. Jacob Street – messuage, garden, orchard and barn near the River – 53a. Jeremiah Norris 28a. Thomas Hurle 13a. George Young – 14a. James Tudgay 4a.' (These last three tenants all having houses and land 'near the river'). 'John Wyndham esq.-34a. Jane Jeffrys - house and garden adjoining Home Field. Alice Hayes 17a. Jane Marshment – cottage and garden nr Sheep Pen Field. The Parsonage' (occupied at this point by Rev. Thomas Howe) '13a.'

John Ladd then proceeds to list the 'Cottagers' none of whom would have had any holding of land, but who would have been allowed to cultivate for their own subsistence the vertical strips on the steep-sided Court Hall which had existed since around 60 AD. Their names were as follows: Daniel Killey, William Thomson, John Brimson, Ruth Chislett, Jos Combs, Edward Combs, Stephen Norrice, Thomas Marshall, William Marshall, Daniel Dyke, Charles Davis, John Holmes, John Sharp, Grace Markey, William Sharp, John Trimby, John Notton. The descendants of at least three of these families – the Combs, Marshalls and Trimbys, were present well into the 20th century.

The survey goes on to list the three members of the parish who held freehold properties – these were: Robert Black 139a.; Peter

Delmey esq. 275a. Robert Ryall 134a.(Peter had presumably earned the title of 'esq' as a pillar of the community who incidentally owned a considerable acreage of land.) Field and down names which appear in their holdings and have not been previously noted are: Newport Down, Cucknell Field, Yerbury Mead, Barley Close, Whitley Farm and Marcomb Coppice.

Finally John Ladd indicates the existing road system: 'A road from Monkton Deverill towards Kingston; A drove way into Church Field; A road between the houses down to the river; A road from the river up to Fox Linch; Down by the river into Sheep Pen Field; A road up through Fox Linch towards Horningsham; A way by Mullens Croft up to the Common Down.' He then summarises the tenantry lands as amounting to 1619 acres and the Freehold lands to 701 acres, giving a grand total – with the roads etc. - as 2698 acres for the parish as a whole.

1750: 'An estate at Kingston Deverill in the county of Wilts is asked £50 per annum, now occupied by Farmer Knight; consisting of a good Farm House with convenient outhouses and about 6 acres of meadow and pasture and 180 acres of arable land lying well together. For the particulars, apply to Mr Solomon Hughes, attorney at Warminster, or Mr Clutterbuck, attorney in Barford, Wilts. The whole estate within 3 miles of Warminster aforesaid'. *Bath Journal* 20 Aug 1750. (Warminster was obviously closer to KD in the mid 18th century).

There follow a number of rather laconic extracts from the 'Coroner's Bills' for Kingston Deverill during this period.

> *1754:* – Nicholas Card of Maiden Bradley found dead under a hayrick..
> *1763:* – Elizabeth Baxter fell into a well and was drowned.
> *1768:* – Moses Todby killed by the overturning of a cart.
> *1771:* – William Hurdle was digging marl in chalk-pit when the chalk fell upon him so he instantly died.
> *1775:* - Emilia Presly hanged herself: lunacy.
> *1780:* John Lucas – killed: accidental death.

(If the coroner failed to submit such reports on his investigations into what might be termed 'suspicious deaths' he would not be paid – hence their description as 'coroners bills').

Also at this time we have a record of the amount of money paid out to the poor of the parish, the Poor Law which legislated for this having been properly codified in the 1580s. 'Poor Laws' in various different guises had existed since the Black Death in the 14th century, but it was not until the 1540s, following the dissolution of the monasteries, that proper consideration was given to the problem of the 'deserving poor' who had hitherto been looked after, where possible, by monks, friars and nuns. From Elizabethan times individual parishes were made responsible for levying taxes from ratepayers to assist poor members of the local community, and these taxes were collected by official appointees, known as 'overseers'. As a practical- if idiosyncratic- example of how the money was distributed, we have the following entry for KD:

1770:- making 6 shirts 2/-
mending Becket's shoes 1/6
half a hundred fagots 7/-
payment for burial of Mary Tribot 14/3
Will Trimby's coat 9/-

These records for the late 18th century reveal that payments were made on a weekly basis and that the total amount on each occasion came to around two pounds. Recurring names are Hurle, Dunford, Trimby and White, and it is evident that some members of previously wealthy families had fallen on hard times.

The 'Kingston Deverill Way Book 1771' states that the sum of £8.2. 4d was paid out for road repairs in that year, and that the price of three pickaxe handles was 1/6 and that 'flint and rubble' cost 6d per load. The village labourers involved were 'John Ruddick, John Marshall, Thomas Collins, John Tudgay and Will Newbury'.

In 1779 Thomas Thynne, 3rd Viscount Weymouth appointed Thomas Davis to the stewardship of Longleat, a promotion which had a profound effect on the organisation of the estate and the ownership and use of land in the surrounding villages. Davis was the son of an excise officer and had received a good classical education in Devizes. At the age of 14 he obtained an apprenticeship in the estate office at Longleat, and by the time he took over the stewardship from his predecessor Simon Cole he was already well versed in the ramifications of estate management. He very shortly produced astonishingly detailed maps of all the local villages, including, in 1782, one for KD which he commissioned to be drawn up by Thomas Webb, a Warminster surveyor, and which is so comprehensive that it is possible to ascertain, with the aid of an accompanying numbered index, the owner or lessee of every acre of ground and every farm, cottage or house. Thus for Kingston Deverill we have a record of who lived in the village 60 years in advance of such knowledge being available nationally through the information disseminated by the 1841 census. [For a reproduction of the 1782 map and an analysis of the attached record of the occupants of the village at the time, see Appendix E].

Thomas Davis (1749-1807), Longleat Steward

Davis produced his map a few years in advance of the Parliamentary 'Inclosure Act' of 1785, and was thus readily able to decide on the appropriate apportionments of land and resulting rents in accordance with the legal requirement for such information. 'Enclosure' in the sense of the taking over of common land or 'open fields' from the poorer members of the community by those with the means to invest in land ownership, had a long history going back to the 13th century, but its apogee was reached in the fifty years between 1770 and 1820. At its worst it resulted in a mass exodus of labour and even in the destruction of small villages – as is epitomised by Goldsmith's poem 'The Deserted Village' (1770). At the other end of the scale it resulted in a massive increase of farming productivity – both in the growing of crops and the nurture of livestock – and at least for those villagers who could afford to rent a piece of well-cultivated land from a local owner it meant for them an end to 'subsistence' farming.

Fortunately for the Deverill villagers very little common land was lost, not least because the property owners or lessees did not require enclosed land on a permanent basis for their sheep which grazed on the downs on land which was uncultivable anyway, although the flocks were often brought down to the valley for folding and shearing. Where hardship existed as a result of higher rents, both Viscount Weymouth and Thomas Davis attempted to ameliorate the lot of the poorer members of the community throughout the valley. In fact, Thomas Davis, rather than his employer, was the prime mover in respect of virtually all matters concerning the running of the Longleat estate, including any dispute which might arise, since the Viscount was heavily involved elsewhere as a distinguished politician – a career which culminated in his elevation to the Marquisate of Bath in 1789.

1780: 'KD land tax assessment: warrant appointing William Reynolds & James Dyer as collectors for the parish.' The Dyers were the tenants of Manor Farm during this period and the most influential family in the village. A memorial tablet to a number of them, including James, may be seen on the south wall inside the church, behind the organ.

At this point it is relevant to point out that the ownership of land was subject to a strictly imposed Land Tax, and that this had been the case since an appropriate law was introduced in 1692. Over the following century a highly sophisticated system of collection was instituted based on quotas for each individual county, with a variable assessment for each town and village within the total amount required, the rate being 4s in the pound on the property valuation. In 1745 a freeholder's liability for tax was linked for the first time to a voting entitlement, and in 1780 a further act enforced this requirement and resulted in a comprehensive recording system which, for the following

90 years, allows the historian to establish just how much was paid into the exchequer by individual landowners throughout the country.

The assessment for Kingston Deverill drawn up on 17th May, 1780, and for which Messrs. Dyer and Reynolds had been appointed as collectors, was as follows:

Name of Proprietor	Name of Occupiers	Sums assessed £s
Lord Weymouth	James Dyer for Broad-dean Farm	7. 7
do.	do. for part of Butcher's Mead	1
Revd. Mr Massey	for part of the Parsonage in his own hands	4. 15
do.	do. for part of Butcher's Mead	1
Richard Woodyer, Gent.	John Knight for Blackhalls	3. 12
William Blake	do. for William Blake's leasehold	1. 3
Lord Weymouth	do. for late Tudgays	3

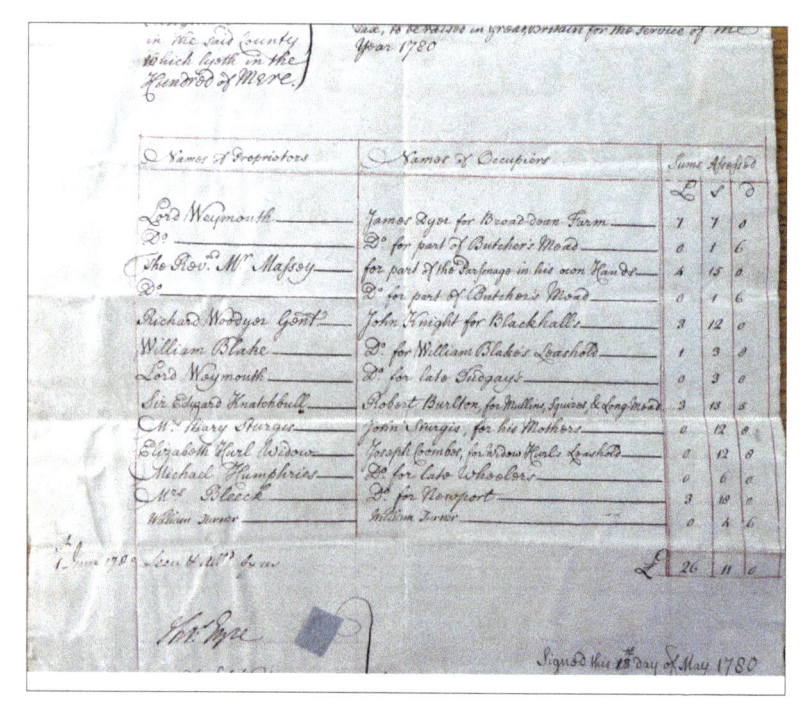

Land Tax Return for Kingston Deverill, 1780 (detail)

Sir Edward Knatchbull	Robert Burlton for Mullins, Squires, & Long-Mead	3. 13
Mrs Mary Sturgis	John Sturgis, for his Mothers	12
Elizabeth Hurl,	Widow Joseph Coombs, for Widow Hurl's Leasehold	12
Michael Humphries	do. for late Wheelers	6
Mrs. Bleeck	do. for Newport	3.18
William Turner	William Turner	4
		£ 26. 11

It will be noticed that at this relatively early stage in the Thynne family's proprietorship of the Manor they owned only 28% of the land in Kingston Deverill, and that there were nine other freeholders. As will be seen at the latter end of this run of detailed Land Tax records (1826), the proportionate ownership of land is very different.

Many of the family names which occur in this assessment as substantial property owners are also listed by John Ladd in 1748, and doubtless a number of their predecessors had lived in the valley from very much earlier times.

Newport still exists as a house name (it was originally a farm) and the Humphries family is commemorated by the listed house called 'Humphreys Orchard'.

Prior to the final enclosure agreement of 1785, the following are examples of the discussions which took place between Thomas Davis and the inhabitants of KD on the subject of property ownership:

1782: 'Schedule of arable land belonging to George Townsend, Lucy Norris and Robert Hurle.

Petition to the inclosure commission by William Blake, Michael Humphreys, William Gerrett, Lucy Norris, George Young, Mary Bleek, Robert Hurle, the revd. M. Massey, Sarah Ryde, William Slade and the Duke of Somerset clarifying certain allotments concerning the enclosure award.

Public notice by Thomas Davis inviting KD landowners to attend a meeting at the home of Farmer Dyer [Manor Farm] on 3 Apr in favour of, or against, the proposed KD inclosure bill.' This represents a fairly democratic injunction.

After the various changes in land ownership brought about by the 1785 Act had been agreed, it would seem that major construction works were put in place throughout the village, if the following Longleat record is any guide:

1785-1787: 'Bills with vouchers submitted by Henry Sturgis, David Hobbs, Thomas Hurle, Charles Brown, James Brazier and John Howell for the carrying stones and lime, stone-cutting, carpentry, payment of labourers, the provision of food and drink and other expenses relating to the widening of the road and the building of the new bridge at KD in accordance with the direction of the inclosure commissioners.' The so-called 'new bridge' (in all probability there was not an 'old' one at the eastern end of the village) is the one which still exists – if occasionally repaired as a result of an argument with a passing tractor – beside 'Bell House', the original school building with its bell still in situ.

The allocation of land and its ownership, together with the layout of the village, is neatly summarised in the relevant entry in the 'Wiltshire Enclosure Awards' volume of the Wiltshire Record Society as follows:

> Award 21 Nov 1785. Commissioners – Richard Richardson of Devizes; Thomas Fricker of Longbridge Deverill; Richard Bloxham of West Dean. Surveyor – Thomas Webb of Warminster, since deceased.
> Lord of Manor: Thomas Thynne, Viscount Weymouth.
> Rector: Millington Massey.
> Area: 2,509a. King's Hill, Cucknell Field, Rodmead Field, Peasecombe, Cow Down, Church Field, North and South Down, Upper and Lower Dean Bottom, West Field, Court Hill, Kilton.
> Allotments: Rector of KD 350a; Viscount Weymouth 1,507a.;(including William Blake 23a; Thomas Davis 153a; [The Longleat steward had granted some land to himself]; Michael Humphry 23a; John Marvin 111a; Henry Sturgis 22a; George Townsend 23a;John Blake, Philip Garrett, William Garrett, Thomas Humphry, Robert Hurle, John Hurle, Lucy Norris, Elizabeth and Rachel Oborne, William Reynolds, William Turner, George Young)

THE SOCIAL SCENE

[the acreage allotted to these last names is not indicated – presumably they all had small, but equal, pieces of land]; William Ballard 128a; Mary Bleek 115a; Peter Delme 234a; William Slade 151a; trustees of Crey's Charity School; dean and chapter of Oxford; dean of Salisbury.

[Oxford and Cambridge colleges owned, and still own, areas of land, small and large, throughout the country, and it is evident that Christ Church, Oxford owned some land in the village at this time. As another local example, Queen's College Oxford has had from the 15th century an interest in land and property at Upton Scudamore. As to the mention of the Dean of Salisbury, it is not known for how long he had an interest in land in KD, but at this time his acreage was leased to William Chafyn Grove, owner of the manor house at Zeals, and whose family founded the preparatory school of the same name in Salisbury]. 'Fencing ... to be at expense of proprietors.' [Surprisingly the Dyer family at Manor Farm are missing from this schedule. Perhaps the surrounding land was taken for granted as being a part of the Longleat estate.]

'Tithes: exonerated by grant of land to rector.
Roads: 8 public roads,1 public road and private carriage way [presumably the entry to the rectory], 1 public bridle way, 3 public footpaths, 4 private roads.
Finance: Viscount Weymouth empowered to charge £433 on certain lands to defray expenses. The rector also empowered to charge for erecting new buildings.'

Thus – together with the 1782 map -we have a very complete picture of the village as it stood at the end of the 18th century, and there are now only a few local events to record in the 1790s, before we enter the 1800s.

[For a copy of the 1782 map which designates a number to each house, and to which is appended a key giving the name of the owner or tenant, see Appendix F].

1791: Around this time the first Trade Directories make their appearance, and in this year the 'Universal British Directory of Trades

& Manufactures' records under Warminster: – 'The Deverills are very small villages and have seldom any regular manufactory, but are principally served by the neighbouring clergy, excepting BD which is a Rectory: the present incumbent is Rev. Mr Massey of Warminster.'

1793: Thomas Davis receives national recognition for his outstanding contributions to effective estate management when he is nominated by the newly formed Board of Agriculture to compile the agricultural survey of Wiltshire. This he accomplished by the following year when his findings were published under the title 'A General View of the Agriculture of Wiltshire'. In 1807 he was asked to produce an updated version, but he died in that year and his son took on the work of a new edition which was published in 1814 and included a dedicatory preface to his father.

1794: 'Rents collected from William Abraham, Stephen Collonce, Joseph Coombs, William Tudgay, William Luckless, Sam Matthews, Edward Casson, John Ruddick, Robert Vallice and Samuel Vallice – collected by Henry Sturgis (bailiff).' Some of the descendants of these villagers appear in the census returns from 1841, others disappear for all time following the desperate situation of the poorer members of the community in the 1820s and 30s.

1796: 'Thomas Pittman, labourer, and George Townsend, yeoman, both of KD for begetting a bastard child on Mary Phillips of the same place, spinster. Robert Ryall, Robert Hurle, George Townsend – jurors.' This extract from the Quarter sessions and Assizes for the year is slightly confusing in that George Townsend's name seems to appear as one of the accused and amongst the jurors. It may be that he has brought the case against Thomas Pittman – but if this were so he should certainly not be a juror. Otherwise we are up against a question of disputed paternity – rather more difficult to resolve in the days before DNA testing.

1798: 'On Tuesday a fire broke out at KD which consumed 4 or 5 houses and did very considerable damage.'[*Salisbury Journal*, 2 July].

The early years of the 19th century saw the introduction of national census returns, these being gathered once every ten years, as they still are. At first these were only 'Enumeration Returns' and omitted the names of individual residents. In 1841 these latter details were included with their ages, but not as yet any indication of how they were employed. From 1851 this information was also included, and it is now possible to view all these records in detail up to 1911, an embargo on publication of the full records being placed for a period of 100 years after each census return. (An analysis of the eight returns for KD between 1841 and 1911 will follow at the appropriate moment in this history, and the author also holds a record of every name mentioned.)

1801: Population of KD – 292.

1802: 'George Dyer pays the half-year's rent of £44 for his farm but objects to local building work and rejects the recommended necessity of repairs to Great and Little Farm.'

1807: Thomas Davis, the eminent steward of Longleat dies. Thomas Thynne the 2nd Marquis of Bath who had succeeded his father in 1796, closes the house as a tribute and together with his brothers and hundreds of tenants attends the funeral. Davis's major interest and enthusiasm was in the preservation of existing woodland and in the management of forestry for future generations – particularly in the circumstances of the pressing need for wood for ships during the Napoleonic War, and the resulting depredation of local forests. KD possesses its own very visible memorial to him in the band of woodland which embraces Court Hill.

Davis was succeeded in the position of steward by his eldest son, Thomas Davis, junior.

1811: Population of KD – 285.

22 July: 'Joseph Abraham has run away from his wife and family and left them chargeable to the parish of KD. Whoever will give such information as may lead to his being taken under the care of me, the undersigned Overseer of the said parish of KD shall receive 1 guinea reward. The said Joseph Abraham is about 38 years of age, five foot five and five or six inches high, of pale complexion with full eyes, and is by profession a Thatcher'. Henry Sturgis, bailiff. [*Salisbury Journal*]

1814: The 'Way Warden's' account for this year indicates that John Tudgay was paid 13/6 for 9 days work on the village roads.

1815: The battle of Waterloo ended the Napoleonic wars, but also marked the beginning of a rapid decline of agricultural investment and activity, a decrease in the value of farms and in opportunities for employment in rural areas. Recession set in, many farms became untenanted and the tenants of those that remained were forced to reduce the wages of their employees who in turn could not afford the high price of bread which resulted from a series of Corn Laws designed to protect landowners from cheaper imported grain. Thomas Davis (junior) fought an uphill battle against the problems besetting the Longleat estate and the villagers, but saw power shifting to the towns and away from the countryside. The enclosure system which had been manageable in the days of his father, was now blighting the lives of the poorer members of the community, and the effectiveness of the Poor Law which in different forms had offered protection to indigent families over the centuries was now waning, since few could now pay the taxes which the operation of the Law entailed.

> *1817:* Rose and Crown, Kingston Deverill, Wilts. To Innkeepers etc. To be sold by auction by A. Darknell, on the premises, on Tuesday 1st day of July 1817 at six o'clock in the evening, subject to such conditions as will then be produced (unless privately disposed of by private contract, in which case due note will be sent – all that desirable and well established INN called ROSE & CROWN, and three stables, cart house, piggery, garden and paddock and all pasture land near adjoining, situated at Kingston Deverill aforesaid now in the occupation of Mr. Tudgay, held by lease under the most Honourable the Marquis of Bath, subject to the small quit rent of 3s per annum. KD is six miles from Warminster, 8 from Frome, 10 from Shaftesbury and 18 from Salisbury. For further particulars apply to The Anchor, Mere, Wilts.[*Salisbury Journal*].

The Tudgay family may well have experienced a falling off in trade.

1821: Population of KD – 328.

1822:'Singular phenomenon. On Monday se'n-night during a thunderstorm, a particularly dark and heavy cloud was observed by the inhabitants of Kingston Deverill, Wilts, on the west of the village: it sent forth a kind of spout, of a much lighter colour, in an oblique direction towards the earth. After various bendings and contortions like those of the proboscis of an elephant, though no wind was stirring in the lower regions, it extended itself rapidly in length and as it approached nearer the earth, its motion resembled that of a pendulum, but still increasing in celerity of vibration, till the lower end reached the hill on the S.W. of the village, between it and Mere and not above half a mile distant from the church of Kingston Deverill. It now exhibited the singular appearance of a transparent tube of about 3 feet in diameter at the lower end where it touched the ground, but much greater at the upper end where it joined the cloud from whence it proceeded, and certainly considerably more than a mile in length. The 2 ends appeared nearly stationary, but the middle part still remained flexible, and bending in all directions, sometimes almost to a right angle. The spectators, who were numerous, were naturally alarmed and expected some catastrophe, at least a sudden discharge of water by means of the spout, which in the vale where the village is situated, might have been attended by very serious consequences: but no such circumstance occurred. It continued for upwards of 20 minutes, during which it moved, being drawn perhaps by the motion of the cloud, over a field of wheat in a rather zig-zag direction towards the church, for about 150 yards. In addition to the external motion above mentioned, the spout appeared to those who had the best opportunities of observing it, to be internally agitated as if by a current of air or some other fluid rushing down it in a spiral direction; while at the lower end a cloud of dust or smoke was thrown up to some height in the air. Some of the spectators imagine it to have been dust blown up by a strong wind from the spout, while others describe it as a thick smoke or steam. It had in its slow progress almost reached the inclosures near the church, when it suddenly disappeared. It was remarked that another cloud was at that moment approaching the upper part of it. No noise or rushing was heard. The young wheat over which the spout passed was now washed by a darker colour than the rest of the field, and this appearance remained visible for several days; the next storm of rain, however, restored it to its original colour'.

This remarkable event –inexplicable at least in the context of the Deverill valley rather than the American mid-west – so vividly, not to say colourfully described in the Salisbury Journal, might well have been viewed in retrospect by the villagers as presaging the disastrous decade of near famine and violent rioting which was to follow.

Bull Mill at Crockerton

1824: In this year the 'Bull Mill' in Crockerton was taken over by a silk-spinning enterprise from Frome under the management of George Ward. As mentioned earlier, the mill had from the earliest times specialised in the wool trade, and this had been greatly expanded in the late 18th century by the Everett family who also added a number of new buildings. Sadly the mill became dormant by 1841, perhaps as a result of the riotous disturbances of the 1830s, but was revived later as will be seen.

1826: William Cobbett (1763 – 1835) the radical reformer, visits Wiltshire at the end of his perambulations around the country, during which his reports on the desperate situation of the rural labourer are serialised in the 'Political Register' and later published in his 'Rural Rides' (1830). He travels the length of the Avon valley and is amazed by its beauty and also its 'sufficiency' –in 'the wool, the milk, butter, eggs, poultry and game ... ample, and much more than ample for the provision for all wants, other than those of mere food and drink.' But he remarks with scathing irony that little of this is available to the working man under the prevailing agricultural system: -'What do the labourers get? To what fare has this wretched and most infamous system brought them? Why is a family of five allowed to have, at the utmost, only about 9s a week. This makes only £23. 8s a year, for food, drink and clothing, fuel and every thing, whereas I allow £62.6s.8d a year for the bare eating and drinking, and that is little enough' After visiting Salisbury Cobbett turned west along the Wylye valley, remarking on the dilapidated state of the cottages and parsonages as he rode through the villages. The nearest he came to KD was Warminster, which he described as 'A very nice town, everything belonging to it is solid and good. There are no villainous gingerbread houses running up, and no nasty, shabby-genteel people; no women traipsing around with showy gowns and dirty necks ... it is a great cornmarket, one of the greatest in this part of England, and here things are still conducted in the good, old, honest fashion'. But if all appears well in the town, what of the labourers who are largely responsible for the townsfolk's prosperity? 'What injustice, what a hellish system it must be to make those who raise it skin and bone and nakedness, while the food and drink and wool are almost all carried away to be heaped on the fund-holders, pensioners, soldiers, dead-weight, and the other swarms of tax-eaters! If such an operation do not need putting an end to, then the devil himself is a saint'. Cobbett went on to become MP for

William Cobbett (1763-1835) possibly by George Cooke, oil on canvas, circa 1831

Oldham and was involved in both the Reform Act of 1832 under the prime ministership of Lord Grey and the Amendment to the Poor Act of 1834 under William Pitt the Younger. The former act saw the abolition of the so-called 'Rotten Boroughs' – those small communities such as Hindon and Heytesbury who were represented by two MPs at Westminster – and also increased the number of those who were eligible to vote, from 500,000 to 800,000. The latter act reduced the ability of local taxation systems to allow the poor to stay in their own homes by means of subsidy from their own communities, and effectively condemned them to removal to a state-funded workhouse. Cobbett was pleased with the decision about the 'Rotten Boroughs' the existence of which he despised, but was bitterly opposed to other aspects of the acts which he saw as not improving the conditions of life for the poor in any way. Sadly he did not live to see the Act of 1845 repealing the Corn Laws, since this did eventually make a distinct difference to the affordability of rural life.

1826 is also an appropriate year in which to look once again at the Land Tax assessments for the village and to compare them with those given for 1780.

Name of Proprietor	Names of Occupier	Names or Description of Estates or Property	Sum Assessed and not exonerated
Marquis of Bath	William Dyer	Great Farm	29. 5. 9
do.	do.	Mervins or Gilberts	2. 0 10
do.	do.	Lamberts	4. 13. 4
do.	do.	Becketts	8. 2
do.	William Rogers	Delmes	13. 9. 4
do.	John Phillips	Black Heath	4. 1. 8
Rev. John Thynne	James Compton	Parsonage	9. 6. 8
Hugh Rabbitts Esq.	William Rawlings	Keepenses	6. 8. 0
do.	do.	Long Mead	10. 0
do.	do.	Townsend	1. 18. 0
Henry Sturgis	Henry Sturgis	Bellenses	18. 8
do.	do.	Ellings	1. 13. 4
do.	do.	Blakes	1. 10. 8
Marquis of Bath	J.C Wookey	Foakes	3. 15. 4

Name of Proprietor	Names of Occupier	Property	Sum Assessed
do.	do.	Young	1. 3. 4
do.	do.	Norris	1. 5. 8
Michael Humphreys	do.	Humphreys	1. 15. 0
Trustees of Hornings-ham School	William Tudgay	Horningsham School	1. 10. 0
Robert Mitchell	Robert Mitchell	Longs	7. 0
Robert Foster	Robert Foster	Fosters	15. 2
J E Mifflen	William Mifflen	J E Mifflens	4. 8
John Tucker	John Tucker	Tuckers	18. 8
Marquis of Bath	Henry Sturgis	Walters	5.10
Humphreys	Tho's Humphreys	Humphreys	3. 6
			87. 8. 4

The Land Tax assessment for 1780 indicated that the Thynne family at Longleat owned some 28% of the land in Kingston Deverill at that time. The assessment for 1826 is, however, very different in that the Marquis of Bath now owns almost 70% of the local acreage – a proportion which will steadily increase throughout the 19th century. The number of independent landowners in the village remains much the same – ten as against nine in 1780. What is interesting is that seventeen of the twenty-four listed properties retain the names of their previous owners, that 'Broad-dean Farm' is now 'Great Farm', and that four properties have taken on the names of their new owners (no mention of 'late' so-and-so as in the 1780 assessment). 'The Parsonage' is inevitably similarly described, but the most interesting appearance in the assessment is that relating to the portion of land owned by Horningsham School. The ownership in question dates back to 1698 when a certain Jeremy Crey of Horningsham conveyed a barn called Keepens and its surrounding fields to his son John and his heirs in perpetuity, in order that the rent from the KD property should provide funds for what became known as 'Crey's Charity', the purpose of which was 'to provide for three good and discreet schoolmistresses that should teach to read in the parish of Horningsham, for instructing those poor boys and girls of the parish whose parents were not able to keep them in reading'. At this point and for many subsequent years, Horningsham had no school as such, and the schoolmistresses taught in their own homes. The charity continued, however, even after Horningsham School was set up in 1845 (five years after the school in KD) and was still functioning in the early 20th century when the land –in a different area of the village after the enclosure act of 1785 – was rented by William Stratton. (As will be noticed, the name 'Keepens' is still preserved in the 1826 assessment, and it is interesting that it refers to a piece of land purchased by Mr and Mrs Rabbitts, on which the Methodist Chapel was later erected. As pointed out in the previous chapter, the solicitor acting for Rev.Henderson, when he wished to purchase the property exactly 100 years later, was unable to establish contact with any of the Rabbitts' descendants.)

1828: On 8th December of this year the Salisbury Journal states that the 'Crown Inn', occupied by Robert Mitchell, is again up for sale. The sale goes ahead later in the month, but the new owner, George Cross, stays for less than two years, putting the pub on the market again in October 1830.

1830: This was the year of the 'Swing Riots' which pitted rural labourers against their landowning employers as a result of the former being now almost entirely dependent for their livelihood on the latter. This resulted from a combination of circumstances which derived from the enclosure acts of the previous century, and the recession brought about by the recent war. In order to maximise their limited profit the landowners reduced their labour force by means of mechanisation, and in particular the introduction of the horse-powered threshing machine. This infuriated already half-starved labourers, and after writing letters of complaint to local farmers over the signature of a mythical 'Captain Swing', the peasantry of East Kent began the destruction of threshing machines and other farm property, and the burning of hayricks. These actions spread swiftly through the southern counties in the late autumn and winter of 1830, and came as close to KD as the village of Hindon. Details of what happened locally are to be found in a book entitled 'Warminster Common' by William Daniell, a self-appointed Methodist preacher, who for over forty years ministered to the poor of the area and was highly revered. His report on the riots reads as follows:

> Nov 27. This week has been a week of sad terrible desolation, such as the oldest man living never knew. The labouring classes of society have assembled in large riotous mobs in several adjoining counties, and they have burned the corn and destroyed the farming machinery in every direction. They have levied contributions where they chose and nothing it seems could resist them. The storm came so near to us as Heytesbury (three miles off): then God mercifully stopped it - twenty of the rioters were secured by the cavalry and taken to prison. But it was in the neighbourhood of Hindon (only ten miles off) where it raged in all its fury; there the mob daringly attacked the cavalry and a regular military engagement took place. One of the mob was shot dead on the spot, another was found dead in the adjoining wood; one or two others, they say, have since died of their wounds, several have had their hands and fingers chopped off; about a hundred, it is supposed, are wounded more or less. Twenty-nine prisoners were taken to Salisbury gaol – the waggon which conveyed them was covered in blood from their wounds. It appears that this has, for the present, diverted the storm: the rioters have all dispersed. I heard the Heytesbury prisoners say to some of our poor, as they were conveyed through the town 'We were coming over to help you'. The Hindon rioters had fixed the hour when on the above fated day they had intended to be at the Deverills (only three miles off) and that the Deverill labourers had agreed to join them and proceed to Warminster, beginning at the Common.. These, together, would have composed probably a thousand persons armed with scythes, reap-hooks, axes, sledges, clubs etc. all elated with their hitherto uninterrupted success.

Given the repressive measures adopted by the government towards the rioters it could be said that the Deverill villagers had a fortunate escape both from the prospect of prison or even death at the hands of the military. As it turned out, the Hindon prisoners were shortly released and the Wiltshire riots were quickly forgotten. It was a different matter across the county border in Dorset, however, where the Tolpuddle Martyrs are still remembered.

1831: population of KD 380. It might appear surprising that in the light of the desperate poverty of the times there should be an increase in the population of the village as compared with the numbers 10 years earlier, but in remote parts of rural England there was nowhere else to go to find work, whereas in the industrial Midlands and the North the situation was very different.

1837: This was a disastrous year for the Thynne family at Longleat. The death of the 2nd Marquess on 27th March had been preceded by that of his eldest son Thomas on 16th January, and a further tragedy followed when the 3rd Marquis, Henry, died on 24th June. This left Henry's widow, Harriet, in sole charge during the minority of her son John Alexander who was only 6 when his father died. It is evident that the Marchioness did a marvellous job as patroness of the villages – a task made the more onerous on account of the terminal illness of her steward, Thomas Davis junior. As we have seen earlier, she instigated the renovation of KD church and made a generous contribution to its rebuilding between 1842 and 1847.

1841: We now reach the year of the first national census, an analysis of which is set out below. (Incidentally, when looking at the ages given in these censuses it should be recognised that they are not always precisely accurate, the enumerators sometimes rounding them up or down if they were uncertain of their own records or of the information given them by their interviewees.)

1841 Census Analysis

1. Population:
    405
2. Age groups:
    under 13: 157
    teenagers: 39
    20-35: 117
    36-50: 44
    51-65: 39
    66-79: 6 -William Toogood 68 (Agricultural Labourer),
        MaryToogood, William Stone 70 (Mason),
        William Rawlings 74 (Yeoman), Mary Stone 75,

THE SOCIAL SCENE   *181*

        Mary Sturgis 75.
    80 +: 3 - Hannah Snelgrove 80, William Trimby (Shepherd) 82,
        Thomas Trimby (Shepherd) 90.
3. Households:
    71
4. Occupations
    Agricultural Labourers: 69 (including 2 fourteen-year olds).
    Farmers: 4 – James Wookey (57), John Compton (55),
        William Rogers (45), John Rawlings (42)
    Shepherds: 3 – Thomas Trimby (90), William Trimby (82),
        William Rabbatt (46)
    Bakers: 3 – John Andrews (55), Thomas White (40),
        Joseph Tudgay (35)
    Yeomen: 2 – William Rawlings (74), James Compton (50)
    Coal Carrier: – William Carpenter (60)
    Preacher (Ranting) [i.e. Primitive Methodist]: – William Nation
(?age illegible)
    Carpenter: – George Humphreys (56)
    Carrier: - Henry Lampard (20)
    Independent: - Mary Sturgis (75)
    Shopkeepers: 2 – William Harwood (40), Henry Sturgis (30)
    Innkeeper: – John Lampard (60)
    Tailor: – John Dismore (35)
    Clock Manufacturer: – John Lampard (25)
    Thatcher: – Edward Marshall (30)
    Masons: 3 – William Stone (70), Thomas Stone (35), William
    Stone (15)
(Note that the Rector of Kingston Deverill is not mentioned in the 1841 census. The incumbent at the time was the Hon. Charles Thynne, a member the Marquis of Bath's family and resident at Longleat. He was rector between 1837 and 1845.)
5. Prominent Family Names
    Brimble – 29 members:
    Marshall – 29
    White – 24
    Tudgay – 19

Trimby – 17
Compton – 12
Stone – 12
Rawlings 12
Pressley – 11

This census enables us for the first time to assess the overall social make-up of the village – the name, sex and age of each individual villager, the number of farms and shops and labourers together with all the disparate traders whose job it was to serve the community. The information given is so obviously invaluable to the historian as to make a disastrous nonsense of the 21st century questioning about the continuation of the 10-yearly census return .

The three members of the Stone family are well-named as 'masons' and it is remarkable that two Trimbys are still described as shepherds at the advanced age of 82 and 90.

(Incidentally, John Lampard the Innkeeper – who also apparently made clocks in his spare time – was the landlord of the 'Rose and Crown' situated by the ford. It should also be noted that no teacher is mentioned: the school, founded in the previous year, was hardly under way).

1843: On 1st February of this year the KD ' Friendly Society' was founded and held its first meeting at the Crown Inn – doubtless 'timed' and under the eagle eye of John Lampard. In setting up this Society, KD was following the lead of many communities in the early nineteenth century in providing welfare, insurance and financial relief for the poorer members of society following the diminution of the ability of the long-standing Poor Laws to provide appropriate assistance. The members of 'Friendly Societies' always met in pubs, and received benefit if agreed and required, in exchange for a small subscription.

1848: Kelly's Directory (founded in the 1830s) provides for the first time a useful interim update on some aspects of the village social scene. It gives the population as numbering 402, and - as recorded earlier - it mentions the existence of the 'National School' for the first time and introduces the following list of 'traders' which may be compared with those appearing in the 1841 census:

> Compton James – Farmer; Emmanuel Trimby – Shopkeeper; Joseph Tudgay – Shopkeeper and Shoemaker; William Weaver – Farmer; Thomas White – Post Office; James Wookey – Farmer and Parish Clerk; Miss Elizabeth Earle – mistress in National School; Henry Garrett – Blacksmith; Henry Lampard – 'Crown Inn'; John Rawlings – Farmer; Stephen Rawlings - Farmer; William Rawlings – Farmer; William Rogers – Farmer.'

The number of farmers has now gone up to six, although two of them, Stephen and William may well be John Rawling's sons and working on the same farm. Compton James is probably the son of John Compton who is mentioned in the census. Two shopkeepers are listed, but both are different from the 1841 duo, and the Crown Inn is now run by John Lampard's son.

1849: The lease of the 'Bull Mill' at Crockerton is auctioned by the Marquis of Bath and purchased by Charles Jupe who, following the lead of the previous owner, George Ward, runs it as a silk mill. Jupe also ran a similar mill in Mere and, as will be seen, provided work both at the mills and at their homes for a large number of Deverill girls over the next 35 years.

1851 Census Analysis

1. Population:
   398
2. Age groups:
   Under 13: 124
   Teenagers: 66
   20-35: 82
   36-50: 79
   51-65: 28
   66-79: 16 - Ann Abraham 66 (Widow: Pauper), Mary Spencer 68 (Pauper), JamesTrimby 68 (Pauper). Henry Ford 68 (Agricultural Labourer), Sophia Humphreys 70, Sarah Harwood 72, (Pauper), William Carpenter 72 (Pauper), Ann

Carpenter 72 (Pauper), George Garnett 73 (Pauper), Martha Garnett 73 (Pauper), Henry Garratt 73 (Pauper), George Coombs 74 (Pauper), Susan Riddick 75 (Pauper), Mary Garratt 75 (Pauper), Elizabeth Trimby 77 (Pauper), Mary Marshall 77 (Widow: Pauper).

80+: 3 William White 80 (Landed Proprietor), Mary White 80, William Tudgay (Master Shoemaker) 82.

3. Households

90 (In this census no houses in the village are named, although at the end there is the following note: 'Two houses building. One house uninhabited)'.

4. Occupations

Agricultural Labourers: 88 (including 1 ten-year-old, 1 eleven-year-old and 2 thirteen-year-old boys and 1 fourteen-year-old girl).

Farmers: 3 – James Wookey 42 (40 acres – 5 men and 2 boys); James Compton 62 (349 acres – 10 labourers), William Weaver 52 (1011 acres – 22 labourers).

Farm Bailiff – William Brown 54.

Rector – David Malcolm Clarke 42, (he had been appointed in 1845)

Landed Proprietors: 6 – Henry Sturgess 43, Joseph Sturgess 46, Thomas White 54, William White 80, George Humphreys 65 (and Edmund Clarke 34 – registered as a visitor to his brother, the rector).

Schoolmistresses: 2 – Emma Cozner 22 (Mistress at Parochial School, living in Rector's house), Sophie Sturgess 20.

Victualler – John Borleston 29.

Master Shoemaker – William Tudgay 82.

General Dealer – Joseph Brimble 22.

Master Baker – John Andrews 62.

Bakers: 2 – Emmanuel Trimby 42, Joseph Tudgay 49.

Laundress – Mary White 42

Apprentice – Henry Trimby 15.

Masons: 3 – Thomas Stone 47, Joseph Stone 20, Lewis Fletcher 46.

Cordwainer – William Harwood 50.
'Carpenter's Wife' – Henrietta Tite 25.
Silk Spinners: 7 – Sarah Marshall 15, Louisa Marshall 14, Mary Marshall 14, Eliza Fletcher 18, Mary Fletcher 14, Maria Nash 17, Leah Brimble 11.
Coal Carriers: 2 – John Carpenter 42, Stephen Collins 48.
House Servants: 5 – Mary Jane Smith 16, Ann Ford 22, Elizabeth Presley 34, Eliza Hall 36, Elizabeth Eames 21 (the latter two employed by the Rector).
Charwoman – Elizabeth Marshall 30.
Dressmaker – Ann Harwood 45
Solicitor's Articled Clerk – Josiah Bryant 18 (visitor)
Blacksmith – Philip Orchard 30.
'Farmer's Daughter' – Sarah Rawlings 35.

5. Prominent Family Names
Marshall – 39 members
Tudgay – 36
White – 30
Brimble – 28
Coombs – 24
Presley – 21
Trimby – 19
Carpenter – 17
Ford – 14
Ruddick – 14

It is interesting that this census reveals that the population of the village has diminished slightly since 1841 but that the number of households has increased from 71 to 90, indicating perhaps that more houses have been built and that there is less crowding, or that there has been a change in enumeration practice which now distinguishes when more than one household lives in one dwelling. It is also notable that the 'occupations' listed show that the village is remarkably self-sufficient. 'Shopkeepers' are absent, but there is a 'Victualler' and 'General Dealer' to add to the three bakers, and you can have a dress made or laundered (the latter by the appropriately-named Mary

White) your horse shod, your coal delivered, your shoes mended and your children taught by two schoolmistresses. Charles Jupe who had taken on the lease of Bull Mill at Crockerton in 1849 and converted it into a silk factory, has persuaded seven young KD girls to work there, or to spin at home, and there are no less than 88 agricultural labourers, including some very young boys and one 14-year-old girl. The 'cordwainer', William Harwood, will be making shoes –as will the elderly Master Shoemaker, William Tudgay – but his output might have included footwear of a more luxurious stamp, since his title is distinctly anachronistic and derives from the high quality leather produced in Cordoba in the middle ages. A carpenter is surprisingly absent and is replaced in the 'occupations' list by 'carpenter's wife'. It is distressing to see so many 'paupers' – no less than 13 – amongst the more elderly members of the community. They will all be dependent on financial help from the parish, and perhaps in some cases from the newly-constituted 'Friendly Society'.

Kelly's Directory for 1855 indicates that John Burleton is now the innkeeper at the 'Crown', and the same source for 1859 records that he remains the pub owner in that year.

At some point in the 1850s the family of George Pope moved to KD as tenant of one of the larger farms. With his wife Mary Ann, two daughters Julie and Ellen, and two sons Samuel and James he took on the responsibility of a 2,300 acre establishment and gave employment to no less than 50 men and 20 boys. All looked set fair for a thriving enterprise, but tragedy soon followed, as this extract from the Salisbury and Winchester Journal for November 10th, 1860, reveals in graphic detail:

MELANCHOLY DEATH FROM DROWNING.---Mr George Pope of Kingston Deverill came by his death in a very sudden and melancholy manner on Monday last. The lamented gentleman, it appears, left his home on horseback about mid-day as was his custom, and after spending about an hour and a half in riding round his farm and in giving different directions to his labourers, he dismounted, tied his horse up in the vicinity of some new buildings, and proceeded on foot across some fields in the direction of others of his labourers. There is a dead well in one of the fields through which he had to pass; this was partially covered in, and it is supposed by many that he must have either walked across the well unwittingly, and have been precipitated into it by the giving way of some portion of the imperfect covering, or that on examining the well for some purpose he accidentally slipped into it and was drowned. The family of the deceased on finding that the time at which he usually returned home had long since elapsed, became somewhat uneasy, and sent to neighbouring houses to enquire for him. No one had seen him but a shepherd boy, who said at three o'clock in the afternoon he saw him walking across the fields. Further search was made, and after a time it was found that the insecure covering of this old well had been much displaced , and on looking down a hat was seen swimming on the top of the water. Grappling irons were immediately procured, and in a few minutes the worst fears of all were realised. The deceased was found to be quite cold; indeed, he must have been in the water for several hours. The well is about 40 feet deep and contains 30 feet of water. An inquest was held by George Sylvester Esq., coroner, on the following Wednesday morning, when a verdict of 'Found Drowned' was returned. The deceased gentleman was universally respected as a kind master and a good and hearty neighbour, and his loss is most severely felt.

It is known that Mary-Ann and her family struggled on for a while since they appear in the 1861 census, but by 1871 they have gone and the probability is that the farm was acquired by the Stratton family at some point after they took on the tenancy of the Manor Farm in 1865. It is an evocative tribute to the victim of the tragedy that the designation 'Pope's Farm' has been retained.

1861 Census Analysis

1. Population
   373
2. Age Groups
    Under 13: 96
    Teenagers: 53

20-35: 88

36-50: 67

51-65: 50

66-79: 17 - Elizabeth Carpenter 68 (Silk weaver). Joseph Trimby 69 (Farm labourer), Katherine Abrams 70, Mary Tudgay 70 (widow-pauper), Mary Bramble 70 (Pauper), Rachel White 72, Lucy Bramble 73 (Silk Factory), George Riddick 74 (Farm labourer), George Humphreys 75 (Carpenter), John Andrews 76 (Farm labourer), Ann Marshall 77 (Widow), Marie Higgins 77 (Lodger), James Trimby 78 (Farm labourer), Ann Tudgay 78, (Pauper), Henry Ford 79 (Pauper), John Tudgay 78 (Farm labourer).

80+: Sarah Harwood 81, Betty Trimby 93.

3. Households

89 For the first time, in this census, some house names appear There are only three, however - 'Newport Farm'- occupied by William Ransom., (This is the farmhouse later known as 'Marvin's'). 'The Crown Inn' – occupied by John Boulton – landlord and farmer, and 'The Parsonage' – occupied by the Rector, David Malcolm Clarke.

4. Occupations

Farm labourers: 85 (including 1 ten-year-old, 1 eleven-year-old and 2 fourteen-year-olds).

Farmers: 3 – William Ransom 54 (Newport Farm: 460 acres, 9 men 7 4 boys): John Boulton 40 (also landlord of the 'Crown Inn'; Mary Ann Pope 55 (widow: 22,300 acres, 50 men &20 boys).

Farm Bailiff :– Josiah Grant 40.

Rector: – David Malcolm Clarke 52 (occupying 'The Parsonage').

Coachman: – Edward Prince 16.

Blacksmiths: 2 – Robert Payne 50, Henry Trimby 25

Shepherds: 11 – John Brown 60, Joseph Mabbett 56, William Portnell 47, Charles Brown 28, Elisha Portnell 19, Alfred Pressley 17, John Tudgay 16, Tom Pressley 15, Charles Fletcher 14, John Coombs 14, Henry Ford 13.

Shepherd Boys: 4 – James Pressley 10, William Carpenter 10,

Andrew Coombs 10, George Marshall 8.

Agent: – Henry Festing 28.

Servants: 14 – Martha Garrett 42, Betty Pressley 40, Sarah Marshall 26, Fanny Carpenter 25, Eliza Pressley 14, Sophie Ford 23, Ann Bursdon 21, Elizabeth Eames 21, Jane Day 20, Hannah Pressley 19, Ann Cable 18, Ellen White 18, Martha Matthews 16, Jane Marshall 14.

Cooks: 2 – Ann Jacobs 40, Eliza Howe 47 (Rector's cook).

Carpenter: George Humphreys 75.

Teacher: Leah Pressley 20.

Masons: Lewis Fletcher 50, Joseph Stone 30.

Silk Workers: 17- Lucy Bramble 73, Elizabeth Carpenter 68, Elizabeth Pressley 30, Ellen Bramble 22, Louis Marshall 22, Elizabeth Tudgay 22, Harriott Carpenter 20, Ann Riddick 20, Martha Pressley 20, Emily Pressley 15, Mary Ann Coombs 15, Emily Coombs 14, Hannah Portnell 13, Emma Carpenter 12, Maria Marshall 12, Agnes Trimble 12, Nesta Tudgay 11.

Carters: 2 – Edward Carpenter 17, Joseph Newbury 57.

Mealman: - Bingham Creed 40

Baker: - Emmanuel Trimby 53.

Gamekeeper: - Thomas Northeast 25.

Grocers: - George Tudgay 47, Charles Rabbets 53.

Cordwainer: - David Tudgay 15.

Laundress: - Mary White 50.

Fish Dealer: - Joseph Bramble 32.

Thatcher: - Edward Marshall 58.

Governess: - Mary Marshall 27.

5. Prominent Names

Marshall 55 members

Trimby 36

Tudgay 35

Pressley 24

Carpenter 20

Coombs 20

Bramble 17

Ford 15

White 14

The fact that this census mentions only two 'paupers' amongst the elderly members of the community might indicate that employment opportunities in the village have distinctly improved. Indeed we now have no fewer than 15 shepherds (including the four young boys) and 17 silk-workers, as opposed to only 7 ten years earlier. Some new 'occupations' have also appeared: there is a Coachman, the youthful Edward Prince who was presumably employed by the rector, a 'Fish Dealer' Joseph Bramble (someone reasonably unique it might be imagined in a land-locked county in the 19th century), a 'Mealman' with the unlikely name of Bingham Creed who supplied food for the animals, and a 'Governess' Mary Marshall – though who employed her is a matter of conjecture, particularly since Rev. Clerk had no small children. It will also be noticed that the Marshall, Tudgay, Trimble and Carpenter families still dominate the village.

In this year a highly detailed coloured map of 'The Manor of Kingston Deverill' was produced at Longleat –and, incidentally, it was also recorded that 'The Living is a Rectory valued at £324'.

1865: Harrod's Directory records that John Lampard is now the occupier of the Crown Inn, combining this role with that of the village wheelwright.

1871 Census Analysis

1. Population
   324
2. Age groups
   Under 13: 102
   Teenagers: 41
   20-35: 58
   36-50: 47
   51-65: 50
   66-79: 20 – Joseph Mabbett 66 (Shepherd), Jane Garrett 66, William Draper 66 (Agricultural Labourer), Elizabeth Tudgay 66 (Shopkeeper), Charlotte Brimble 66, Sheila Carpenter 67(AL), Thomas Marshall 68 (AL), Philip Garrett

68 (Shepherd), Lewis Fletcher 68 (Stone Mason), Adam Trimby 68. (AL), Wiiliam Coombs 69 (AL), Stuart Clerk 69 (Rector'swife), Harriet Newbury 70 (Pauper), Lucy Ford 70 (Pauper), Matthew Marshall 70, Charles Harris 71, Dinah Trimby 71, James Marshall 74 Thatcher, Alice Edwards 74 (Pauper).

80+: 6 – Mary Barnes 82, Joseph Tudgay 83 (Pauper), John Tudgay 85 (Pauper), Betty Trimby 85 (Pauper), George Humphreys 85 (Carpenter), Maria Higgins 88 (Pauper).

3. Households

82 Some houses, streets and village areas are named – as follows: 'Newport House', 'Kingston St.', 'Monkton Road', 'New Cottages', 'National School', 'Whitepits', 'Primitive Methodist Chapel', ' New Buildings', 'Higher End', 'Village', 'Post Office', 'The Rectory', 'Church of St. Mary, 'Manor Farm', 'Wesleyan Methodist Chapel', 'Bradley Road'.

4. Occupations

Agricultural Labourers: 66 (including 1 boy of 9, 1 aged 11, 1 aged 12, 1 aged 13, 2 aged 14, a 13-year-old girl and Martha Presley 29.).

Farmers: 2 – William Ransom, Newport House 63 (517 acres, 10 men & 7 boys); William Stratton 36 – widower – (2017 acres, 40 men and 20 boys).

Rector: - David Malcolm Clarke 68.

Farm Bailiff: - Charles Pretty 37.

Silk Workers: 13 – Matilda Trimby 11, Sarah Jones 13, Annie Trimby 13, Mary-Jane Trimby 13, Sarah Brimble 13, Louisa Coombs 14, Annie Presley 15, Lucy Jones 16, Fanny Brimble 16, Jane Marshall 20, Elizabeth Riddick 20, Mary Trimby 21, Jane Tudgay 23.

Police Constable: - George Pike 36.

Groom:- Thomas Tuckwell 44.

Blacksmiths; 2 – George Burgess 42, Henry Trimby 35.

Dressmaker: - Julie Marshall 22.

Shepherds; 5 – John Marshall 15, Joseph Mabbett 66, Henry Mabbett 16, Samuel Trimby 53, George Tudgay 25.

Agricultural Engine Driver: - John Lyne 26.
Tailor: - James Curtis 42.
Carpenter: - George Humphreys 85.
Seamstress: - Harriet Curtis 32.
Dairyman: - Obed Giles 29.
Servants: 9 – Emily Coombs 24, Alice Coombs 20, Eunice Marshall 30, Jane Biddicombe 30, Emma Draper 21, Martha Garrett 53, Eliza Noakes 19 (Rectory), Harriet Tapsell 29, Elizabeth Miles 19 (Manor Farm).
Laundresses: 2 – Mary White 62, Ann Presley 58.
Thatcher: - James Marshall 74.
Carter: - Moses Brimble 33.
Shopkeepers: 2 Emmanuel Trimby 63 (Retired), Henry Carpenter 53.
School mistress: Georgina Callaghan 29 (Board School).
Stone Masons: 3 – Lewis Fletcher 68, Joseph Stone 41, Henry Richards 22.
Mason's Boy: - Aaron Abraham 13.
Gardeners: 2 – James Newbury 36, Absalom Trimby 44.
Gamekeeper: - Henry Oakley 40.
Grocer: - Henry White 46.
Baker: - George Tudgay 58 (also Courier).
Postmistress: - Elizabeth Tudgay 66 (also Shopkeeper).
Cook; - Anne Goring 34 (Manor Farm).

5. Prominent Family Names
   Marshall – 50 members
   Trimby 40
   Tudgay 33
   Coombs 24
   White 18
   Brimble 15
   Carpenter 14
   Presley 11

The number of farms has now fallen to two, with a consequent reduction in employment for agricultural labourers from the figure of

85 in 1861 to 66 ten years later. There are also now only 5 shepherds as opposed to 15, and there is the ominous appearance of John Lyne as the driver of an 'Agricultural Engine'. William Stratton arrived on the scene as the tenant of Manor Farm in 1865, and the family is celebrating their 150th anniversary in residence as I write (2015). The silk workers are still numerous, according to this census, and are now controlled – presumably together with other members of the community - by a new figure on the beat, Police Constable Pike. There's still a Stone amongst the masons and Mary White is continuing to launder, though now with some help. For the first time servants appear in substantial numbers, so there must be some wealthier people about – but at the other end of the scale there are now more paupers than was the case in 1861. It is also interesting that the 'Crown Inn' is no longer mentioned in this census and it seems that the innkeeper, John Lampard, moved at some point in the 1860s to the 'Angel' in Mere where he appears in the 1871 census for the town. Since his family includes a daughter aged 8 who was born in KD, and a second daughter aged 5 who was born in Mere, the conclusion is that the 'Crown' closed its doors for the last time in around 1865. From this point, and for the next hundred years, the KD villagers were dependent on the King's Arms (later called The New Inn) at Monkton for their alcoholic intake and related social life. (The latter pub is still sometimes remembered by its original title 'The Tipling (sic) Philospher', and the building's use as an 'alehouse' under that title derives from a lease granted to John Philips of Monkton by Thomas Thynne, Viscount Weymouth – later the 1st Marquis of Bath – in 1776. The lease passed through various hands – John Philip's brother, Henry, in 1794, James Dredge in 1808, William Dredge in 1814, Jeremiah Francis in around 1830 and Stephen Carpenter in 1859, - by which time the 'Philosopher', tippling or not, was no longer in evidence).

The mention of the existence of a 'Primitive Methodist Chapel' as well as a 'Wesleyan' version is interesting, since there is no other reference to its establishment (although the 1841 'Ranting' preacher was perhaps a Primitive Methodist), so it may have been fairly short-lived. We have already encountered in Chapter 2 the take-over of the Wesleyan Chapel by the Primitive Methodists in 1903.

Very soon after his arrival at Manor Farm, William Stratton built – at his own expense – the road which bypasses the New Inn at MD. His arrival also coincided with a run of wet seasons and steadily decreasing prices for agricultural produce due to increasing imports from the new colonies. Parties of emigrant farm workers from the Deverill villages were organised and assisted by Lord and Lady Bath, and most of these went to Canada.

In 1875 Kelly's Directory has the following entry:

> Private Residents: Rev. Clerk; William Stratton .Commercial Traders: James Curtis – Shopkeeper; James Long – Butcher; William Stratton – yeoman, Manor Farm; Henry Trimby – Blacksmith; George Tudgay – Shopkeeper, Carrier and Post Office Receiver; Charles Pullin – Farmer, Newport Farm. Letters arrive from Warminster at 8.40 a.m. dispatched at 5 p.m. on Sundays at 1045 a.m.. The nearest money order office is at Mere.

It is interesting that the Directory describes both Rev. Clerk and William Stratton as 'private residents' (whilst incidentally later naming the latter as a 'yeoman') Since they neither of them own the properties in which they live the reference can only be to the fact that they have 'private means'. This, however, seems not to apply to the new farmer on the block, Charles Pullin, who has taken over from William Ransom at Newport Farm. George Tudgay, described in the census as a 'courier', is now a 'Post Office Receiver' – combining this post with shopkeeping and baking – and we are also given the details of how the postal service works as to the timings of deliveries and collections. In addition the village has acquired a butcher in the person of James Long.

In 1878 another Directory, Owen's, the village population is stated to number 337 (a net gain of 13) and gives George Tudgay an actual 'post office' – although this would also double as his shop.

1881 Census Analysis

1. Population

277

THE SOCIAL SCENE

2. Age Groups
   Under 13: 104
   Teenagers; 34
   20 -35: 35
   36 – 50: 48
   51 – 65: 28
   66 – 79: 25 – Hannah Marshall 66, Christopher Holland 66 (Gardener), George Trimby 66 (AL), John Marshall 67 (AL), William White 69 (pauper), George Tudgay 69 (Baker and Grocer), Ann Harris 69, James Presley 69 (AL), Elizabeth Draper 70 (Widow), Elizabeth Garrett 70 (pauper), John Tudgay 70 (Independent), Martha Marshall 72, Benjamin Trimble 72 (pauper), Jane Presley 73, Isabella Williams 73, Ann Harwood 74, Mary White 74, Charlotte Trimble 75, Elizabeth Tudgay 75, Susannah Holland 75, John Carpenter 76, Lewis Fletcher 77, Philip Garrett 77 (pauper), Sheila Carpenter 78, Adam Trimby 78 (pauper).
   80+ 3 – Diana Trimby 81, James Marshall 83 (pauper), Alice Edwards 84 (pauper).
3. Households
   71. Some new designations now appear:- 'Bradley Road', 'Prospect Lane', 'Pope's Farm', 'Higher End'; 'New Farm House', 'Marvin's Farm', 'Lower End'.
4. Occupations
   Agricultural Labourers: - 35
   Master Dairyman – Henry Westcombe 57
   Dairyman – Ernest Westcombe 19
   Retired Grocer – Emmanuel Trimby 71
   Shepherds: 4 – Oliver Marshall 11, Joseph Hunt 25, Henry Ruddick 36, William Kerley 38
   Blacksmith – Henry Trimby 45
   Carters: 5 – Charles Marshall 28, William Newbury 34, Thomas Marshall 43, Frederick Ruddick 51, James Townsend 60
   Grocer – James Curtis (Greenwich Pensioner)
   Wesleyan Preacher – Robert Mabbi 46 (also AL)
   Road Contractor – John Carpenter 35

Rector – Thomas Kingsbury 58 (Prebendary of Sarum)
Servants: 8 – William Reid 40 (Chelsea Pensioner – Rectory), Elizabeth Reid 34 (Rectory), Emily Holt 29 (Rectory), Emma Trimby 16, Anna Tudgay 16, Lilly Curle 14 (Stratton's Farm), Lorna Webb , Ross Dyer 18 (Marvins)
Baker and Grocer – George Tudgay 69
Gamekeepers: 2 – Stephen Ruddick 54, George Coffinio 47
Shopkeeper – Henry White 56
Coal Merchant – Joseph Stone
Rectory Coachman – James Newbury 46
Gardener – Christopher Holland 66
Pond Maker – James Long 61
Seamstress – Harriet Ford
Assistant School Teacher =- Elizabeth Ford 26
National School Mistress – Anne Gilbert 18
Farm Bailiff – Charles Presley 49
Farmers: 2 – William Stratton 46 (2149 acres, 29 men 6 boys), Charles Pullen 43 (Marvins: 877 acres, 9 men, 5 boys)
Cook – Sarah Woods (Stratton's Farm)
Groom – Thomas Tuckwell 56
Builder – Henry Tuckwell 15
Agricultural Engineer - John Lyne 26
Independent – John Tudgay 70
Charwoman – Betsy Marshall 64
Hawker of Pig Meat – Edward Mills 50
Thatcher – John White 64
Thatcher's Assistant – Frank White 12
Laundress – Frances Howell 59
Police Constable – Henry Harris 32

5. Prominent names
    Marshall- 38 members
    Trimby 29
    Tudgay 26
    White 17
    Carpenter 16
    Kerley 13

In the 10 years since the previous census the population of KD has dropped by 47, mostly in the age-groups 20-35 and 51-65, and it is particularly significant that the number of agricultural labourers has almost halved, from 66 to 35. There are now only 7 girls working in the silk industry as opposed to 14 in 1871, and it is obviously the case that there are serious employment difficulties for young people. The servant population has remained much the same, however. The Rector, Thomas Kingsbury (who came to KD in 1879 following the death of his predecessor David Malcolm Clerk) has three, plus a coachman; the Strattons have two and there are also two at Marvin's Farm. At the other end of the scale there are six members of the community who are described as paupers, but remain at home in the care of their families rather than being sent to the workhouse.

There are now no fewer than five 'carters', although only one blacksmith was now available to tend the horses, when previously there had been two. George Tudgay is still running his shop (and possibly the post office) and his financial success is perhaps indicated by the reference to his retired brother John, aged 70, as being 'independent'. For the first time there is mention of a Coal Merchant, a 'Hawker of Pig Meat' and a 'Pond Maker' – the latter's responsibility being the excavation and lining of round ponds (popularly known as dew ponds) in the chalk for the benefit of the sheep.

It is interesting to find both a Chelsea Pensioner (William Reid) and a Greenwich Pensioner (James Curtis) living in the village at the same time. William (a retired soldier) would have been entitled to live at the Chelsea Hospital and James at the Royal Hospital, Greenwich (the Chelsea Hospital's naval equivalent) if they were unmarried, but they both chose to live elsewhere, and were nonetheless entitled to draw their service pensions.

In 1889 Kelly's Directory records that the Post Office is run by John Carpenter and that mail is received at 9.30 and dispatched at 5, except on Sundays when there is a receipt of mail at 10 but no dispatch. Postal Orders are issued at the PO, but not paid. Joseph Stone now combines his job as a coal merchant with that of a Carrier and with the assistance of John White runs a service to Warminster on Tuesdays,

Thursdays and Saturdays. The Greenwich Pensioner James Curtis is still a shopkeeper as is Henry White; James Long continues to dig ponds and Henry Trimby remains at his forge. The Westcombe father and son 'Dairyman' team have been replaced by Francis Oborne, but the farmers William Stratton and Charles Pullen remain in harness, albeit 8 years older.

1891 Census Analysis

1 Population
    231
2 Age Groups
    under 13: 60
    teenagers: 38
    20-35 : 49
    36-50: 38
    51-65: 32
    66-79: 12 – Henry White 66, Sarah White 68, Thomas Tuckwell 69, (Dairyman's assistant), John White 69 (AL), John Marshall (AL), James Long 71 (AL), Rachel White 72, Edward Carpenter 73 (AL), John White 74 (Carrier), Martha Garrett 76, Benjamin Brimble 78, Charlotte Brimble 79.
    80+: 2 - Philip Garrett 87, (retired Shepherd), Martha Marshall 90.
3 Households
    57 – There is a distinct diminution in the number of registered households in this census as compared with that of 1881, and many houses are described as unoccupied.
4 Occupations
    Dairyman – William White 32
    Dairyman's assistant: 2 – John White 13, Thomas Tuckwell 69
    Cheesemaker – Lottie White 21
    Agricultural Labourers: 46
    Midwife – Elizabeth Kerley 60
    Road Contractor – John Carpenter 45
    General Labourer – William Carpenter 73
    Grooms: 2 – George Carpenter 17, George Penthicest (?) 21

Rector – William Moore 40 *
Cooks: 2 – Elizabeth Carpenter 21 (Rectory), Emily Whatley 19, (Manor Farm)
Housemaids: 2 – Rose Carpenter 19 (Rectory), Rosaline Hodge 19, (Manor Farm)
Nurse – Martha Hallett 23 (Rectory)
Grocers: 2 – Henry White 66, Harriet Curtis 52
Grocer's Apprentice – Herbert Galpin 15
Glass Fitter – Arthur Stone 21
Agricultural Engine Driver – Charles Stone 38
Shepherds: 5 – George Stone 16, Henry Ruddick 41, William Ruddick 18, Philip Garrett 87 (ret'd), William Kerley 62
Gardener – James Day 32 (Pope's Farm)
Thatcher – Thomas Hill 45
Laundresses: 2 – Emily Hill 43, Louisa Marshall 58
Assistant Teacher, National School – Elizabeth Ford 41
Errand Boy – Henry Coombs 14
Gamekeeper – Abraham Garrett 31
Silk Workers: 10 – Bessie Coombs 10, Elizabeth Trimby 13, Julia Markey 16, Sarah Marshall 24, Georgina Tudgay 17, Amelia Coombs 23, Sabina Marshall 24, Matilda Ruddick 25, Clara Tudgay 27, Elizabeth Hibberd 28
Blacksmiths: 2 – Henry Trimby 55, Albert Lyon 40
Organist & Elementary Certificate Mistress – Catherine Kneller 39
Farm Bailiff – Benjamin Galpin 43
Dressmaker – Elizabeth Garrett 50
Farmers: 3 – William Stratton 56, Charles Stratton 24, Charles Pullin 50
Governess – Ethel Forster 26 (Manor Farm)
Parlourmaid – Julia Everett (Manor Farm)
'Boots' in Hotel – Ernest Howard 21
Housekeepers: 2 – Jane Farthing 50, Ellen Pullin 30
Engine Fitter – Thomas Lyon 34
Carrier – John White 74
Carpenter – Henry Maxfield 36

Police Constable – Arthur Matthews 36
(* William Moore took over from Thomas Kingsbury as Rector in 1885)
5. Prominent Family Names
Marshall – 19 members
White 16
Trimby 15
Carpenter 14
Stone 10
Kerley 9
Tudgay 9

In the 10 years since the 1881 Census the population of the village has again dropped significantly, there being 46 fewer inhabitants. Those aged between 66 and 79 now number 12, as opposed to 25 and the 30 – 35 age group has been reduced by 14. The most significant reduction, however, is in the number of children under 13 in the village – 60, down from 104, indicating that many families have moved away. Strangely the agricultural labourers have increased in number, as have the silk workers and a number of new 'occupations' have appeared – two laundresses, a midwife, a governess, an organist, a glass fitter, a governess a nurse and a cheesemaker. (Incidentally, it would be interesting to know what kind of cheese Lottie White was making, as she worked with her two brothers William and John in the Dairy, but almost certainly it was something 'local' rather than the once-famous Wiltshire Loaf, a product of the north of the county and which had long since been overtaken by cheeses from Gloucester and from Cheddar, for the reason that the coming of the railway to Chippenham meant that it was more profitable for the Pewsey Vale farmers to send their fresh milk directly to London. Jane Austen, who mentions Wiltshire cheese in 'Emma' (1816) would not be alone in being pleased to know, if she were here today, that the 'loaf' is once more in production at a dairy farm in Brinkworth). Martha Hallett, the Rectory nurse, would have had the responsibility of looking after Rev Moore's four surviving children, and would perhaps have heard them tell of their elder brother Urban, who died tragically at the age of

9 and who is notably commemorated in the church.

There are again five shepherds, (although one of them, Philip Garrett is 87 and officially 'retired'), and 2 farmers - Charles Pullin and William Stratton, the latter now assisted by his son.

Also in 1891, Charles Jupe, the director of the silk factory at Bull Mill in Crockerton decided to move north to Malmesbury to take over a business there, leaving the running of the local concern to his son Isaiah. This was a disastrous decision for the community, since Isaiah was incapable of efficient management, with the result that the mill closed in 1894 putting many individuals in the valley out of work.

Kelly's Directory of 1895 reveals that Harriet Curtis is still running her shop – and that James Long, who disappears from the 1891 census, continues in his occupation as pond-maker at the age of 75. There are now two 'carriers' – Henry Meaden and Joseph Stone - replacing the 74-year-old John White mentioned in the previous census and rather surprisingly working on his own. Henry Trimby remains as the Blacksmith and Henry White is now a Shopkeeper whilst his son William continues to run the dairy.

The Directory of 1899 mentions much the same occupational team, with the addition of Henry Merfield who is described as the Parish Clerk.

1900 is the year in which piped water first reached the Upper Deverills. Its installation was instigated by the Marquess of Bath and at first could only be used by the farming community.

1901 Census Analysis

1. Population
   175
2. Age groups
   Under 13: 44
   Teenagers: 19
   20-35: 47
   36-50: 15
   51-65: 30
   66-79: 15 – James Newbury 66 (AL), William Stratton 66 (Farmer), - Marshall 68, Richard Matthews 68 (Pensioner),

James Mather 68, Sarah Ruddick 68, Moses Tudgay 68, Elizabeth Kerley 68, John Draper 69 (AL), Joseph Stone 70, William Marshall 70, Josiah Trimby 71, William Keley 72, Thomas Tuckwell 73 (Cattleman), James Long 78 (Pond Maker).

80+: 5- James Trimby 81, Rachel White 82, Robert Mather 84, Edward Carpenter 87, Mary Trimby 87.

3. Households

48 – Another reduction in the number of occupied houses.

4. Occupations

Dairywoman – Rachel Court 65

Cheesemakers -2: Emily Court 35, Ellen Court 15

Dairyman and Cattleman – Charles Court 61

Farm foreman – William Chant 57

Cattlemen- 7: Thomas Chant 14, Edward Chant 16, Thomas Trimby 19, Thomas Tuckwell 73, - White 48, Herbert Newbury 25, Arthur Marshall 35

Nurse/silk Worker – May Riddick 60

Shepherds – 6: Henry Riddick 16, William Marshall 70, Walter Penney 40, John Pearce 55, George white 27, George Trimby 31

Agricultural Labourers – 17

Shopkeepers – 2: Harriet Curtis 63, Jemima White 64

Pensioners – 2: Richard Matthews 68, Edward Carpenter 87

Carters – 6: Walter Penney 17, George Newbury 54, George Feltham 25, John Feltham 27, Silas Marshall 24, James Marshall 30

'Cook Domestic' – 3: Sara Draper 27, Kate Reeves 22 (Rectory), Matilda Kilford 25 (Manor Farm)

Schoolmistress – Beatrice Perrin 35

School Assistant – Rose Draper 19

Blacksmiths -2: Henry Trimby 65, Richard Howell 55

Clergyman C of E – Edmund Caudwell 35*

Retired Merchant – Robert Matthew 84

Housemaids – 4: Alice ? 17 (Rectory), Agnes Baker 15 (Rectory), Hannah ? 20 (Manor Farm), Fanny Carpenter 17 (Manor

Farm)
Road Constructors -2: John Carpenter 50, William Carpenter 33
Sub-Postmistress - ? Carpenter 18
Groom – Frederick Foot 26
Assistant Groom – Arthur Carpenter 15
Pondmaker – James Long 78
Gamekeeper – Abraham Garrett 42
Stockman – William Trimby 48
Bailiff – Benjamin Galpin 54
Farmers – 2: William Stratton 66, Charles Pullin 60
Carrier – Frederick Newbury 26
* Edmund Caudwell was appointed Rector in 1900 and remained in office until 1903.

Prominent Family Names
Marshall 21 members
Trimby 14
Carpenter 11
Penney 11
White 9

The population of the village has again dropped, this time dramatically - the figure of 175 comparing with 231 in 1891. The number of teenagers has been halved to 19, and those aged between 36 and 50 reduced from 38 to 15. These figures reflect the reduction in employment opportunities in the valley – the 1894 closure of the Silk Factory being just one example – and the resulting removal of many of the younger members of the community to the towns. Nonetheless, the numbers in the farming community still hold up reasonably well, with 17 'agricultural labourers', 7 'cattlemen' and 6 shepherds, assisted doubtless by the 6 'carters' and the single 'carrier'.(The occupation 'Carrier' as distinct from 'Carter' is mentioned for the first time in the 1891 census, and the official difference between the two activities is that the 'Carrier' transported heavier goods – and sometimes people – between a village and a town and often combined these responsibilities with that of a 'shopping agent', purchasing requested goods and charging a commission, whereas a 'Carter' was involved with the transport of lighter goods within the confines of the community. Doubtless the distinction was often blurred). Harriet Curtis continues to run her shop and James Long is out on the downs pondmaking at an advanced age, but the dairy has been taken over from the Whites by the Court family. Seven young people are employed domestically at the Rectory and Manor Farm and it is only May Riddick who is described as a 'silk worker' – but this was doubtless a response to the census inspector which involved the past rather than the present. The Marshall family is the only one to keep its numbers up – the remaining previously prominent family groups having fallen away.

Kelly's Directory for 1903 simply mentions the arrival of William Henderson as Rector in that year, and indicates that there is a new 'Carrier' in the village, Fred Newbury. The 1907 version notes that Emma Tudgay is now running the shop and that Henry Trimby, now aged 71, remains the village blacksmith.

1911 Census Analysis

1. Population
    176
2. Age Groups
    Under 13: 56
    Teenagers: 20
    20-35: 40
    36-50: 40
    51-65: 19
    66-79: 16 – Thomas Howell 66 (retired blacksmith), Elizabeth Pearce 66, Richard Matthews 68 (Army pensioner, Sgt.), Annie Trimby 68, Charles Pullin 69 (Farmer), Eliza Tudgay 69, Elizabeth Marshall 74, Sarah Newberry 74, Eliza Marshall 74, Martha Marshall 74, Henry Trimby 75, Anne Stone 75, Aaron Combs 75, William Stratton 76 (retired Farmer), Moses Tudgay 77, William Marshall 78 (farm labourer –retd.)
    80+: 1 – Thomas Tuckwell 87 (farm labourer – retd.)
3. Households
    46 – Dairy House and Dairy Cottage are mentioned for the first time and 'Pope's Farm' is now described as 'late Pope's'. There

has been as slight rise in the number of resident households, but many houses are still unoccupied.

4. Occupations

Dairyman – Charles Court 41

Domestic Help - Jane Kim 25

Cowmen: 3 – James Wilson 43, Thomas Trimby 29, William Trimby 58

Under Cowman – George Wilson 16

Farm Labourers: 13 – Samuel Wilson 14, Herbert Newbury 35, Ernest Marshall 32, Charles Newbury 37, Arthur Carpenter 23, Herbert Marshall 41, Stanley Marshall 13, Wilson Day 21, Arthur Pearce 13, Arthur Trimby 32, Henry Fletcher 65, Aaron Combs 75, Herbert Gibbs 41

Cowboy – Frederick Wilson 13

Organist – Arthur Daintree 60 (widower from Islington)

Carrier – Frederick Newbury 36

Carters: 6 – George Newbury 33, William Whatley 24, George Carpenter 36, James Marshall 40, Arthur Marshall 45, Frank Carpenter 29

Shopkeeper – Emma Tudgay 60

Shepherds: 4 – Charles Barter 54, George Pearce 40, John Pearce 33, Ernest Morgan 30

Schoolteacher (Elementary) – Gertrude Harding 22

Rector – William Henderson 45*

Gardeners: 2 – Henry Helps 44 (Rectory), James Day 52, (late Pope's)

Housekeeper – Eliza Helps 42 (Rectory)

Page – Arthur Sollis 14 (Rectory)

Post Office/Road Contractor – John Carpenter 65

Road Labourer – Arthur Stone 40

Waggoner – Walter Pearce 17,

Farm Bailiffs: 2 - Benjamin Galpin 64, John Howell 32

Gamekeeper – Arthur Garrett 51

Barmaid – Beatrice Garrett 21

Cook – Margaret Garrett 18, (Manor Farm)

Housemaid – Margaret Fletcher 18 (Manor Farm)

Parlourmaid – Rossalta Curtis 21 (Manor Farm)
Coachman- Robert Guy 51
Farmer – Charles Pullin 49
*William Henderson was Rector from 1903 – 1926

5. Prominent Names
Marshall – 25 family members
Pearce 17
Newbury 13
Garrett 11
Carpenter 10
Wilson 10

Remarkably the population has stabilised during the past decade, the total number of villagers remaining the same, the only major decrease being amongst the 51-65 year-olds, the increases appearing amongst the children and those aged between 36 and 50. The six 'carters' are now joined by a youthful 'waggoner', and the Rector, William Henderson, has acquired a 'page' – duties unspecified – and a married couple, Henry and Eliza Helps, who are well-named as his assistants in the house and garden. Emma Tudgay is now running the village shop.

Kelly's Directory for 1915, lists John Carpenter as sub-postmaster, Richard Stratton at Manor Farm and Charles Pullin at Newport Farm, Walter Brashier (assistant overseer), Charles Court (Dairyman), Marshall Herbert (shopkeeper) Harry Scott (gamekeeper to the Marquis of Bath) and Frederick Carey (Sexton). It also describes the Methodist Chapel as 'disused'. The 1920 edition elevates Walter Brashier to the headmastership of the school, and mentions the following newcomers – Gregory Stafford 'farmer' at Marvin's Farm, Reginald Cook as farm bailiff and Fred Newbury as the shopkeeper.

As mentioned earlier, there is a one hundred year embargo on detailed access to the census returns as far as members of the general public are concerned, so from the end of the First World War we are dependent upon the annual Electoral Rolls, other local records, in so far as they have been preserved, and upon living memories. Some more recent events have been recorded in earlier chapters concerning the school, the church and the history of farming, but given the absence in particular of relevant PCC and Parish Council minutes, remaining information in the context of this 'social scene' chapter is sparse.

We have the population figures, however, and these show a consistent diminution – 164 in 1921 and 152 in 1931 – and in between these dates the gradual withdrawal, as stated earlier, of the Longleat patronage and land ownership as a result of the First World War. No census was taken in 1941, and from 1934 population figures for the two adjoining villages, Kingston and Monkton were assessed together, giving a combined total in 1951 of 252, the KD total being roughly half that figure.

The Electoral Registers for the years between 1919 and 1958 reveal that many of the 'traditional' families remain in the village – the figures for 1919 including 6 Carpenters, 6 Marshalls, 6 Newburys, 9 Trimbys and 3 Tudgays, for 1937 9 Marshalls, 8 Newburys and 6 Trimbys, and for 1958 5 Marshalls, 4 Newburys and – again – 6 Trimbys. Later these numbers dwindle, leaving only isolated representatives of these long-standing village families – with the exception of the Trimbys whose numbers remained at 3 until 1994.

Kelly's Directory, in its County series, continued for a few more years (it's town and city editions were published until 1974) - and from the 1923 edition we can establish that Reginald Cook remained as the farm bailiff, that Fred Newbury was still the shopkeeper, but that Walter Brashier was replaced at the school by Phoebe Garland. In 1931 Messrs. Cook and Newbury are still where they were, George Carpenter is now the Sexton, Clifford Hayes a 'poultry farmer' and Richard Stratton a JP.

At some point in the 1930s a local resident, Emily Gibbs (nee Coombs), (1870 – 1958) wrote a fascinating memoir which reminisces about 'ancient' KD customs. Her essay can be found at Appendix G.

The Directory for 1935 describes the 'principal landowners' as the Marquess of Bath, R. Stratton JP, J.M Stratton, S.R White OBE JP, and William Hinton. Clifford Hayes continues as a poultry farmer, William Newbury is a 'carrier' (perhaps a strange term to encounter in the mid-twentieth century) and Edgar Perrett Jn. is the Farm Bailiff. In 1935 the innkeeper at Monkton is John Howell, and Phoebe

Garland, the retired headmistress now lives at no.91 in that village. In the following year, the new headmistress, Dorothy Richards and her husband Edward are in residence at the School House.

The final directory, published in 1939, appears to list only those of relative independent means, namely Richard Stratton, Fred Newbury (smallholder), William Newbury, who continues as a 'carrier', George Carpenter who combines confectionary sales with the running of the Post Office, Alan James Lynn of Marvins and Miss H.M Inman who is living at Hedge Cottage. (In common with all other local trade directories, Kelly's ceased their County series publication with the advent of the Second World War).

At this point, we are confronted by the absence of detailed documentary evidence of the social life of the village and its inhabitants – but with a few fascinating exceptions. One of these is in the form of three typewritten sheets held at the History Centre, and the information they reveal indicates that whatever was happening elsewhere in the world, the people of Kingston Deverill were ready to handle anything which might befall in the event of a German invasion in 1940.

Invasion Committee
    Mr R Stratton Chairman
    Miss Mather Vice- Chairman
    The Rev C Heath Caldwell
    Mr Lister
    Mr Frampton
    Mrs Lynn Allen

A R P Head Warden	Mr Allard
Food Officer	The Rev Heath Caldwell tel.no. Sutton Veny 78
Home Guard	O.C. Lieut.Com. Lister Warminster 8
Police Divisional HQ	Warminster 3
Longbridge Police	Sutton Veny 53
Maiden Bradley Police	M.Bradley 257
Mere Fire Engine	(only to be called if communications with Warminster fail).

Home Guard HQ Club Room, Monkton
Invasion Committee HQ Manor Farm., Kingston M.Bradley 11
Official Notice Board Home Guard, Kingston (key with Mr Shadwell)
The Mortuary   The Old Chapel, Kingston (key with Dr.Lynn Allen)
Food Office Church Street, Westbury   Westbury 124
Parish Animal Steward   Mrs Legg
Medical Officer of Health Dr.Blackley Warminster 351

Kingston Deverill

WVS Representative	Mrs Lynn Allen
Chief Housewife	Miss Beckwith
Billeting Officers	Miss Herbert, Miss Mather
ARP Wardens	F. Legg, A.Trimby
Stretcher Bearers	A. Day. W.Pearce, E.Marshall

Stirrup Pumps & Buckets F. Legg, Manor Farm, Mrs Bassett, Dr.Lynn Allen Miss Mather
First Aid Point   Dr. Lynn Allen 'Marvins' (unofficial)
First Aid Boxes   The School, F. Legg (also 2 stretchers), Miss Mather
Red Cross   Mrs. Lynn Allen, Miss Beckwith, Mrs Preston, Mrs Eggleton, Mrs Noble
Messengers   D. Weeden, Mrs Crichton, Miss Herbert, I.Fear, W. Newbury Miss M. Carpenter
Arrangements for Refugees   Newport Barn (to be used till billeted)
Sanitary Arrangements   In charge of Mrs E Marshall
Cooking   Mrs E Newbury, Mrs J Pearce, Mrs J Carpenter, Mrs Legg, Mrs Brand, Mrs V Raynes, Mrs Noble
Baking   Miss A Smith, Mrs J Newbury, Mrs Brand
To Look after Children   Mrs Perrott, Mrs B Gibbs, Mrs N Carpenter, Mrs Brand Miss Taylor
Boiling Kettles Available   Mrs Green, Mrs Fryer, Mrs J Newbury, Mrs J Pearce Mrs Lemon, Mrs B Trimby, Mrs Gibbs (senior), Mrs G

Carpenter
Food Supplies   Cups and mugs for 50 people, 4 Tea pots, 2 Jugs, 2 Basins (at the School). Stores at Newport – key at Manor Farm. Miss Druce in charge. Miss Pitt. Extra flour stored in both shops. At Newport: - 66 tins biscuits, 168 lbs. Sugar, 6 doz. tins of Beans, 30 lbs. Tea, 96 tins Evaporated Milk, 70 lbs. Margarine, 240 tins Corned Beef

Centre for distribution of milk and meat   Lambing Yard

Picks and Shovels available Manor Farm, J Carpenter, G Carpenter, F Legg, C Newbury, E Marshall, Miss Mather

Wheel Barrows   Manor Farm, J Carpenter, G Carpenter, E Marshall, Mrs Bassett, E Trimby, Miss Mather

Long Ladders   Manor Farm & Miss Mather

School Children   If alarm comes in school hours children will be kept in school till roads are safe, and then taken to their homes by Mrs Preston, Miss Taylor and Miss Herbert

Mere Schoolchildren   Thelma Garrett, Thelma Fear, Eunice Bryant, Thomas Baggs, Betty Matthews, Morley Cummings, Raymond Pearce, Ronald Pendue, John Wisbech. Mere arranges for transport when roads are safe, otherwise beds are are provided at the new Rest Centre. [This entry refers to older KD children who are at school in Mere].

The Battle of Britain apart, given the elaborate precautionary measures drawn up by the people of Kingston Deverill, it is hardly surprising that the German High Command decided against an invasion in the autumn of 1940. They simply had to ask themselves how they might fare when encountering a defensive system which included eight boiling kettles and 96 tins of evaporated milk. In the event - rationing, the blackout and the later appearance of American troops apart - the closest the village came to the evidence of war was the spectacular crash of a German bomber on King's Hill, and the appearance of Italian POWs in brown uniforms working on the hedges and ditches of a farm rented by the Strattons in the village of Zeals (and seen occasionally in KD according to two of the evacuees who came to the school).

THE SOCIAL SCENE

A number of notable events which took place in the village during the war, in the late forties and the two decades that followed, are mentioned in the school's logbook, but the rather significant arrival of mains electricity supply to the village in 1947 is omitted, as is the distribution of Coronation mugs in 1953.

Also in 1947 a film entitled 'House of Darkness' 'starring' John Stuart, Leslie Brook and George Melachrino with his orchestra, was made at the Rectory, which doubled for the occasion as a 'haunted house'. The filming was enlivened by the presence of a number of villagers who were recruited as extras. After the war the Rectory was divided up into flats and these were successfully rented out during the following 30 years, until the building was purchased by Robert and Judith Brown in 1982.

Old Rectory (Kingston House)

In the mid nineteen-fifties there was a violent storm which badly damaged the church windows, and the task of rescuing the glass and re-leading it was entrusted to Arthur Fear. He and his wife Nellie had moved from Maiden Bradley in 1945 and in that year set up a Post Office at no.20 KD, the postal service having previously operated from Whitepits Farm, the home of Jack Carpenter and his wife Marjorie. In 1957 Arthur purchased the converted Methodist Chapel from Lancelot

The Methodist Chapel

Shadwell and set up a small shop – an 'east end' establishment which paralleled the 'sweet shop' at the 'west end' of the village, run by Edie Day – whilst continuing to run the postal service. Meanwhile no.20 became the main village shop run successively by the Pilbrow, Peters, Goldsmith and Thomas families – the most prominent owner being Liz Peters.

THE SOCIAL SCENE

Before it became a private house, post office and shop, the Methodist Chapel had undergone a series of different manifestations, the most interesting of which was its existence as a Handicraft Centre. The instigator of this was Lancelot Cayley Shadwell who moved with wife Mary to KD in 1937, building himself a home called Barley Close just by the ford in the river. Shadwell (1882 – 1963) was a published poet but made his name as a ceramicist, running a highly successful pottery in Broadstone, Dorset until the business was overcome by the effects of the depression in the late 1920s, after which he worked for some years with the renowned Bernard Leach in St.Ives. Shortly after his move to the village he bought the derelict Chapel and set up the Handicraft Centre with the idea that local people would come there and both make and display their individual craftwork The popularity of the establishment was such that very soon various items were put up for sale and the Centre found itself pressed to fulfil the orders which it received. In 1948 Heal's of Tottenham Court Road staged an exhibition in which three items from the KD Handicraft Centre were included, and thereafter set up a standing order for its products. There was a particular demand for Rushwork, and Robin Toogood who delivered bread to cottagers in KD remembered the bundles of Hampshire rushes which were stacked outside the chapel doors. Shadwell also had a passion for the construction of model boats, and the foundations of the brick harbour he built for them can still be seen near the ford. Shadwell's son died in the war, and a dedicatory plaque

The Shadwell plaque

was constructed in his memory. This was preserved by Arthur Fear when he bought the Chapel (which he renamed as 'Rodney House') and the plaque is now to be found on the outside wall nearest the road. It reads as follows: 'This Handicraft Centre is established as a lasting memorial to Lancelot Rodney Cayley Shadwell, Flying Officer RAF Bomber Command, who did not return from the great raid on Essen, Germany on the night of April 3rd 1943. Per Ardua ad Astra.'

KD Football Team, 1936/37
back row: T Green, Mr R Stratton, B Castle, A Marshall, J Newbury, C Clifford, Capt Hayes, R Gray, D Thomas; front row: B Newbury, Richardson, B Newbury, L Newbury, B Stone, Hill

Later, the Chapel housed a succession of men's, women's and youth clubs, some of which fed into to the local football and cricket teams. Football gradually disappeared, but cricket continued to thrive and its popularity was enhanced when the pitch was substantially rehabilitated in 1977.

As previously stated, the population statistics from the time of the 1961 census represent a combination of the figures for both Monkton and Kingston, which makes sense considering that the villages are so close to each other. These statistics give the numbers

KD Football Team, 1946/47
back row: R Stratton, J Day, Len Newbury, T Haywood, R Gray, C Munday, L C Shadwell, W Newbury; front row: Len Smith, G Keate, J Pearce, J Kent, R Clifford, M Marsh, G Clifford

as 209 for 1971, 233 for 1981, 267 for 1991, 255 for 2001 and 248 for 2011: in other words they have remained fairly static throughout the past forty years, with the population of the two villages roughly equally divided.

The Upper Deverills Village Hall which houses many events including dinners, exhibitions, art classes, quiz nights, lectures, committee meetings – and since 2013 monthly pub nights – was erected next to the cricket pitch in 1954, and became the HQ for the local branch of the Women's Institute in 1956. In this same year, members of the WI (Mesdames Baird, Gray, E. Blitso, Cooper, Stratton, Taylor, Rich, Joy, Light, Maidment, Dufosee, Toop and M.Blitso) put together a remarkable 'Scrapbook' which is a treasure-trove of photographs and memoirs. The valley is greatly indebted to the compilers of this invaluable document, which is now preserved at the History Centre.

With the closure of the Monkton pub in 1966 and the shop in KD in 1991, the Upper Deverills Village Hall and the Church are

Village Hall – built in 1954

Village cricket – 1960s

now the only establishments where the community can come together.

1958 saw the arrival in the village of an eminent musician Dr W.K Stanton, who took up residence in the house by the ford previously occupied by Lancelot Shadwell. Dr Stanton had been a chorister at Salisbury Cathedral, continued his education at Lancing College and then was appointed as head of music at Reading University. Early in his career he had some success as a composer, with a published oboe quintet and a choral piece entitled 'The Spacious Firmament' which was performed at the Three Choirs Festival at Hereford in 1936. At the time of his move to the village he had recently retired from his final post as Professor of Music at Bristol University. He retained his connections with Bristol, however, and brought groups of singers and instrumentalists from the university to give concerts in the valley. During the 1960s he was an influential figure on the management committee of the Bournemouth Symphony Orchestra at a time of financial crisis.

Dr W. K. Stanton with visiting musicians

In the early 1970s the farmworkers' cottages opposite the old post office were constructed. Later in that decade and in the early 80s two extraordinarily heavy snowfalls are remembered, and on both occasions (as was the case in 1947) the village was cut off from the outside world for a week. A more memorably significant event was the erection in 1988 of a beacon on the summit of Cold Kitchen Hill to mark the 400th anniversary of the defeat of the Spanish Armada. This

Cold Kitchen Hill Beacon

tall and notably sturdy iron structure was constructed by Beaumont Chimneys of Mere and erected by the villagers. The beacon was 'fired' for the first time that year and has lit up the night sky on many subsequent occasions – at the millennium, on the 50th anniversary of the Queen's Accession in 2002, at her Diamond Jubilee in 2012 and to commemorate the 70th anniversary of both VE Day and VJ

Day in 2015. Also at the millennium all three churches in the valley were redecorated and KD church's woodwork was skilfully refurbished and restored by Peter Patrick. The churches at KD and LD were also equipped with highly effective floodlighting.

Whilst on the subject of the churches, it should be mentioned that they have enjoyed a succession of fine organists, the most recent being Professor Charles Taylor who undertook the task for 8 years between 1992 and 2000, and John Budgen who took over in the millennium year and (at the time of writing) is still in office.

1982 saw the publication of the book entitled 'The Deverill Valley', the inspiration for which was Colonel Jack Houghton-Brown who farmed at Pertwood. The book was edited by Frederick Myatt and comprises a series of excellent essays on the history of the valley by Bernard Hunt, John Peddie, Richard Stratton and Bruce Watkin.

In 2005 another splendid 'valley' book appeared under the title 'The Deverills Wonderful Water'. This lavishly illustrated production was instituted by the Deverill Valley and Crockerton WI with the encouragement of Lady Bath, and the research group comprised Pepita Smith, Sylvia Titt, Roy Andrews, June Baggs, Elizabeth Harvey, Janet Budgen, Les Wood, Margaret Bottomley, Jill Russell, Shirley Weedon, Pat Wood and Helen Bingham. A free copy was delivered to every household in the Upper and Lower Deverills and Crockerton in January 2006.

Also in 2006 there was a notable 'visitation' from the Bishop of Salisbury, David Stancliffe, who came up with the exotic idea of what might be described as a 'Eucharist on Wheels', the first part of the service to take place at Longbridge Church, the middle section at Brixton and the actual communion celebration at Kingston. Thanks to the churchwardens' brilliant organisation it all went according to plan, the congregation dutifully traversing the Deverill valley and finding themselves herded into the churchyard at the end of the service by a humorously threatening bishop's crook in order to receive a final blessing. In 2015 another bishop's visitation took place – this time involving the dedication of an extension to the Kingston churchyard.

Activities on the secular side of village life throughout the Deverill valley are almost too numerous to mention and are comprehensively detailed in the excellent monthly Parish Magazine, currently edited by Judy Munro. Some of these events have already been described, but particularly notable in addition are the regular group visits to the Salisbury Playhouse and occasional classical and jazz concerts, plays and pantomimes in the local churches and barns. Following an earlier manifestation in the 1970s, a highly successful Deverill Valley Festival took place in May 2014 comprising professional drama groups, an orchestra, chamber ensembles, a choir, a masterclass, a brass band and lectures on a variety of subjects. A variation on this Festival is planned for 2016, both events mentioned being run by Richard Munro.

For many years the Upper Deverill's Village Hall Committee has taken the responsibility for organising a number of annual events, all of which are widely appreciated. These include the Village Fete with its competitive classes for flowers, produce and crafts, and the star attraction – the Dog Show. There is also a Duck race on the river, various lectures and quizzes, a music night, celebratory dinners to mark the Harvest and Remembrance Day – and the ever popular 'Nine Lessons' Christmas Carol Service which also involves accompanying instruments and organ and the usual provision of mulled wine (to a secret recipe) and mince pies.

It will be evident from the final pages of this chapter that the 'social scene' has recently become much more inclusive as far as the five villages of the valley are concerned. This was inevitable following the closure of two churches, three schools, several shops and at least one pub over the years, and the obvious easing of travel access. I hope it will be understood that, for earlier years, the detailed history of each individual Deverill village is an absorbing separate issue, particularly up to the time of the 2nd World War, and that it is for this reason that I have had to confine most of my research to the village in which I live.

Manor Barn (interior)

Manor Barn (interior)

Kingston Deverill (Summer)

Kingston Deverill (Winter)

Appendix A
Kingston Deverill Clergy

John Cockerill; Rector 1302 – 1334.
William Aldebourne; Rector 1334 – 1361.
Thomas Rae; Rector 1361 – 1375.
Roger Typell; Rector 1375 – 1390.
Robert Neel; Rector 1390 – 1407.
John Blounham; Rector 1407.
Adam Usk; Rector 1407 – 1419.
Thomas Smyth; Rector 1419-1421.
John Hurleq; Rector 1421 – 1425.
Robert Symmys; Rector 1425.
Robert Wedingham; Rector 1425 – 1472.
Thomas Aleyn; Rector 1472 – 1511.
William Ravyn MA; Rector 7 Sep 1511 – 1 May 1516. Patron - John Atyate.
Roger Roe; Rector 1 May 1516 – 29 Dec 1534. Patron – Peter (from Horningsham).
Richard Dudd; Rector 29 Dec 1534 – 15 Dec 1549. Patrons – Edward Stourton & John Fitzjames.
Thomas Drinkell (otherwise known as 'Trynelle' or 'Tryngull') Rector 15 Dec 1549 – 1562. Patron – Walter Cure.
Johannes Butte; Curate 1553.
William Nettulton; Curate 1553.
Anthony Forrest; Rector 17 May 1562 – 16 Dec 1576.
Edmund Lillie; Rector 16 Dec 1576 – 6 June 1589 (resigned). MA, DD. Fellow of Magdalen College, Oxford 1563, Vice-Chancellor of Oxford University 1585 – 1593, Master of Balliol College 1580 – 1610. Buried at St. Mary's, Oxford.

Richard Wills; Stipendiary Curate 1578.
John Fletcher; Stipendiary Curate 1579.
John Morgan; 'Minister' 1586, Stipendiary Curate 1588-1590.
Guy Clinton; Rector 6 June 1589 – 28 March 1616. MA.
Edmund Vernon; Rector 28 Mar 1616. MA Brasenose College. BD.
Thomas Newland; Rector 25 Feb 1617 – 15 Jun 1643. MA Christ's College, Cambridge.
Thomas Aylesbury; Rector 15 Jun 1643 – 29 Jan 1661. MA, BD.
John Berjew; Rector 29 Jan 1661 – 1682. MA. (Died 16 July 1688).
Edmund Ludlow Coker; Rector 24 Sep 1682 - ?1698. Trinity College, Cambridge. MA Hart Hall, Oxford. (Born Hill Deverill and Curate there).
H. Coker; Rector ?1698 – 1706. (Brother of Edmund).
John Drew; Rector 26 Feb 1706 – 17 Apr 1727. BA Oriel. (Born in Stourton and combined the living of KD with Stourton and Gasper. Buried KD).
Benjamin Coker; Rector 1728 – 16 Mar 1742. MA King's College, Cambridge. (Brother of Edmund and H. Coker).
Thomas Howe; Rector 16 Mar 1742 – 23 Nov 1770. MA Aberdeen. (Married Frances White of Tattington Place, Suffolk. Died in Great Wishford).
Edward Burnett; Curate 7 July 1752. MA. (Later Rector of Walton Chapel, Street; died 25 Oct 1768).
Millington Massey: Rector 23 Nov 1770 – 6 May 1808. BA St. John's College Cambridge. MA, BD. Chaplain to Viscount Weymouth 1768 – 1783. (Also Rector of Corsley 1768 -1774, and Vicar of Warminster 1773-1808). Responsible for the removal of the Stone Trilithon - probably 'Egbert's Stone', as mentioned in the Anglo-Saxon Chronicle for the year 878 - to the ford below the village, c. 1790. Lived at Warminster.
William Slade; Curate 24 Sep 1797. BA Queens College, Oxford. (Also Curate at Brixton Deverill).
John Davis; Curate 13 Jun 1802.
Charles Philott; Rector 1808 -1813. MA Christchurch, Oxford. (Later Perpetual Curate at Frome).
Josiah Thomas (1782 – 1820); Rector 1813-1820. MA St. John's

College, Cambridge.

Thomas Heathcote; Stipendiary Curate 1814.

John Offer; Stipendiary Curate 1818.

Henry Bridgeman; Rector 1820-1823. MA Trinity College, Cambridge. Archdeacon of Bath 1817-1820.

Lord John Thynne, (1798 – 1891), third son of 2nd Marquis of Bath. Rector of Kingston and Longbridge Deverill 1823-1837; Sub-Dean of Lincoln Cathedral 1823 - 1831. Sub- Dean of Westminster 1836 – 1881. MA St.John's College, Cambridge. (Married Anne Constantia Beresford 2 March 1824. Buried in Westminster Cloisters).

James Downe; Curate 1824. MA.

Joseph Griffith; Curate 1825.

John Brigstock; Curate 1831. MA Jesus College, Oxford.

William Gale; Curate 1832. MA Pembroke College, Oxford.

Lord Charles Thynne (1813-1894), eighth son of 2nd Marquis of Bath. Rector 1838 -1845; later Sub-Dean of Canterbury Cathedral; seceded to Rome 1852; returned to C of E 1886. MA Christ Church,Oxford.

W.W. Gale: Curate 1838.

David M Clerk; Rector 1846 – 1879. Also Prebendary of Wells Cathedral 1840-1893. LLB St. John's College, Cambridge. (Responsible for moving the Trilithon from the Ford to the Rectory Garden, c. 1856.)

Thomas Kingsbury; Rector 1879-1885. Also Canon of Salisbury Cathedral. MA Trinity College, Cambridge. On his retirement he and his sister Martha presented the church with an organ which is still in use. The organ was built by Forster and Andrews of Hull and cost £500.

William Moore; Rector 1885-1898 (Benefice combined with Monkton Deverill from 1892). BA St. John's College, Oxford.

Edmund Caudwell; Rector 1899-1903. BD St.Mary Hall, Oxford

William Henderson; Rector 1903-1927. (Kingston Deverill Rectory vacated in 1925 as 'too large' for Rev. Henderson's family requirements.) MA St.Catherine's College, Cambridge. (Rumoured to have died of a heart attack in the street at

Warminster, following an earlier argument with his cook).

Between 1925 and 1975 the Rector of KD resided at BD Rectory.

Robert Cooper Fugard; Rector 1927-1939. Ordained in Duluth, USA.

Cecil Heath Caldwell; Rector 1939 -1948. (Benefice now combined with both Monkton and Brixton Deverill, the incumbent residing in the BD rectory).

Thomas Teague; Rector 1948-1954. MA University of Durham

Giles Martin Spinney; Rector 1954-1982. MA Christ's College, Cambridge; Wycliffe Hall Oxford. It was during his ministry that two important changes took place. Firstly, in 1970, the church of St. Alfred the Great in Monkton closed its doors (becoming a private house 5 years later). Secondly in 1972, the church of SS Peter & Paul at Longbridge Deverill joined the existing triumvirate of churches under one rector, following the retirement of the last incumbent at Longbridge, Rev Ivor Williams. Giles Spinney stayed on at Brixton rectory for 3 years, but moved in to the new (and still existing) Longbridge Rectory in 1975.

Michael Ernest Hinton; Rector 1982-1987. MA Kings College, London. (The arrival of Rev Hinton coincided with the closure of the church of the Assumption at Hill Deverill. It became a private house in 1985).

Philip Richard Morgan; Rector 1987-1994. MA Wadham College, Oxford.

Charles Nicholas von Benzon; Rector 1995-2000. Solicitor; Southwark Ordination Course. Resided at 6, Homefield Close, Longbridge – the current Rectory. (The Deverills became part of the Cley Hill Benefice in 1995)

Canon Antony Watts; Rector 2000-2007. MA Kings College, London. Sarum and Wells Training College. (From 2002 the Cley Hill Benefice became a 'Team Ministry' and the assistants to Canon Watts were WPM Hughes, CS Owen, N Payne, A Wadsworth and AJR Yates. From 2004 the team was joined by Canon Richard Askew – MA Brasenose College, Oxford; Canon Treasurer at Salisbury Cathedral (1983-1990); Rector Bath Abbey (1990-2000)).

Norma Payne; Team Vicar 2008- 2010; Team Rector 2011-2013. Bristol University. Assistant, Rev. Di Britten.

Pauline Reid; Team Rector 2014- . Eastern Region Ministerial Training Course; MA in Pastoral Theology.

Appendix B
Kingston Deverill WW1 War Memorial

The men behind the names

There are seven names on the First World War Memorial in Kimgston Deverill Churchyard. What follows in an attempt to make them less anonymous.

1. Walter Dunford

Walter was born in 1895 and was the fourth son of Charles and Amelia Dunford. Charles (b.1859) was a farmer, and he and his wife (b.1854) lived at Manor Farm, Monkton Deverill. In addition to Walter they had four sons: William (b.1884) Ernest (b. 1886), Percy (b.1889) and Harry (b.1898). They also had four daughters: Emma (b. 1887), Julie (b. 1891), Amy (b.1893) and Lily (b.1896).

Walter enlisted at Warminster, initially as a Private (28448) in the 11th Reserve Cavalry Regiment. Later he transferred (as Private 16826) to the 1st Battalion, Hampshire Regiment. He died of wounds on 1st September 1915 and is buried in Grave 11 at St. Acheul French National Cemetery in Amiens.

2. Percy Garrett

Percy was born in 1892 and was the eldest son of Abraham and Catherine Garrett. Abraham (b. 1860) was a gamekeeper, and he and his wife Katherine (b.1859) lived in KD. Percy had a twin sister, Winifred, an elder sister Beatrice (b.1890 and described in the 1911 census as a barmaid) – and a younger brother William (b.1896).

Percy enlisted at Bradford-on-Avon as a Private (203611) in 1/4th (TF) Battalion of the Duke of Edinburgh's (Wiltshire) Regiment. He died on 20th September 1918 whilst serving in Egypt, and is buried in Grave 0245 in Cairo War Memorial Cemetery.

APPENDICES

3. William Grevitt

William (his surname is incorrectly spelt as Grevatt on the War Memorial) was born in 1879 in the village of Thursley in Surrey. His parents Robert and Ellen had married earlier in the same year and William was the first of six boys. He was a farm boy in his teens and in 1899 joined the Queens (Royal West Surrey) Regiment as Private 6196. He married Bessie Mary Larkham in 1913 at Kingston Deverill Church – Bessie living at that time at Teffont Magna with her father Alfred who was a maltster. William was killed in the Battle of Gheluvelt on 31st October 1914 and his name appears amongst the missing on the Menin Gate.

4. Edwin Lewer

Edwin was born in Horningsham in 1888 and was the second son of William and Sarah Ann Lewer. William (b.1852) was a gamekeeper and he and his wife (b.1862) lived at Forest Cottage, West Woodlands, moving later to The Hollies, East Woodlands. They had three other sons – George (b.1887), William (b.1897) and Frederick (b.1899), and two daughters – Mary Jane (b.1893) and Rose (b.1895). Edwin became a wheelwright and is listed as living as a lodger with the family of George Primmer at Alexander Cottage in Quidhampton in the 1911 census.

Edwin enlisted at Devizes, and became a Lance-Corporal (10261) in the 1st Battalion of the Duke of Edinburgh's (Wiltshire) Regiment. He was killed in action on 2nd September 1915 and his name appears among the missing of the Wiltshire Regiment on Panel 53, Ypres (Menin Gate) Memorial.

5. Frank Mabbett

Frank was born in 1886, the second son of Alfred (b.1864), railway engine driver, and Emily (b.1865). In the 1901 census the family is registered as living at Earls Road, Portswood, Southampton, and as well as Frank (who is described as an 'office boy') it comprises three other sons – Alfred (b.1885), a 'draper's assistant', William (b.1889) and Albert (b.1891) – and two girls – Clara (b.1896) and

Edith (b.1899). The date of the family's move to Southampton is not clear, but it is almost certain that Frank's father, Alfred, lived in Church road, Brixton Deverill, as his family is registered as living there in 1871. Frank married in March 1905 and at some point went to Northamptonshire, since at the time of his death his wife Ada is described as living at Upper St., Kettering.

Frank enlisted at Northampton as Private (27315) in the Northants Regiment, later transferring, also as a Private (3011762) to the 4th Battalion, Suffolk Regiment. He died on 25th April 1917 and is listed among the missing on Bay 4 at the Arras Memorial.

6. Herbert Poolman

Herbert was born in Monkton Deverill in 1885 and was the eldest son of Andrew (b. Poole, 1850) and Mary (b. Chitterne, 1850). Andrew was a wheelwright and had two other sons – Alfred (b.1886) and Godfrey (b.1889). There were also two daughters – Elizabeth (b.1880) and Harriet (b.1882). At the time of Herbert's death his wife, A.M. Poolman, was living at Codford St.Mary.

Herbert enlisted in Devizes, and became a Sergeant (6146) in the 2nd Battalion of the Duke of Edinburgh's (Wiltshire) Regiment, later transferring, also as a Sergeant (45197) to the Durham Light Infantry. He died on 23rd January 1917 and is buried either at the Communal Cemetery at Le Quesnoy or at the Communal Cemetery at Valenciennes (St.Roch) – his military records mentioning both sites.

7. Albert Tudgay

Albert was born in 1877 and was the only son of Thomas (b.1837) – 'agricultural labourer' – and Eliza (b.1841). He had three sisters – Clara (b.1864), Georgina (b. 1874) and a twin, Linda. (In the 1891 census Albert is also listed as an agricultural labourer).

Albert was a driver (T4/110349) in the RASC and was amongst 49 officers and men who were drowned when the vessel in which they were embarked, the HT (Hospital Transport) 'Cameronian' was torpedoed and sunk off Alexandria on 2nd June 1917. His name is commemorated amongst nearly 1000 lost at sea, on the Chatby Memorial, Alexandria.

Appendix C Architect's Plans for Church Restoration, 1842

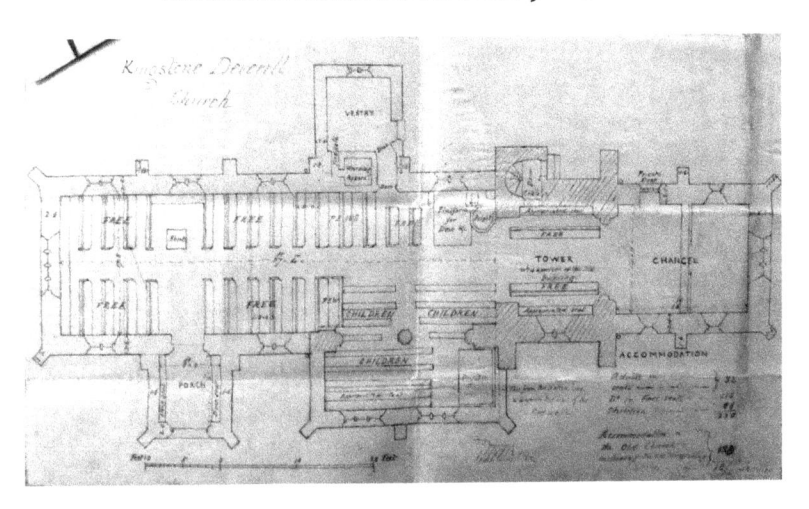

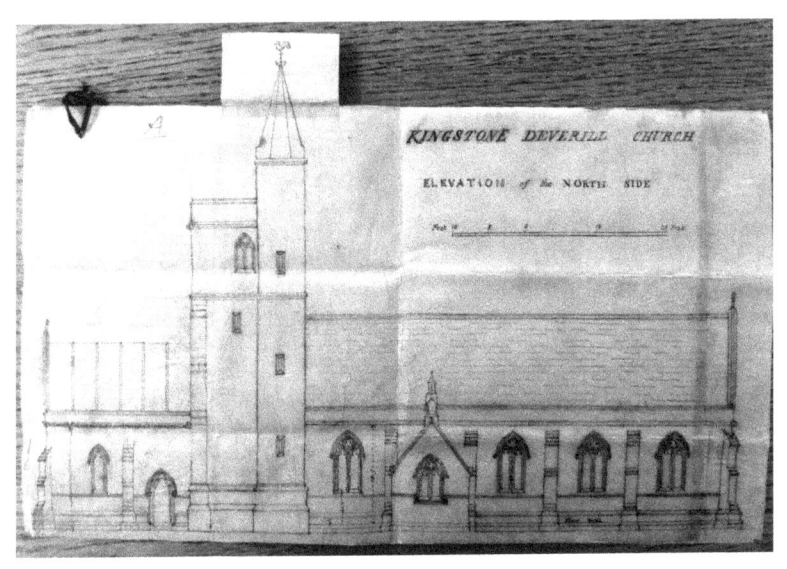

Appendix D
KD School Admissions 1949 – 1969

(Children resident in KD except where indicated)

1949
David Bartlett MD
David Reid
Phyllis Sutton MD
Stephen Burke BD
Pauline Hill
David Stratton
John Dufosee MD
Grahame Matthews

1950
Leonard Burke BD
Edwin Jones MD
Victor Jones MD
Raymond Castle MD
Valerie Nutting MD
ChristinaTrappes
Philip Lyles `
Pat Kinnersly
Paul Fairclough BD
Terence Cowling
Rosemary Hines
Anthea Danby
John Carpenter BD
Rosemary Boyes BD

James Woolgar

1951
Anthony England
Sandra Howson
Derrick Stanley
Margaret Baker
Patrick Dibben MD
Kenneth Lewis
Ann Reeves
Ralph Reeves
Clarence Williams
Irene Dufosee MD
George Murray
Anne Hodgson MD
Timothy Smith MD
Margaret Hazeldene MD

1952
Jennifer Carpenter
Marie Jones MD
Peter Stratton
Barbara Trollope
Jane Legg MD
Joyce Mason

APPENDICES

Ann Middleton BD
Ann Beer
Peter Beer

1953
Christopher ?Celer MD
Christine Orr
Colin Reeves BD
Brian Wooster
James Castle MD
Keith Marsh MD
Timothy Smith MD
Robin Lemon MD
Karen Fuller
Elizabeth Gunnell BD
Denise Hinton
George Gunnell BD
Judith Legg MD

1954
Shirley Light MD
Colin Garlick MD
John Reeves
Brian Stephens
Mary Gadd
Yvonne Stephenson
Jacqueline Gallop
Judy Gallop
Christopher Reed BD
Sally Reed BD
Timothy Spinney BD
Pamela Simms

1955
Christopher Wrixen MD
Jane Every BD

John Every BD
Tony Musselwhite BD
Ruth Phillpotts BD
Anne Veal
Andrew Gallop
Rosie Gadd
John Gunnell BD
Derek Jackson
Ivor Jackson

1956
Christopher Kent
David Everett HD
Nigel Smith BD
Nichola Smith BD
Sally Price
Simon Price
Richard Maggs HD
William Rich MD
Alan Light MD

1957
Peter Allard BD
Duncan Gray
John Thomas
Susan Mawson BD
Charles Skiller
William Skiller

1958
Davina Trollope
Susan Kent
Elizabeth Allard BD
Robert Allard BD
Nigel Orr
Christopher Wilson BD

Peter Wilson BD
Graham Woolf
Simon Mawson

1959
Carol Dunford Maiden Bradley
John Pennell BD
Elvira Pennell BD
Stephen Allard BD
Paul Austin
Richard Drake MD
Michael Molyneux BD
Mary Henbury BD

1960
Timothy Gallop
Elizabeth Hembury BD
Malcolm Hill
Diana Reeves
Terry Stevens
Richard Fuller

1961
Raymond Dix MD
Rachael Thomas
Peter Friederich MD
Rodney Dix MD
Michael Dennett BD
Angela Gray
Sally Pedley
John Winter MD

1962
June Orr
Philippa Pedley
Anthony Marchmont MD

Alan Marchmont MD
Sally Allard BD

1963
Richard Dix MD
Douglas Titt MD
Alison Gray
Judith Gray
Roderick Gray

1964
Debra Marshall BD
Lynne Morley
Henry Vatcher Wishford
Clifford Dix
Ronald Dix MD
Christopher Drake MD
Heather House MD
David Fuller

1965
Belinda Gray
Malcolm Stokes BD
Jennifer Butler BD
Colin Woolf
Elaine Kent
Lynda Nubbert MD

1966
Anthony Nubbert MD
Kevin Gray
Margaret Titt MD
Peter Collins MD
Paul Collins MD
Elizabeth Vivien MD

1967
Michael Giddings
Martin Giddings
Valerie Cockburn
Andrea Ruddle MD

1968
Audrey Bell BD

Catherine Bell BD
Caroline Silk MD
Brian Collins MD

1969
Jean Drake MD
Caroline Gallop
Martin Swaffham MD

Appendix E
KD Field Names

It is interesting to compare the field names which appear in surveys or on maps dating from the 18th century with those names which are current today. The fields or areas of downland which are shown on the 'Map of the Manor of Kingston Deverill, Belonging to the Right Hon the Lord Viscount Weymouth Situate in the County of Wilts' published in 1748 are named as follows:

Home Field, Sheep Pen Field, Under Kilton, Averil Court Hill, The Cow Down, Dean Bottom, Peascombe, Mullens Croft, Church Field, Brook Furlong, the Common Down, Fox Linch, Swort Furlong, Rodmead, Rodmead Field, Cucknell Field, Marcomb Field, Hilcomb Field.

To these may be added those fields which are mentioned in John Ladd's 'Survey of the Manor of Kingston Deverill' dating from 1749:

Kingsale, Walbury, Forerudge, Down Leze, Broad Mead, Dean Layes, Little Mead, Hescomb Field, Hescomb Coppice, Frampton, Billey, Marcombe Copse, Tonguecomb Wood, Wheeler's Close, Long Half, Sheelds, Bidcomb, Killen, King's Hill, Newport Down, Yerbury Mead, Barley Close.

The Land Tax returns for the period 1780 -1826 yield two further names:

Keepenses, Butchers Mead

David Stratton tells me that many of these 43 named fields no longer exist, primarily for the reason that they have been absorbed into larger fields –or downland areas. Those which are still current – albeit in some cases with a slightly altered title are:

Sheep Pen Field (now Shepton Field), Kilton, Averill Court Hill (now Court Hill), Cow Down, Dean Bottom (now Dane's Bottom),

Church Field, Rodmead, Cucknell, Marcombe Field (now Marcombe Wood), Hescomb Field (now Hiscombe), Billey (now Bitley), Tonguecombe Wood (now Truncombe).

Three field names ; Peasombe, Fox Lynchets and Broad Mead have only very recently vanished from view.

In a brief essay on the subject written for the Parish Magazine by Richard Stratton in the 1960s a number of additional names are mentioned, and particular emphasis is placed on their historical significance.

> Every field and wood has a name and it seems to me to be a pity to live in the country without knowing the names of the fields adjoining, or in the sight of, one's house. ...Many field names reflect previous ownership. Examples are Seagrams, Coleman's Piece, Pope's Ground, Slades, Humphrey's Orchard (and Farm) and Dunford's Down.
>
> We have the birds to thank for Peewit's Gorse, Larksdown and Cuttie's Lynch.
>
> The copse at the bottom of Keysley Lane containing the bridleway is Whiteman's Acre ... and the field above is called Hopabout. The combe behind Whitecliffe House is Boar's Bottom and the steep country at the end of that farm once earned the name Abyssinia.
>
> In Kingston we are continually reminded of the passage of King Alfred by the field names – Knight's Field, Court Hill, Dane's Bottom and King's Hill, whence can be viewed the cement works chimney near Edington'.

Appendix F
1782 Map and key to the occupants of the numbered buildings

1.Late William Smith; 3. J & T Trimby (tenant); 4. William Abraham (t); 5. William Notton (t);12. Thomas Humphrey (t);13. Stephen Long & Peter Delme; 16. Thomas Davis (t); 20.Henry Sturgis (t); 23. Henry Sturgis (T); 24. Parsonage house and homestead; 27. William Garrett (t) house, garden and orchard; 28. William Reynolds (t) house, garden, close of meadows. 30. Kingston Deverill Great Farm, home, homestead etc. Lord Weymouth. 32. George Townsend (t); 33. Michael Humphrey (t); 36. John Mervin (t) house, farm and orchard; 40. Mary Bleek, house barn, studio etc; 41. George Townsend (t); 42. John Mervin (ten); 43. Michael Humphrey (t) & barn; 44. Philip Garrett (t) house and Smith's shop; 50. William Turner (t); 52. John Parsons (tenant of Mary Bleek); 57. Robert Hurle (t); 61. William Slade; 62. Feoffees of Horningsham School – house etc. exchanged to William Slade; 63. William Slade; 66. Elizabeth & Rachel Oborne (t); 68. Elizabeth & Rachel Oborne (t); 70. George Young, house and shop (t); 71. Lucy Morris (t); 74. Peter Delme, house, barn, stables, homestead – called Bodenham's Farm; 75. John Blake (t); 76. Thomas Davis (t); 77. ~~Thomas Davis (t), signed to Joseph Coombs; 79. Henry Sturgis (t); 89. Late Bartley, now Robert Bulliton; 90. Late Bartley, now Robert Bulliton; 91. Elizabeth and John Marshall; 92.Edward Smith and John Stone, at the Whitepits; 93. William Reynolds (t); 94. Samuel and Robert Vallis; 95. Samuel Norris; 96. Joseph Coombs; 97. Paul Matthews..

A number of the houses marked on the 1782 map remain in the 21st century, and of these the Listed Buildings are as follows: Hedge

APPENDICES   *239*

Cottage, Marvins, Humphreys Orchard, Barn at Manor Farm, Pope's Farmhouse and Flat, and nos. 35, 36, 38 & 39 KD. Also Listed are Kingston House (which replaced the Parsonage in 1858) and Keysley Farmhouse (off the map). The earliest extant building is the Manor Barn, some of whose timbers have recently been dated to 1407.

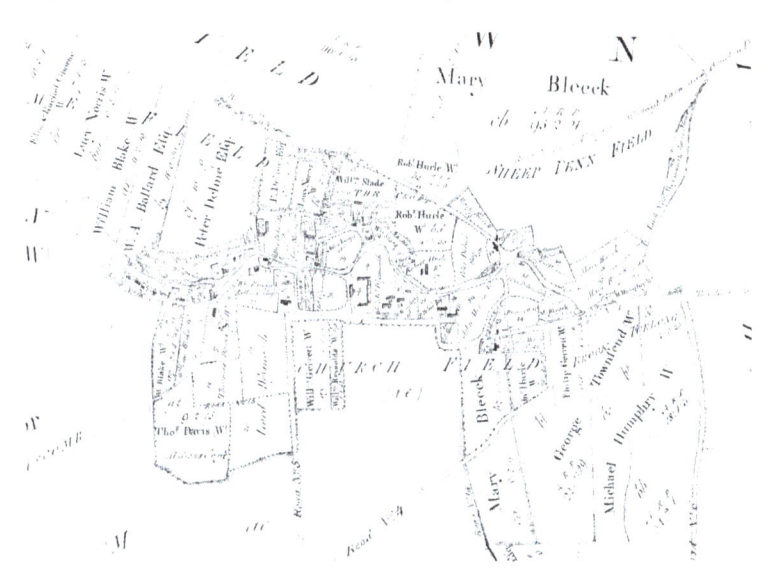

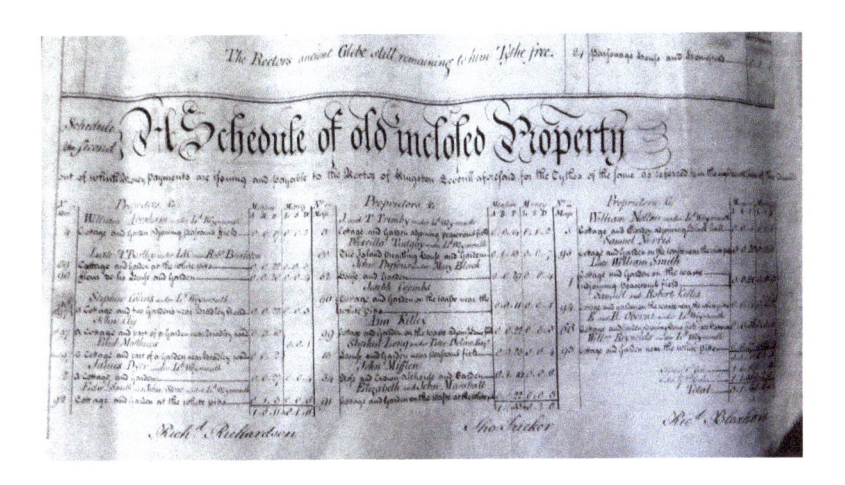

Appendix G
Old Village Customs of Kingston Deverill

(by Emily Gibbs* (nee Coombs) 1870 – 1958)

One of the old customs of this village was the Whitsun Festival, held on Whit Tuesday. There were two Friendly Societies and each met at their headquarters – one in the Schoolroom and the other at the New Inn. Headed by a Brass Band they marched in procession with their banners to the church, where a service was conducted by the Rector. The marchers, wearing rosettes of red and blue ribbons and with red and white ribbons in their hats each carried a flagstaff which was bedecked with the same colours. After the service the procession was re-formed and the marchers returned to their headquarters where a capital spread was awaiting them, the Rector presiding. After doing justice to the good fare a few loyal toasts were proclaimed and responded to and the members then paid a visit to the farm houses, where they always met with a good welcome. Afterwards they marched to the rectory where a good tea was provided for all, followed by dancing, racing and other amusements until the evening shadows lengthened and the company then returned once more to their quarters for supper. A little more dancing and music then brought the day to a close. It was a great day of rejoicing for old and young – old friends met and all care and worry was cast aside for one day in the year.

The advent of the National Insurance signed the death warrant of most of the old village clubs. I would like to add that, after the departure of Canon Kingsbury from the parish [1885] the old custom of giving the tea on this day was kept up by the late William Stratton.

Another old custom was the Allotment Supper. Each cottager

was the holder of an allotment, and each year at Michaelmas they assembled at the rectory to pay their audits. They then sat down to a well-laden board consisting of roast beef and Christmas pudding – and good beer, the rector always presiding. After the repast the rector gave a speech on different subjects of the day, and the rest of the evening was spent in harmony, everyone thoroughly enjoying themselves and looking forward to the next occasion.

Another tradition was the Christmas Treat at the Rectory, when the choir, the bellringers and schoolchildren met in the old hall, and all were entertained to tea. The bellringers gave a selection on the handbells and the choir and children sang carols. Each of the children then said a verse from the 2nd chapter of St.Matthew and received 1d. Afterwards all assembled round a large Christmas Tree where a sackfull of presents was opened and handed to both adults and children. It was a night very much looked forward to and enjoyed by all.

One other tradition, which I believe is very old is the Sunday Christmas Feast – and it is so-called to this day although it is no longer kept. Years ago, however, it was a time of great rejoicing, and it was, I've been told, something to do with the dedication of the church and it fell on the first Sunday after the 10th of September. It was a day of great festivity, and however poor a family was they always made a Plum Pudding and carried it to be baked in a Bakehouse oven. Hence the name 'Kingston Pudding Eaters'.

*Emily was born in KD in 1870 and was the daughter of Aaron Coombs (an agricultural labourer) and his wife Mary – members of the Coombs family having been resident in the village since the 17th century. In 1895 she married Hubert Gibbs who was born in LD, the couple moving to MD shortly afterwards, and subsequently to KD where they lived at no.63. Emily is reminiscing in the 1920s about the traditions she describes, many of them still in existence in her childhood. She and her husband celebrated their Diamond Wedding in 1955, Hubert dying the following year, and Emily in 1958 after spending the last two years of her life with her family in Southampton.

Appendix H
KD Evacuees

As already indicated in Chapter 3, the School Logbook has the following entries concerning evacuees:

Sep 11 1939 -'27 on register; 6 children on evacuation register'.
Feb 9 1940 -'number on roll 25 +2 evacuees (both present); Jun 19 -'admitted 7 evacuee children from Beckford School, Dornfell St. NW6'.
Jun 20 -'admitted evacuee child. Admitted 4 other evacuated children.' Jul 3 1944 -'admitted one more evacuee (girl)
Jul 26 -'admitted two more evacuee children'
Jul 31 admitted 1 evacuee (boy).

Unfortunately the 'evacuation register' mentioned in the entry for 1939 no longer exists, so it is impossible to establish just who the children were who were sent out of London immediately following the outbreak of war. It might be thought that the London Metropolitan Archives would hold a record of evacuees and their destinations, but circumstances were so chaotic both at this early period of the war and later during the blitz that virtually no details were kept.

As previously mentioned, we know the names of the evacuees who are stated to be present on February 9th 1940 - Joyce and Richard Harbud- and they found themselves accommodated for some time at 69 KD. They were evacuated from Beckford School in West Hampstead as were the seven children who followed on June 19th, but when interviewed they were unable to recall the names of their co-evacuees. As is the case with the Metropolitan Archives, the school holds no records prior to the 1950s, so again a blank has been drawn.

The Admissions Register might, however, hold some clues –

despite the mention of the existence of a separate evacuee document – since a number of entries indicate that the child in question had his or her home in London –or in two cases, from Bristol.

Likely Evacuees ex London

Geoffrey Reid; adm.25/6/40; father Alfred; 68 KD; dob 23/2/30; Westwood Junior School, Sidcup; returned home 4/7/40; re-registered 30/9/40; home again 3/2/41.

Betty Matthews; adm. 2/9/40; father Charles; no KD address; dob 11/8/31; Godwin Road, Forest Gate; left for Mere School 14/8/42.

Joyce Matthews; adm. 2/9/40; sister to above; dob 1/5/35; no other details.

Anne Brand; adm. 11/9/39; father Peter; 14 KD; dob 31/1/34; Gardiner Road, Forest Gate.

John Wilson; adm. 23/9/40; with aunt, Muriel Cork in MD; dob 18/6/30; dep 27/9/40 'guardian left district'.

Jean Lawlor; adm. 30/0/40; Whitecliffe Farm BD; dob 5/1/35; Stoneleigh, Ewell, Surrey; home 15/1/41.

Philip Phillips; adm. 2/11/40; Laurel villas, BD; dob 25/11/33; Childs Hill NW2.

Diane Alder; adm. 12/1/41; dob 27/4/30; father Edward; Keysley Cottage; Bellevue Road, Battersea; Mere Senior School 15/8/41.

Shirley Alder; dob 11/10/33; home 14/8/42 – otherwise as sister above.

Hazel Young adm. 7/3/44; father Jack; 82 MD; dob 7/7/37; Ilford.

William Cooke; adm. 7/10/40; Polden (grandmother) BD; dob 22/11/29; Annunciation School, Edgware; dep 15/8/41 to Avenue Senior School.

Victor Baker; adm. 2/11/40; father Henry; 28 KD;dob 24/11/30; Crampton Road Walworth; dep 14/8/42 to Melksham Senior School.

Possible Evacuees ex Bristol

Brian Fox; adm. 9/11/40; father Henry; Whitecliffe Farm; dob 21/6/35; Victoria Park, Bristol; home 4/4/41.

June Cooper; adm. 28/4/41; father Reginald; 1, Kingston Close; dob 29/9/31; Hannah More School, Bristol; home 17/4/42.

Appendix J
Longleat Estate Map of Kingston Deverill, by John Ladd, 1748

APPENDICES   *245*

Appendix K
Kingston Deverill Old and New Rectories, by Manners and Gill

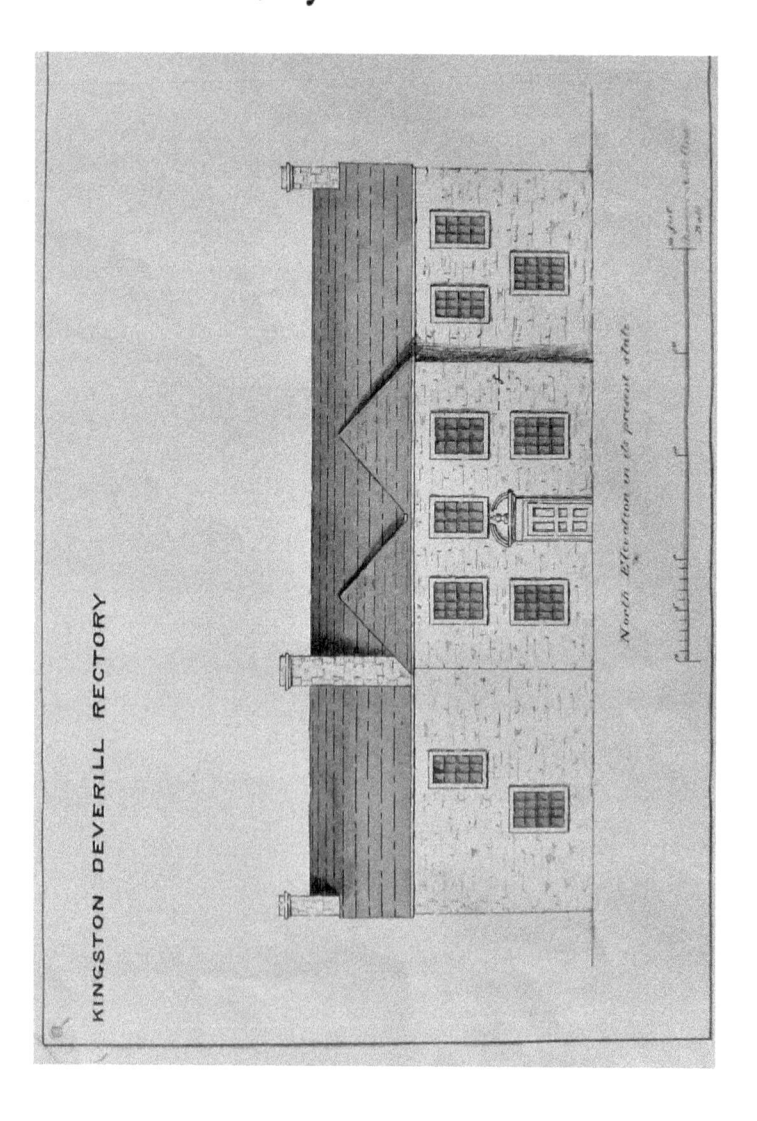

APPENDICES   247

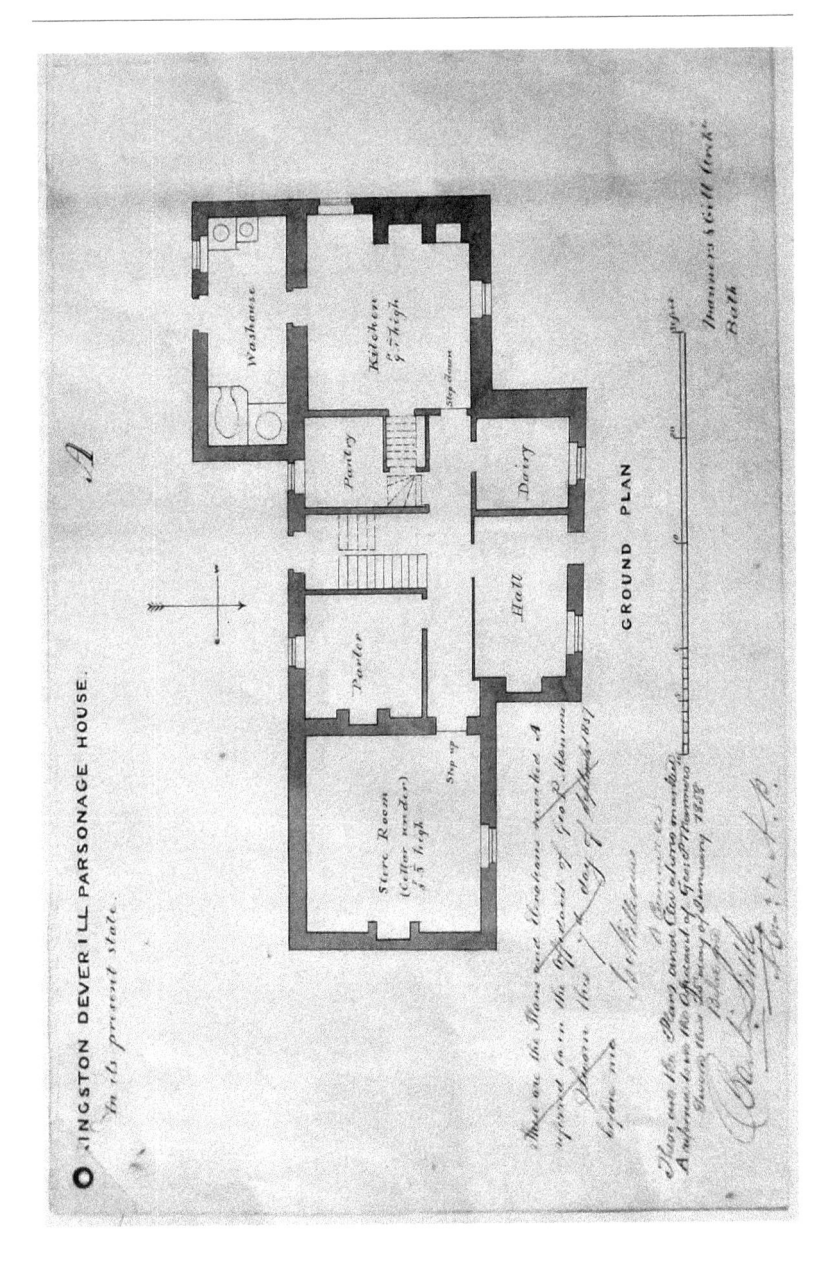

The titles of these architects' drawings are misleading. The elevation on p. 246 and plan on p. 247 relate to the Old Rectory. The elevation on p. 248 and plan on p. 249 depict the New Rectory.

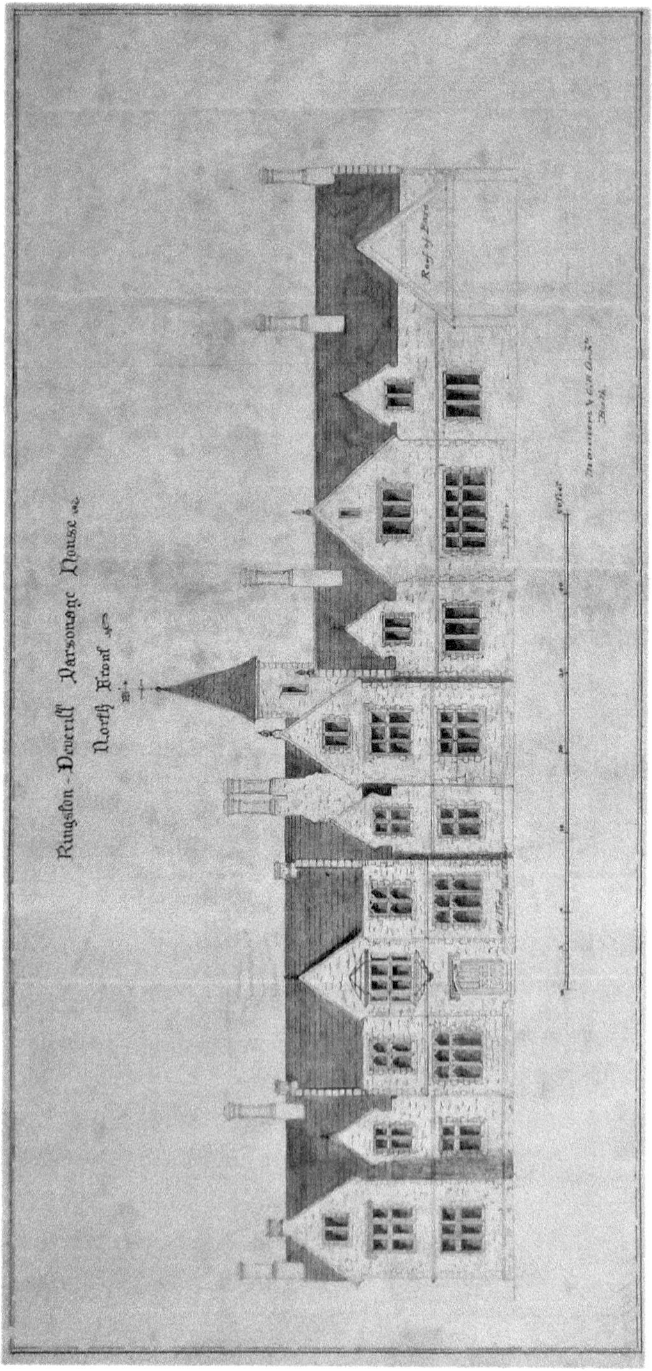
Kingston - Deverill Parsonage House
North Front

APPENDICES

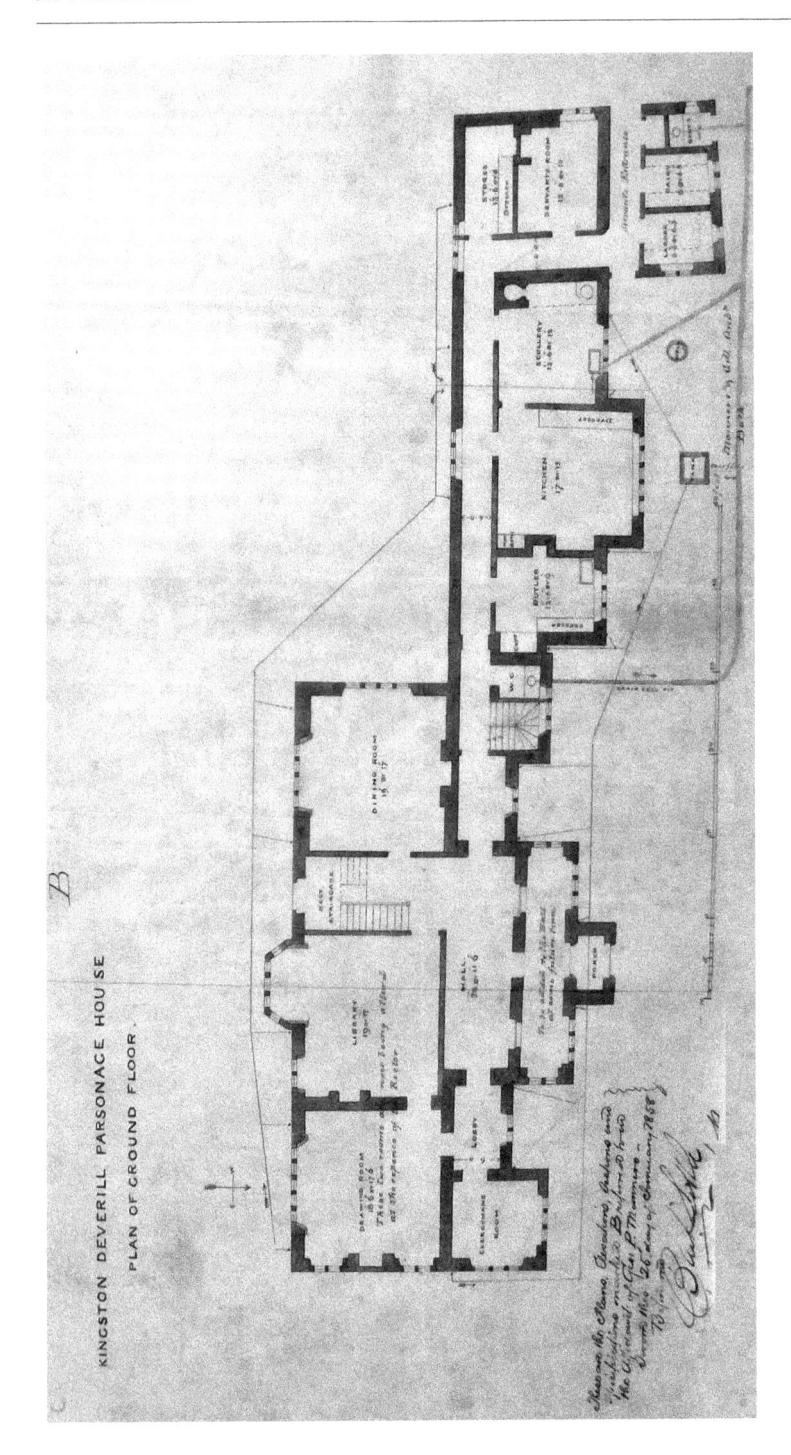

Bibliography

Note: WRS: Wiltshire Record Society; WSHC: Wiltshire & Swindon History Centre, Chippenham

Aubrey, John, *Natural History of Wiltshire.* 1691
Bettey, Joseph (ed.), *Wiltshire Farming in the Seventeenth Century.* WRS vol. 57, 2005
Camden, William, *Britannia.* 1586. trans. Philemon Holland, 1610
Census Returns for Kingston Deverill. The National Archives, Kew
Chandler, John (ed.), *John Leland's Travels in Tudor England.* 1998
Chandler, John (ed.), *Printed Maps of Wiltshire 1787-1844.* WRS vol.52, 1998
Cobbett, William, *Rural Rides.* 1830
Crittall, Elizabeth (ed.), *Andrews and Dury's Map of Wiltshire 1773.* WRS vol.8, 1952
Crowley, D.A (ed.), *The Wiltshire Tax List of 1332.* WRS vol.45, 1989
Dale, Christabel (ed.), *Wiltshire Apprentices and their Masters 1710-1760.* WRS vol.17, 1961
Daniell, William, *Warminster Common.* 1832
Davis, Thomas, *A General View of the Agriculture of Wiltshire.* 1793
Defoe, Daniel, *Tour through the Whole Isles of Great Britain.* 1726
Deverill Valley & Crockerton WI. *The Deverills: Wonderful Water.* Warminster Press, 2005
Electoral Rolls for Kingston Deverill. WSHC
Elrington C. (ed.), *Wiltshire Feet of Fines Edward 111.* WRS vol. 29, 1974
Faculty Papers for the Diocese of Salisbury. WSHC
Farr, Brenda & Elrington, Christopher (eds). Revised Henry Summerson, *Crown Pleas of the Wiltshire Eyre, 1268.* WRS vol.65, 2012
Fowle, J.P.M. (ed.), *Wiltshire Quarter Sessions and Assizes 1736.* WRS vol.11, 1955
Gibbs, Emily, *Old Village Customs of Kingston Deverill.* c.1925
Hicks, Ian (ed.), *Early Vehicle Registration in Wiltshire.* WRS vol.58, 2006
Hoare, Sir Richard Colt, *Ancient History of North & South Wiltshire.* 1819
Hoare, Sir Richard Colt, *History of Modern Wiltshire.* 1822
Hobbs, Steven (ed.), *Wiltshire Glebe Terriers, 1588-1827.* WRS vol. 56, 2003
Hobbs, Steven (ed.), *Gleanings from Wiltshire Parish Registers.* WRS vol.63, 2010
Hunnisett, R.F (ed.), *Wiltshire Coroners' Bills 1752 -1796.* WRS vol. 36, 1987
Johnson, H.C (ed.), *Wiltshire County Records, Minutes of Proceedings in Sessions.* WRS vol.4, 1949
Kelly's Directories of Wiltshire
Kingston Deverill School Logbook 1898 -1969. WSHC
Kingston Deverill School Admissions Register 1931-1969. WSHC
Kingston Deverill Vestry and PCC Minutes 1903-1941. WSHC
Ladd, John, *Survey of the Manor of Kingston Deverill.* 1749

Land Tax Returns. WSHC
Murphy, W.P.D (ed.), *Lieutenancy Papers 1603-1612*. WRS vol.23., 1969
Myatt, F (ed.), *The Deverill Valley*. The Deverill Valley History Group, 1982
Nicholson Engineering, Bridport, *Report on State of Bells in Kingston Deverill Church*. 1997
Nicolson, Adam, *Gentry*. Harper Press, 2011
Pugh, R.B (ed.), *Wiltshire Feet of Fines Edward 1 & 11*. WRS vol.1, 1939
Pugh, R.B (ed.), *Wiltshire Gaol Delivery and Trailbaston Trials*. WRS vol.33, 1978
Ralph, Chris, *The Kingston Deverill Sarsen Stones*. 2000
Ramsay, G.D (ed.), *Two 16th Century Taxation Lists, 1545 and 1576*. WRS vol.10, 1954
Salisbury Journal
Sandell, R.E (ed.), *Abstracts of Wiltshire Inclosure Awards and Agreements*. WRS vol.25, 1970
Sandell, R.E (ed.), *Abstracts of Wiltshire Tithe Apportionments*. WRS vol.30, 1975
Sherlock, Peter (ed.), *Monumental Inscriptions of Wiltshire: an edition in facsimile of Monumental Inscriptions in the County of Wilton, by Sir Thomas Phillipps*. WRS vol.53, 2000
Shorto, R. (ed.), *A Little Picture Book of Old Warminster and District*, vols 1 & 2. Coates and Parker 1996/1999
Skinner, John, *Journal of a Somerset Rector, 1803-1834*. ed. Howard and Peter Coombs, The Guernsey Press, 1971
Smith, A.H (ed.), *The Parker Chronicle*. Methuen, 1935
Stratton, Richard, *Farming in the Upper Deverills*. Deverill Valley History Group, 1982
Stratton, Richard, *History of the Hurle Bequest*. 1982
Upper Deverills Parish Plan. 2014
Victoria County History of Wiltshire vol. II: Anglo-Saxon Wiltshire, Domesday... 1956
Victoria County History of Wiltshire vol. IV: Economic History, Agriculture, Industry ... 1959
Victoria County History of Wiltshire vol. XIX: Mere and the Deverills (forthcoming)
Warminster Journal

List of Illustrations

Cover and frontispiece: Watercolour of Kingston Deverill Church, by Chris Littlemore, 2006

p. 9: *The Deverill*, photograph by Alison Cameron
p. 10: *The Deverill Valley in 1897*, Ordnance Survey
p. 11: *Little Knoll* and *Cold Kitchen Hill*, photographs by Julian Wiltshire
p. 12: *John Aubrey*, © National Portrait Gallery, London
p. 12: *Andrews & Dury's map, 1773*, Wiltshire Record Society
p. 13: *Sir Richard Colt Hoare*, National Trust Images, (NT Stourhead)
p. 13: *Sir William Cunnington*, © National Portrait Gallery, London
p. 14: *Colt-Hoare & Cunnington overseeing excavation*, Wiltshire Museum, Devizes
p. 14: *Rex de Charembac Nan Kivell*, National Library of Australia
p. 15: *Bronze Age enamelled horse & rider brooch* and *Early Roman glass bead necklace*, photographs by Alison Cameron: Wiltshire Museum, Devizes
p. 16: *The Emperor Vespasian*, Internet CC
p. 17: *Roman roads*: OS
p. 18: *The Ford*, photograph by Alison Cameron
p. 19: *King Egbert*, Internet (from West façade of Lichfield Cathedral)
p. 19: *King Alfred*, photograph by Julian Wiltshire
p. 20: *Extract from the Anglo-Saxon Chronicle, AD 878*: Master and Fellows of Corpus Christi College, Cambridge
p. 20: *Egbert's Stones*: geography.org.co.uk/photo/2794232
p. 21: *Alfred's Tower*: photograph by Alison Cameron
p. 22: *Queen Edith*: Cambridge University Library, MS ee.3.59
p. 23: *Robert Vernon*: photograph by Alison Cameron
p. 24: *Sir John Thynne* and *Edward Seymour, Duke of Somerset*, © Reproduced by permission of the Marquess of Bath, Longleat House, Warminster, Wiltshire
p. 25: *A view of Longleat, 1675*: Internet
p. 25: *Lieut. General Edmund Ludlow*, © Reproduced by permission of the Marquess of Bath, Longleat House, Warminster, Wiltshire
p. 27: *Sir John Thynne, junior* and *Maria Touchet*, as above
p. 28: *Ordnance Survey Map, 1811*, OS
p. 29: *The Church in 1835, south side*, scanned from reproduction of J. Buckler's etching in KD Church
p. 30: *The Church in 1835, north side*, as above
p. 33: *William Tyndale*, © National Portrait Gallery, London
p. 36: *The 1578 Chalice*, photograph by Robert Shuler
p. 40: *The Bishop's Chair, 1682*, photograph by Alison Cameron
p. 41: *Manuscript of Eleanor Hurle Bequest, 1688*, photograph by Robert Shuler
p. 44: *Bishop Thomas Ken*, © National Portrait Gallery, London
p. 46: *The Third Bell* and *The Bell Mechanism*, photographs by Alison Cameron

LIST OF ILLUSTRATIONS 253

p. 49: *Bishop Shute Barrington,* Auckland Castle Trust, Courtesy of the Church Commissioners

p. 50: *Lord John Thynne,* Dean and Chapter of Westminster

p. 51: *Thomas Thynne, 3rd Viscount Weymouth/1st Marquess of Bath,* © Reproduced by permission of the Marquess of Bath, Longleat House, Warminster, Wiltshire

p. 53; *The Hon. Harriet Baring, 3rd Marchioness of Bath,* as above

p. 57: *Gargoyle* and *The 17th century pulpit,* photographs by Alison Cameron

p. 58: *Altar Coffin Lid,* as above

p. 59: *The East Window,* as above

p. 60: *The West window – late 15th century glass,* as above

p. 61: *The Saxon Font,* as above

p. 62: *Chancel, Altar Cross and Effigy,* photograph by Julian Wiltshire

p. 63: *Kingston Deverill Church,* photograph by Alison Cameron

p. 67: *Flagon,* photograph by Robert Shuler

p. 69: *Organ,* photograph by Alison Cameron

p. 70: *Philip Urban Moore window* and *Amy Stratton window,* as above

p. 71: *Amy Stratton's copper beeches,* photograph by Julian Wiltshire

p. 72: *Kingston Deverill Church choir, 1895,* WI Village Scrapbook, Wiltshire & Swindon History Centre

p. 73: *The Stones in 1924,* Archive of Coates & Parker, Warminster (from pictures selected by Ray Shorto for *'A First Little Picture Book of Old Warminster and District')*

p. 77: *Model T Open Ford Touring Car 1914,* Internet

p. 80: *The War Memorial,* photograph by Alison Cameron

p. 82: *Lantern in Church porch,* as above

p. 83: *The King Alfred banner* and *Madonna and Child,* as above

p. 84: *Baptism Shell,* photograph by Robert Shuler

p. 85: *Brixton Deverill Church,* photograph by Kevin Abraham

p. 89: *School Photo from c.1878,* WI Village Scrapbook, WSHC

p. 90: *Page 1 of School Logbook, 1898,* WSHC

p. 92: *Walter Dunford,* Karen Dunford

p. 93: *The School House,* photograph by Alison Cameron

p. 94: *The School House Bell,* as above

p. 95: *The Headteacher's house,* as above

p. 101: *George V Silver Jubilee celebrations, 1935,* WI Village Scrapbook, WSHC

p. 103: *East Beach, Bournemouth, 1950s,* Postcard, Dearden & Wade Ltd., Bournemouth

p. 105: *The Beckford School, Hampstead,* © Robin Webster; CCA

p. 105: *William Beckford* © National Portrait Gallery, London

p. 106: *Fonthill Abbey in 1823,* Royal Collection Trust/ © Her Majesty Queen Elizabeth II, 2016

p. 110: *Ration Book,* photograph by Alison Cameron

p. 112: *Kingston Deverill School, 1950s,* WI Village Scrapbook, WSHC

p. 113: *Giles Martin Spinney with school group, 1955,* Tim Spinney

p. 115: *Lady Helen Asquith (1980),* courtesy of Lady Clare Asquith, Mells Manor

p. 118: *Kingston Deverill School, 1961,* WI Village Scrapbook, WSHC

p. 121: *Kingston Deverill School, 1968,* as above

p. 128: *Mr William Stratton,* courtesy of the Stratton family, Manor Farm, Kingston

Deverill

p. 131: *Mr Maidment (senior) c.1920,* WI Village Scrapbook, WSHC

p. 133: *Mr Richard Stratton (snr),* courtesy of the Stratton family, Manor Farm, Kingston Deverill

p. 134: *Manor Farm workers, 1930s,* WI Village Scrapbook, WSHC

p. 135: *Mr Grey & Mr Bletso, 1930s,* as above

p. 136: *Mr Dennis Maidment at Keysley Farm, 1930s,* as above

p. 137: *Memorial Service for Richard Stratton, 1950,* photograph by Julian Wiltshire

p. 138: *Mr Richard Flower Stratton,* courtesy of the Stratton family, Manor Farm, Kingston Deverill

p. 139: *David Stratton,* as above

p. 140: *Manor Farm House,* photograph by Alison Cameron

p. 142: *Bateman sprayer:* photographs by Julian Wiltshire

p. 143: *Receding sheep,* as above

p. 156: *Wardour Castle,* astoft.co.uk © Allan Soedring

p. 159: *Daniel Defoe,* © National Portrait Gallery, London

p. 164: *Thomas Davis,* Frontispiece to '*A General View of the Agriculture of Wiltshire*', WSHC

p. 166: *Land Tax Return for Kingston Deverill,* WSHC

p. 174: *Bull Mill, Crockerton,* courtesy of Olivia Clifton-Bligh, Bull Mill House

p. 175: *William Cobbett,* © National Portrait Gallery, London

p. 211: *Old Rectory (Kingston House),* Archives of Coates & Parker Ltd., Warminster (from pictures selected by Ray Shorto for '*A Second Little Picture Book of Old Warminster and District*')

p. 212: *The Methodist Chapel,* photograph by Alison Cameron

p. 213: *The Shadwell Plaque,* as above

p. 214: *Kingston Deverill Football Team, 1936/37,* WI Village Scrapbook, WSHC

p. 215: *Kingston Deverill Football Team, 1946/47,* as above

p. 216: *Village Hall,* photograph by Alison Cameron. *Village Cricket,* WI Scrapbook, WSHC

p. 217: *Dr. W K Stanton,* WI Scrapbook, WSHC

p. 218: *Cold Kitchen Hill Beacon,* photograph by Julian Wiltshire

p. 221: *Manor Barn Interior,* photographs by Alison Cameron

p. 222: *Kingston Deverill (Summer & Winter),* photographs by Julian Wiltshire

p. 233: *Architect's Plans for Church Restoration, 1842,* WSHC

p. 241: *1782 map of Kingston Deverill Inclosures* and *Schedule of Old Inclosed Property* WSHC

p. 246: *Longleat Estate Map of Kingston Deverill, 1748,* © Reproduced by permission of the Marquess of Bath, Longleat House, Warminster, Wiltshire

Index

Aberdeen University, 47
Abstract of Education Returns, 86
Act of Toleration, 40
Act of Uniformity, 39
Admissions Register, 101, 104, 111, 114, App.D
Agincourt, 150
Agriculture Act, 137
Aldebourne, Rev. William, 29, App A
Aldridge, Edward, 44
Aleyn, Rev. Thomas, 151, App A
Alfred (King), 5, 19, 21, 22, 83, 152
Alfred's Tower, 21
Alton Priors, 130
Altrincham, 47
Amesbury, 18, 19, 22
Amiens, 61
Ancient History of North & South Wiltshire, 13
Andrewes, Lancelot (Bishop), 37
Andrews and Dury, 12, 28
Anglo-Saxon Chronicle, 5, 19
Antwerp, 33
Aquae Sulis (Bath), 17
Arthur (King), 18
Arundel Family, 40
Arundell, Lady, 26
Askew, Canon Richard, App A
Asquith, Herbert, 115
Asquith, Lady Helen, 115, 116, 117, 118, 120
Asquith, Raymond, 115
Assize of Clarendon, 146
Athelney, 21
Aubrey, John, 10
Audley, Lord, 26
Augustinian Priory, 23
Austen, Jane, 200
Authorised Version of the Bible, 36
Avalon, 18

Aylesbury, Rev. Thomas, 38, App A

Backwell, 72
Balliol College, Oxford, 36
Bannard E.J & W, 67
Barford St. Martin, 162
Barley Close, 213
Barnard, John, 35
Barnard, Richard, 35
Barnardo, Dr. 99,
Barrington, Shute (Bishop), 49
Bath, 50, 65, 103, 125, 132
Bath & Wells, 44
Bath Journal, 162
Batt(e), John, 35, 41
Batt, Henry, 35
Beacon 217
Beaumont Chimneys, 218
Beckford School, 105, 106, App H
Beckford William, 105
Beckford, Alderman, 27, 105
Bedford, 39
Belgae, 122
Bell Inn, Beaconsfield, 26
Benzon, Rev. Charles Nicholas von, App A
Berjew Family, 40
Berjew, Brune, 31, 41, 43, 44
Berjew, Jane, 31
Berjew, Rachel, 44, 48, 49
Berjew, Rev. John, 38, 39, 49, App A
Berry Pomeroy, 23 (n)
Bishop's Bible, 37
Black Death, 147, 163
Black Earth Field, 102
Blake, Charles, 43, 159, 160
Blake, John, 161
Blake, William, 166 – 168
Bleek, Mary, 167, 169, App F
Blounham, Rev. John, App A

Bodingham's Farm, 43, App F
Bonham, 40
Book of Common Prayer, 35, 38, 39
Boulton, John, 188
Bournemouth Symphony Orchestra, 217
Bowles, William, 66
Boyle, Sir Edward, 120
Boyton, 127, 148
Bradley House, 23 (n)
Bradley Road, 130, 139, 140, 141
Brand, Anne, 108, App H
Brashier, Walter Ernest, 75, 96, 98, 206
Brewham, 21
Bridgeman, Louisa, 50
Bridgeman, Rev. Henry, 49, 50, App A
Bridges, Robert, 130
Bridgwater, 148
Bridport, 45
Brigstock, John, 52, App A
Brimsdown, 10, 13
Brinkworth, 200
Bristol, 125
Bristol University, 217
Britannia, 152
Britten Rev. Di, App A
Brixton Deverill, 5, 9, 17, 47, 79, 81, 82, 85, 96, 109, 114, 115, 119, 128, 148, 153, 157, 219
Broadstone, 213
Buck's Head, 160
Buckler, J, 29
Budgen, John, 219
Bull Mill, 160, 174, 183, 186, 201
Bunyan, John, 39
Burleton, John, 186
Burnet, Edward, 47
Burnett, Edward, App A
Burton Mrs. C.J, 112
Bush, Mr, 76
Butte, Johannes, App A

Cadbury Castle, 16, 18
Caldwell, Rev. Cecil Heath, 81, 82, 106, 107, 208, App A
Callaghan, Georgina, 88, 192
Cambridge, 37
Camden, William, 152

Camelot, 18
Camerton, 65
Canada, 194
Canterbury Cathedral, 87
Canterbury, 63, 64
Carey, Mrs, 76, 106
Carol Service, 220
Carpenter, G, 82
Carpenter, George, 208
Carpenter, Jack 20, 96, 211
Carpenter, John, 74, 132, 197
Carpenter, Mabel, 106
Carpenter, Marjorie, 211
Carpenter, Stephen, 193
Castle Hill, 10
Catherine of Aragon, 32
Caudwell, Rev. Edmund, 72, 91, 92, 202, App A
Census Returns, 171
Census, (1841, 180-2
Census, (1851), 183-5
Census (1861), 187-90
Census (1871), 190-2
Census (1881)), 194-6
Census (1891), 198-200
Census (1901), 201-3
Census (1911), 204-6
Cerdic (King), 19
Chapel of St.Andrew, 29
Charles I, 26
Charles II, 39, 40
Charlton Horethorne, 154
Charnage, 133
Cheddar, 200
Chedworth, Baron, 47
Chelsea Hospital, 197
Chippenham, 134, 145, 200
Choir, 71, 72, 75, 76
Christ Church, Oxford, 169
Christ Church, Warminster, 120
Christ's College, Cambridge, 47
Clarendon Code, 39
Clement VI, 32
Clerk, Rev. David, 20, 53, 56, 57, 64, 65, 66, 67, 68, 73, 87,184, 188, 190, 191, 194, 197, App A
Clerk, John Perkins, 6
Cley Hill, 10

INDEX

Clinton Rev. Guy, 36, App
Cloford, 38
Clove, William, 35
Cobbett, William, 174-6
Cockerill, Rev. John, 29, App A
Cockey, William, 45
Codford, 14
Coke, Thomas, 123
Coker, Rev. Benjamin, 45, App A
Coker, Rev. Edmund Ludlow, 31, 39, 42, 44, App A
Coker, Rev. H, App A
Col Cruachan, 12
Cold Kitchen Hill, 10, 12, 13, 14, 16, 17, 28, 102, 217
Cole, Simon, 164
Collingbourne Ducis, 134
Cologne, 60
Common Reader, The, 66
Compton Chamberlayne, 156
Compton, James, 56, 183, 184
Compton, John, 181
Conventicle Act, 39
Coombs, Aaron, App G
Coombs, Emily, App G
Corn Laws, 172, 176
Corn Production Act, 131, 132
Cornwall, (Earl of), 22
Corporation Act, 39
Corsley, 47
Corton, 154
Court Hill, 18, 20, 47
Coverdale, Miles, 32, 33, 39
Cozner, Emma, 66, 87, 184
Cranmer, Thomas (Archbishop), 32, 34, 35, 36, 38
Crey, Jeremy, 177
Crey's Charity School, 169, 177
Crockerton, 9, 88, 110, 111, 115, 160, 174, 183, 186, 201
Cromwell, Oliver, 26, 155
Cromwell, Thomas, 32, 33, 34
Crown Inn, (*see also Rose and Crown*), 178
Cunnington, William, 13, 14
Curtice, Roger, 43
Curtis, James, 197, 198
Curtis, Mary, 42, 43, 48, 49

Daintree, Arthur, 74, 205
Daniell, William, 178
Dauntsey's School, 111
Davis, John, 47, App A
Davis, Thomas, 125 (n), 163-5, 167, 168-72, App F
Davis, Thomas, Jnr., 171, 180
Day, Edie, 212
Dearmer, Percy, 81
Dee Barn, 139, 140
Defoe, Daniel, 159
Delme, Peter, App F
Denison, Edward (Bishop of Salisbury), 54
Deserted Village, The, 165
Deverill Valley, The, 219
Deverill Valley Festival, 220
Deverills: Wonderful Water, The, 219
Devizes, 155, 164
Devizes Museum, 16
Dodington, Sir Francis, 155
Downe, James, 52, App A
Drake, Richard, 142
Draper, Rose, 91, 202
Dredge, James, 193
Dredge, William, 193
Drew, Rev. John, 44, App A
Drinkell, Rev. Thomas, (*otherwise* Trynelle or Tryngull), 35, 36, App A
Drops of Dew, 79
Dryden, John, 123 (n)
Dubonni, 16
Duck, Son and Pinker, 103, 107
Dudd, Rev. Richard, 32, 33, 34, 152, App A
Dufosee, Miss, 113, 114
Dukes of Somerset, 23 (n)
Duluth, 78
Dunford family, 163
Dunford, Amelia, 92
Dunford, Charles, 92
Dunford, Emma Louise, 92, 93, 96, 97
Dunford, Karen, 93
Dunford, Walter, 92, 97, App B
Dunham Massey, 47
Durotriges, 16
Dyer, George, 171

Dyer, James, 165, 166, 167, 169
Dyer, William 176

Earl, Elizabeth, 87, 183
East Knoyle, 24
Ebble, 147
Edith (Queen), 22
Education Act, 1944, 110
Education of the Poor Digest, 86
Edward III, 146, 147, 149
Edward the Confessor, 22
Edward VI, 24, 34, 35
Egbert (King), 19, 20
Egbert's Stones, 5, 19, 21, 67, 69
Electoral Registers, 206, 207
Elementary Education Act, 88
Elizabeth I, 24, 153
Elliott, Augusta, 75, 94, 95
Emma, 200
English Hymnal, 81
Enumeration Returns, 170
Essen, 214
Ethandun, 5, 19
Evacuees, 104, 105, 106, 107, 108
Exeter, 157

Farley, M.E, 121
Farrington, Robin, 84
Fear, Arthur, 211, 214
Fear, Brian, 109
Fear, Nellie, 211
Festing, Henry, 65
Fishguard, 134
Five Mile Act, 39
Fletcher, John, App A
Flitcroft, Henry, 21
Fonthill, 27
Fonthill Abbey, 106
Fonthill Gifford, 26
Ford, Elizabeth, 88, 196, 199
Forrest, Rev. Anthony, App A
Forster & Andrews, 68
Fosse Way, 17
Freestone, John, 35
French, Robert, 35
Friendly Society, 182, App G
Frome, 45, 54, 134, 172, 174
Fugard, Rev. Robert Cooper, 78, 81, 102, 108, App A

Gale, William, 52, App A
Garland, Phoebe, 98, 99, 100, 102, 207
Garrett, Percy, App B
Gasper, 44
Gatehouse, Edward, 42
General View of the Agriculture of Wilts, 125 (n), 170
Gentleman's Magazine, 29
George III, 21
George V, 95, 101, 102
Gibbs, Emily, 207, App G
Gibbs, Hubert, App G
Gilbert, Anne, 88, 196
Gillingham, 160
Gilpin, H, 74
Glastonbury Abbey, 21
Glorious Revolution, 40
Gloucester, 59, 200
Godalming, 132
Goldsmith, Oliver, 165
Great Bible, 32, 33, 37
Great Farm, App F
Great Wishford, 47
Greenwich, Royal Hospital, 197
Grevitt, William, App B
Grey, Lady Jane, 36
Grey, Lord, 176
Griffith, Joseph, 52, App A
Grove, William Chafyn, 169
Guinevere, 19
Guthrum, 19

Hadow Committee, 99
Handicraft Centre, 213
Harbud, Joyce, 104, 105, App H
Harbud, Richard, 104, 105, App H
Harding & Sons, 68
Harding, Gertrude May, 93, 205
Harriet, Marchioness of Bath, 52 - 54, 57, 63, 65, 67, 180
Harrod's Directory, 190
Hayter, Sam, 63
Heals, 213
Heathcote, Thomas, 50, App A
Hedge Cottage, 106, 208, App F
Henderson, Rev. William, 64, 72, 73,

INDEX

76, 77, 78, 79, 91, 108, 178, 204, 205, 206, App A
Henry II, 146
Henry IV, 25
Henry V, 25, 150
Henry VI, 25
Henry VIII, 23, 32, 33, 34, 151
Hereford, 217
Heytesbury, 13, 145, 176, 179
Hill Deverill, 5, 9, 25, 39, 114, 124, 128, 153
Hindon, 25, 176, 178, 179
Hinton, Rev. Michael Ernest, App A
History Centre, Wiltshire & Swindon, 5, 145, 208, 215
History of Modern Wiltshire, 31
Hoare, Henry, 11, 21
Hoare, Sir Richard Colt, 13, 14, 31, 58, 65, 151
Holland, Philemon, 152
Holman, Herbert Leigh, 83, 84
Holman, Suzanne, 84
Holmes, John, 160
Horner, Katherine, 115
Horningsham, 22, 23, 39, 151, 177, 178
Horningsham School, 177, 178, App F
Hosier, Arthur, 134
Houghton-Brown, Col. Jack, 219
House of Darkness, 211
Howe, Rev. Thomas, 47, 161, App A
Howell, John, 207
Hughes, W.P.M., App A
Hull, 68
Humphrey, George, 188, 191
Humphrey, Michael, 43, 167, 168, 177, App F
Humphrey, Richard, 161
Humphrey, Thomas, 168, 177, App F
Humphreys Orchard, 167, App F
Hunt, Bernard, 219
Hurle Bequest, 41
Hurle Family, 40, 163
Hurlc, Anne, 158
Hurle, Eleanor, 38, 40, 41, 42, 157
Hurle, Elizabeth, 167
Hurle, Marjory, 43
Hurle, Peter, 37, 155
Hurle, Robert, 45, 157, 167, 168, 170, App F
Hurle, Thomas, 161, 168
Hurle, William, 35, 40, 158, 160, 161
Hurleq, Rev. John, App A
Hyde, Edward, (Duke of Clarendon), 39
Hymns Ancient & Modern, 106

Inclosure Act, 164
Incorporated Society of Building Churches, 55
Inman, Miss H.M., 208
Iscalis, (Charterhouse), 17

James I, 36
James II, 40
Jupe, Charles, 183, 186, 201
Jupe, Isaiah, 201

Kanengisser, Peter, 60, 61
Keble, John, 52
Kelly's Directory, 88, 97, 182, 186, 194, 197, 201, 204, 206 – 208
Ken, Thomas, (Bishop), 44
Keysley Down, 126
Keysley Farm, 98, App F
Kiddell / Liddill, William, 43
Kilmington, 9, 11, 112, 160
Kingett, June Mary, 104
King's Arms (see also New Inn, and *Tipling Philosopher),* 193
Kings Hill, 28, 210
Kingsbury, Martha, 68
Kingsbury Rev. Canon Thomas, 68, 196, 197, App A, App G
Kingsettle Hill, 21
Kingston Deverill Way Book, 163
Kingston House, 20, 211, App F
Kivell, Rex de Charembac Nan, 14, 16
Kneller, Catherine, 70, 199
Knight, John, 48
Knox, John, 86

Ladd, John, 160-62, 167, App J
Lampard, Henry, 183
Lampard, John, 181- 183, 189
Lancing College, 217
Land Tax, 165 - 167, 176, 177

Lander, Charles, 41, 42
Langland, William, 149
LEA, 113
Leach, Bernard, 213
Lead Road, 17
Leadley, Francis, 64
Leigh, Vivien, 83, 84
Leland, John, 151
Leversedge, Deborah, 43
Lewer, Edwin, App B
Liddill/ Kiddell, William, 43
Lillie, Rev.Edmund, 36, App A
Lincoln Cathedral, 52
Lisieux, 22
Little Knoll, 10
Lleyn sheep, 142
Local Education Authority, 113
Lokyer, John, 35
Lollards, 31, 148
London Metropolitan Archives, App H
Long Knoll, 10, 11
Long Parliament, 25
Longbridge Deverill, 5, 9, 10, 24, 65, 88, 129, 132, 137, 219
Longleat, 23, 24, 26, 27, 44, 47, 51, 66, 87, 145, 155, 160, 163, 164, 177, 180, 181, 190, 207
Lord's Hill, 136
Ludlow (Family), 23, 24, 39, 47, 51, 66
Ludlow, Lt. Gen. Edmund, 25, 26, 152, 156, 157
Ludlow, George, 25
Ludlow, Henry, 25
Ludlow, William, 25
Lye, 145
Lynn, Alan James, 208

Mabbett, Frank, App B
Madonna and Child, 83, 84
Magdalen College, Oxford, 36
Maiden Bradley, 23, 99, 112, 114, 115, 119, 132, 152, 211
Maiden Castle, 16
Malines, 84
Malmesbury, 155, 201
Manners & Gill, 52, 53
Manor Barn, App F
Manor Farm, KD, 7, 57, 132, 139, 140, 187, 193, 194, 206, 209, 210, App F
Marlborough, 155,
Marler, Thomas, 37
Marvin's Farm, 27, 196, 197, 206, 208, App F
Mary I,, 36
Massey, Rev. Millington, 20, 47, 48, 168, 170, App A
Mather, Mrs., 103
Matthew Bible, 32, 33, 37
Maxfield, Beatrice Alice, 92, 93, 94
Maxfield, Fred, 74
Maxfield, James, 58
Melachrino, George, 211
Melksham, 134,
Mells, 115
Mendip Hills, 17
Mere, 9, 11, 22, 28, 41, 42, 64, 83, 103, 111, 112, 118, 119, 124, 136, 145, 153, 160, 172, 173, 183, 218
Merino sheep, 144
Mervin. John, App F
Mervyn (Family), 26, 27
Mervyn (Sheriff of Wiltshire), 26
Mervyn, Sir James, 26, 27
Mervyn, Lucy, 26
Methodist Chapel (*see also* Wesleyan Methodist Chapel), 64, 178, 206, 211, 213
Michell, Cuthbert, 35
Monkton Deverill, 5, 9, 21, 24, 28, 40, 47, 80, 81, 82, 83, 92, 106, 108, 109, 114, 115, 124, 128, 129, 153, 157, 162, 193, 207, 214
Moore, George (Brother), 64
Moore, Philip Urban, 70, 200
Moore, Rev.William, 68, 72, 90, 199, 200, App A
More, Sir Thomas, 32, 33
Morgan, John, App A
Morgan, Rev. Philip Richard, App A
Morris, William, 105
Munro, Judy, 220
Munro, Richard, 220
Myatt, Frederick, 219
Mycenae, 16

INDEX

Nadder Valley, 127
National Schools, 182
National Society, 86
Natural History of Wiltshire, 10
Neel, Rev. Robert, App A
Nettulton, William, 35, App A
New Birth, The, 79
New Inn, MD (*see also Tipling Philosopher*), 74, 128, 194
Newbury, Charlie, 132
Newbury, Dorothy (nee Nobbs), 108, 111, 114, 116, 117
Newbury, Fred, 208
Newbury, William, 163, 208
Newcastle, 58
Newland, Rev. Thomas, 37, 38, 153, App A
Newman, John Henry (Cardinal), 52
Newport Farm, 167, 188, 191, 194, 206
Newson, Minnie, 92
Nicholson Engineering, 45
Nobbs, Dorothy, 107
Novello's, 72,

Obourne, Elizabeth, 31
Obourne, William, 31
Offer, John, 86, App A
Oldham, 176
Olivier, Laurence, 84
Ordnance Survey, 28
Osmund, (Bishop), 29
Owen, CS App A
Owen's Directory, 194
Oxford, 26, 36, 37

Parish Magazine, 220
Parsonage, 48, 49, 67, App F
Patrick, Peter, 219
Payne, Rev. Norma, App A
Pearce, Mrs. 116
Peasants Revolt, 148
Peddie, John, 219
Penny Annie, 91, 92
Penruddock, Colonel, John, 156, 157
Penruddock's Rebellion, 156
Perrin, Beatrice, 91, 202
Pertwood, 219
Peters, Liz, 212

Petter and Lister, 133
Philips, Henry, 193
Philips, John, 193
Phillimore, Robert, 56
Phillips, William, 43
Philott, Rev.Charles, 49, App A
Piers Plowman, 149
Pilgrimage of Grace, 34
Pilgrim's Progress, 39
Pitt, William (The Younger), 176
Plowden Report, 120
Plowden, Lady, 120
Political Register, 174
Poll Tax, 149, 150
Poole, 17
Poolman, Herbert, App B
Poor Law, 163, 182
Pope, George, 186
Pope, Mary Ann, 185, 187, 188
Pope's Farm, 187, 204, App F
Poton, Edward, 153
POWs, 210
Presley, Leah, 88, 189
Preston, Ivy, 107
Primitive Methodist Chapel, 193
Primitive Methodists, 64
Priory for Black Canons, 23
Prisoners of War, 210
Pullin, (Pullen) Charles, 194, 196, 198, 199, 203, 206
Pusey, Edward, 52

Queen's College, Oxford, 47, 169

Rabbits., Mr. & Mrs., 64
Rabbitts family, 178,
Rabbitts, Hugh, 176
Radstock, 127
Rae, Rev. Thomas, App A
Ramsbury, 148
Randolph, Very. Rev. John, (Dean of Salisbury), 80
Ransom, William, 188, 191, 194
Ravyn, Rev. William App A
Rawlings, John, 181
Rawlings, Stephen, 183
Rawlings, William, 183
Reading University, 217

Reform Act, 176
Reid Rev. Pauline, App A
Reid, William, 197
Remmesbury, William, 147
Richard II, 149
Richards, Dorothy Ivy, 101, 102, 104, 208
Richmond, 59
Ridgeway, Frederick, (Bishop of Salisbury), 96
Roe, Rev.Richard, 32, App A
Rogers, John, 32
Rogers, William, 181, 183
Rome, 64
Rose and Crown, 160, 172, 182, 186, 188, 193
Rose, Robert, 35
Rotten Boroughs, 176
Roundway Down, 155
Rowney, Noel, Dean of Salisbury, 169
Rural Rides, 174
Ryall, Robert, 170
Ryall, Thomas, 43

St. John's College, Cambridge, 47, 64
St. Helena, 115
St. Ives, 213
Salisbury, 146, 147, 150, 155, 156, 172, 175, 179
Salisbury Cathedral, 68, 109, 119, 148, 217
Salisbury Journal, 160,170, 171, 174, 178, 186
Salisbury Museum, 102
Salisbury Playhouse, 119, 220
Savoy Conference, 38
Saxton, Christopher, 11 (n)
Schliemann, Heinrich, 16
School Logbook, 72, 76, 89, 90
Scottish Education Act, 86
Selwood, 5, 11 (n), 19, 21, 151
Semley, 134
Semley School, 96
Seven Years War, 21
Seymour, (Family), 23
Seymour, Edward, 1st Duke of Somerset, 23, 24, 34
Seymour, Jane, 24

Seymour, Percy, 18th Duke of Somerset, 80
Seymour, Webb, 10th Duke of Somerset, 167
Shadwell, Lancelot, 212, 213, 217
Shadwell, Rodney, 214
Shaftesbury, 172,
Shaw, Martin, 81
Siminson, Mr, 76
Six Articles, 34
Skinner, Rev. John, 65, 66
Slade, William, 47, 48, 49, App A
Smissen, Poppy, 119, 120, 121
Smithfield Market, 132, 149
Smyth, Rev. Thomas, App A
Somerset (Dukes of), 23 (n)
Songs of Praise, 81, 106
Sorviodunum (Salisbury), 17
Southampton, 150
Spacious Firmament, The, 217
Spinney, Rev. Giles Martin, 84, 113, App A
Spinney, Tim, 84
Stafford, Gregory, 206
Stancliffe, David (Bishop of Salisbury), 219
Stanter (Family), 22, 23, 150, 153
Stanter, Alexander, 151, 152
Stanter, Roger de, 25
Stanton, Dr. W.K., 216, 217
Statute of Labourers, 147
Stockton Wood, 127
Stonehenge, 112,
Stoolball, 112
Stourhead, 13, 21
Stourton, 44, 151
Strasbourg, 84
Stratton family, 96, 187
Stratton, Amy, 70, 71
Stratton, Arthur, 130
Stratton, Charles, 199
Stratton, David, 7, 139, 142
Stratton, Michael, 108
Stratton, Pamela, 112, 113
Stratton, Richard (Snr) 41, 76, 78, 106, 110, 133, 137, 207, 208
Stratton, Richard (Jnr), 71, 111, 112, 113, 114, 138, 219, App E

INDEX

Stratton, William, 70, 71, 74, 75, 91, 95, 98, 128, 130, 131, 178, 191, 193, 194, 196, 198, 199, 203, 206, App G
Street, 47
Stuckey & Co., 54
Sturgess, Henry, 184
Sturgess, Joseph, 184
Sturgess, Sophie, 87, 184
Sutton Veny, 115, 121
Swing, (Captain), 178
Swing Riots, 178
Symmys, Rev. Robert App A

Tanswell, A, 98
Taylor, Professor Charles, 219
Thatcher, Margaret, 150
The Common Reader, 66
The Deserted Village, 165
The Deverill Valley, 219
The Deverills: Wonderful Water, 219
The New Birth, 79
The Spacious Firmament, 217
Thomas Rev. Josiah, 49, 86, App A
Three Choirs Festival, 217
Thynne (Family), 23, 24, 27, 41, 55, 145, 160
Thynne, Alexander, Viscount Weymouth, 75
Thynne Rev. Lord Charles, 52,63, 64, 65, 87, 181, App A
Thynne, Henry, 43
Thynne, Henry Frederick, 3rd Marquess of Bath, 180
Thynne, Sir James, 26, 156
Thynne, Lady Joan, 27
Thynne, Rev. Lord John, 50, 51, 52, 65, 87, 176 App A
Thynne, Sir John, 1, 2, 26, 23, 24, 25, 26, 27
Thynne, John Alexander, 4th Marquess of Bath, 52 (n), 64, 130, 180, 194
Thynne, Thomas, 26, 27
Thynne, Thomas, 1st Marquess of Bath, 51, 180, 193
Thynne, Thomas, 1st Viscount Weymouth, 45,
Thynne, Thomas, 2nd Marquess of Bath, 87, 171, 172, 176, 180
Thynne, Thomas, 3rd Viscount Weymouth, 163, 165, 166, 168
Thynne, Thomas Henry, 5th Marquess of Bath, 75 – 78, 81, 201, 206, 207
Tipling Philosopher (*see also New Inn* and *King's Arms*), MD, 74
Titt, John Wallis, 131
Tolpuddle Martyrs, 179
Toogood, Robin, 213
Totnes, 23 (n)
Touchet, Maria, 26, 27
Tour of the Whole Island of Great Britain, 159
Tractarian Movement, 52
Trimby, Alfred, 75
Trimby, Peter, 43
Trinity College, Cambridge, 68
Trowbridge, 64, 111, 130
Trynelle/ Tryngull, Rev. Thomas (otherwise Drinkell), 35, 36, App A
Tudgay, Albert, App B
Tudgay, George, 194, 195
Tull, Jethro, 122
Tyndale, William, 32, 33, 37
Typell, Rev. Roger, 31, 148, App A

Univeral British Directory of Trades & Manufactures, 170
Upton Scudamore, 169
Usk, Rev. Adam, App A

VE Day, 218
Venta Belgarum (Winchester) 17
Vernon (Family), 22, 23, 29
Vernon, Rev. Edmund, App A
Vernon, John de, 23
Vernon, Sir Robert de, 22, 23
Vespasian, Titus Flavius, 16
Village Fete, 220
Village Hall, 215
Vilvoorde, 33
Vindocladia (Badbury), 17
Virgil, 123
VJ Day, 218
Vowles, Mr, 76

Wadsworth, A, App A

Wailes, William, 58
Walton Chapel, Street, 47
War Memorial, 80, 92
Warburton, Rev. 88
Warburton's Census of Wiltshire Schools, 87
Ward, George, 174, 183
Wardour Castle, 26, 40, 155
Warminster, 9, 10, 47, 49, 64, 68, 74, 76, 78, 103, 108, 111, 112, 113, 125, 127, 131, 132, 134, 136, 152, 160, 162, 170, 175, 179, 197
Warminster Common, 178
Warminster Journal, 77, 78, 130
Waterloo, 172
Watkin, Bruce, 219
Watts, Canon Antony, App A
Weaver, William, 56, 57, 183, 184
Wedingham, Rev. Robert, App A
Wells Cathedral, 64
Werner, Mrs. V, 118, 120
Wesleyan Methodist Chapel (*see also* Methodist Chapel), 64, 87
West Hampstead, App H
West Lavington, 111
Westbury, 19, 21
Westly, Ephraim, 43
Westminster Abbey, 52
Wheat Act, 135
Wheeler, Mrs. C, 88
Wheeler, Sir Mortimer, 16
White, Frances, 47
White, Thomas, 184
White, William 183, 184
Whitecliff, 151

Whitecliffe Down, 13
Whitepits, App F
Whitepits Farm, 211
Whitsun festival, App G
Wilkins, Miss, 76
William & Mary, 40, 44
William the Conqueror, 22
Williams, Ralph Vaughan, 81
Wills, Richard, App A
Wilson, Harold, 119
Wilton, 141
Wiltshire & Swindon History Centre, 5, 145, 208, 215
Wiltshire Archaeological & Natural History Society,, 68
Wiltshire Record Society, 5, 145
Wincanton, 132, 159
Winchester, 37, 148
Wishford, 115
Women's Institute, 76, 215
Women's Institute *Scrapbook,* 215
Womens Land Army, 136
Woodlands Manor, 83
Wookey, James, 181, 183, 184
Woolf, Virginia, 66
Wootton Bassett, 134,
Wycliffe, John, 31, 33, 148
Wylye (river), 9, 152
Wylye Valley, 175

Yarnfield Gate, 11 (n)
Young, Mr, 87

Zeals, 169, 210